The Selected Witter Byn.

Witter Bynner, 1937

THE
SELECTED
WITTER
BYNNER

Poems,
Plays,
Translations,
Prose,
and
Letters

University **Edited**

of **by**

New Mexico Press **James**

Albuquerque **Kraft**

for Brooks and Elizabeth, and for Lynn and Eduardo

© 1995 by the University of New Mexico Press
All rights reserved.
First edition

Library of Congress Cataloging-in-Publication Data
Bynner, Witter, 1881–1968.
[Selections]
The selected Witter Bynner : poems, plays, translations, prose,
and letters / edited by James Kraft. — 1st ed.
p.   cm.
Includes bibliographical references.
ISBN 0-8263-1607-7
I. Kraft, James. II. Title.
PS3503.Y45A6   1995
811'.52—dc20   94-33013
                                                              CIP

Designed by Milenda Nan Ok Lee

Published with the support of The Witter Bynner Foundation for Poetry.

Contents

Acknowledgments

I wish to express special thanks to The Witter Bynner Foundation for Poetry for their support of this book, for permission to reprint the material in this book, and for their support of the research I originally completed for the five-volume *The Works of Witter Bynner* (1978–1981). I am also grateful to the MacDowell Colony and the Millay Colony for the Arts for their fellowships to write the biography of Witter Bynner and this book. Special thanks go to Paul Horgan, who first introduced me to the work of Witter Bynner and encouraged me in a study of Bynner's writing and his life. Pat McDonald, who has served as my assistant throughout my research on Bynner, has been a great support.

Introduction

This anthology is intended to present a representative selection of Witter Bynner's best poetry, plays, translations, prose pieces, and letters. They have been chosen to reflect Bynner's writing career and to act as a companion to the biography *Who is Witter Bynner?* Bynner wrote more than thirty volumes of poetry and prose over the more than fifty years of his professional career from 1907 to 1960. *The Selected Witter Bynner* is the only book that represents all aspects of his writing in a single volume.

The anthology presents the material within each section chronologically as it was published. A few poems Bynner rewrote slightly and republished in subsequent volumes. This anthology always includes the last version of the poem, but includes the poem as part of the volume where it was first published. In this way, the reader can see the progression of Bynner's poetic work, but Bynner is always represented by the version he considered his last and, presumably, his best. The few poems included here in the uncollected section were either published in magazines and never in a book, or exist only in manuscript in the Houghton Library at Harvard University, where most of Bynner's archive is now located.

There are two exceptions to this chronological presentation. Even though *Spectra* was published in November 1916 and *Grenstone Poems* in September 1917, the selections here from *Grenstone Poems* appear before those from *Spectra*. The reason is really chronological: virtually all the poems in *Grenstone* were written before the poems in *Spectra*. *Grenstone Poems* represents what Bynner wrote as a poet during this period. In fact, there were no *Spectra* poems before February 1916 and, as the reader knows, or will discover, they were not written by "Witter Bynner," but appeared under the pseudonym "Emanuel Morgan," in a style different from his up to this point.

The other exception to the chronological presentation is the prose section. Here it seemed more effective to present the prose as it reflects Bynner's life. Much of his prose writing is autobiographical and often written later in life about an earlier period. For example, Bynner published in 1951 *Journey With Genius,* his book on the trip to Mexico with the D. H. Lawrences in 1923. The prose selection from this book appears with the other prose pieces relating to the period of the 1920s.

The location of all work included here is evident as one reads, with the exception of the letters. The source of almost all the letters is the Houghton Library at Harvard University. The few exceptions are noted in the appendix "Location of Letters." Of the more than seven thousand extant Bynner letters only a very small selection could be included here. For a reader interested in the letters, a larger selection appears in *The Works of Witter Bynner: Selected Letters.*

A few words on the editorial procedure for the letters. Early in his life, Bynner wrote most of his letters by hand; after about 1922, he more often dictated to his private secretary, and the letters were typed. Bynner was always a careful writer. There are few slips or errors in his handwritten letters and, until late in life when he had eye trouble, he carefully corrected both the original and the copy of his dictated and typed letters. For the sake of historical accuracy and in order to preserve their original character, the letters are printed as he wrote them. Minor changes were made only for editorial consistency in spelling or style. For example, Bynner sometimes underlined a book title and sometimes put it in quotation marks; in this edition, all titles are printed in italics.

The place from which a letter was sent and its date are given at the start of each letter in a standardized form, regardless of the format in the original. Bynner generally gave address and date in this way, and when he wrote on his printed stationery, which carried the address at the top, he usually included a date to the right. The two exceptions to the procedure used here are given below in the list of symbols and abbreviations found in this work.

All salutations and closings have been omitted except in a few instances where they are intrinsic to the understanding of a particular letter. If two or more letters in succession are addressed to the same person, the addressee's name has been indicated only before the first letter in the series.

The following editorial symbols and abbreviations have been used in editing these letters:

. . . a few words, phrases, or sentences omitted (but not a full paragraph)

***	a paragraph or more omitted
[ ]	material inserted by editor
Santa Fe	This reference at the heading of a letter is to Bynner's house at 342 Buena Vista Road, Santa Fe, New Mexico. The house is at the corner of Buena Vista and College Street—or the Old Santa Fe Trail, as it is now called. The house was assigned various addresses after Bynner began occupying it in 1922, but he lived at the same location throughout his forty-six years in Santa Fe.
Chapala	This reference at the heading of a letter is to Bynner's house in Chapala, Jalisco, Mexico, a town on Lake Chapala, about thirty-five miles south of Guadalajara. Bynner visited Chapala regularly, beginning in 1923, when he accompanied D. H. and Frieda Lawrence, but he did not buy a house there until 1940. Sometime after 1948, the address was changed from 411 Galeana to 411 Madero.
WB	Witter Bynner

Apart from these few symbols used in the letter section, there is little paraphernalia here to intrude on a reader's enjoyment of the writing. Notes exist only when absolutely necessary and are largely restricted to the letter section. Certain names or events in the prose section will not necessarily be known in detail, but the context is clear enough for a reader to know what is taking place. I have given more information in the letter section as the letters often require this to be understood, and the letter section acts as a biographical and historical commentary on the rest of the volume.

Let me illustrate how this occurs. The letters for July 5, 1907 and June 15, 1908 refer to Bynner's association with the Hollywood film director Cecil B. De Mille. Bynner and he were young friends in New York and in 1907 and 1908 wrote plays together. The headnote to the July 5, 1907 letter explains Bynner's efforts to write plays, an extensive if failed effort, and his relationship with De Mille is discussed in that letter and the one for June 15, 1908. This letter also mentions WB's inspiration for a fine poem that came from his time writing in the Maine woods with De Mille. The poem, "The Dead Loon," is included in the "Poetry, Plays, and Translations" section, as are excerpts from three of Bynner's plays: his most famous or notorious play, a one-acter on prostitution called "Tiger," his Greek translation made for Isadora Duncan, *Iphegenia in Tauris*, and his play prompted by Mabel Dodge Luhan, *Cake*. There are in the prose section pieces on "Tiger" and *Iphegenia in Tauris*. In this way there is movement back and forth between the sections with the commentary largely kept in the one section devoted to the letters.

Perhaps a brief biography of Bynner will help orient a reader to Bynner's writing and give a context for what follows. This description should be supplemented by the "Chronology" that is included here and the biography *Who is Witter Bynner?* that serves as a companion volume to this anthology.

Bynner was born in Brooklyn, New York, in 1881 and educated in the public schools in Norwich, Connecticut, and Brookline, Massachusetts. He graduated from Harvard in 1902 and went for the summer to Europe. His first job was as an editor at *McClure's* magazine, then one of the country's most famous magazines for its muckraking journalism and innovative literature. Many important writers, including Willa Cather, were on the staff of *McClure's*, and Bynner learned much about American politics and the writing of literature. He is credited with having introduced A. E. Housman and O. Henry to the magazine, and Ezra Pound in his first American book publication—an eclectic array of writers highly reflective of Bynner's own eclectic nature. He wrote his first book of poems in 1907, *An Ode to Harvard,* and his second in 1915, *The New World,* in praise of the immigrant and a Whitmanesque America.

By 1907 he was living in New Hampshire and traveling throughout the country reading and lecturing, mostly reading the new American poetry and interpreting it. He was engaged seriously in women's rights and equally concerned with the place of the African-American in society. His life was creative and chaotic as he fought his way to an understanding of his poetic character and his role in society, and to an acceptance of his homosexual nature. His main friends were the poets Arthur Davison Ficke, Haniel Long, and Edna St. Vincent Millay, although his friends and acquaintances included Isadora Duncan, for whom he made a translation from the Greek, Augustus St. Gaudens, Carl Sandburg, Carl Van Vechten, John Sloan, Mark Twain, and, briefly, even Henry James.

In 1916 he and Ficke, under the names of Emanuel Morgan and Anne Knish, began writing the Spectra poems, spoofs of the current fads in poetry. The poems were extensively published in magazines, commented on, and published in a book. The hoax lasted almost two years. These poems revealed a new side of Bynner, a freer, more contemporary, more sensual side that was to affect his poetry to the very end of his life.

The next year, he went for the first of two extended trips to China, out of which would eventually come two important translations, one of the major T'ang poets and one of Laotzu, and many essays interpreting the Chinese to Americans. The work he did with Chinese poetry was to shape the direction of his own poetry for the rest of his life. During this period, from 1918 to 1922, he established his residence in Berkeley, taught poetry at the University of California at Berkeley, and became a prominent figure in the Bay Area art world.

Several new volumes of poems were published, now all by Alfred A. Knopf, and his career appeared to be established, but it was not. Bynner's lyric poetry, his orientation to our West and to China, and to the poetry of China, his support of minorities, and his homosexuality seemed increasingly to place him outside the mainstream. He felt he was out of step with the modern poetic world. After much chaotic traveling and uncertainty, he came in 1922 to Santa Fe, almost by chance, and remained in this town, and in his house in Chapala, Mexico, for the rest of his life. He would travel to the East Coast, and went after 1950 three times to Europe, but he had finally found in Santa Fe a community that complemented his nature.

His poems on the American Indian, the Hispanic American, and the Mexican peasant were highly effective poetic portraits of cultures seldom examined. His lyric poems continued to be spare and exquisite at best, but not at all what the poetic world admired. Several volumes appeared over the next years. He wrote many fine essays and a book appeared in 1951 about his relationship with D. H. and Frieda Lawrence, who first stayed in New Mexico in Bynner's house in 1922 and with whom he went to Mexico in 1923.

In 1930, Robert Hunt came to live with Bynner. A man twenty-five years younger than Bynner, bright and volatile, he was Bynner's lover, editor, and companion until he died unexpectedly in 1964. Bynner had his stroke a year later, almost to the day, and remained largely unaware of reality until he died in 1968. He left a small but substantial estate to establish The Witter Bynner Foundation for Poetry to support the work of poets and the awareness of poetry.

Bynner was not a conventional man in what he thought or did, but he was not generally considered unconventional in the style of his poetic expression. He is not thought of as a "modern poet" as, say, Pound, Eliot, or Stevens are, and in certain ways this is correct. Much of what he wrote has a pure lyric quality, and at the start of his career, his writing had a distinctly romantic quality. Yet Bynner was quite modern in certain ways: he was oriented to non-European cultures, particularly to those of the African-American, the American Indian, the Hispanic-American, and the Chinese, and this orientation is clearly evident in his poetry and prose. In fact, his personal orientation was to the American Southwest and to the Orient, and only slightly to Europe. He was a great advocate of Franklin Roosevelt and his politics, and he believed deeply in the idea of democracy as the important principle of government, and as the basis of how one could generously view the world and personally relate to it. He was an early supporter of African-American writers, and in the early twenties gave a poetry prize carrying his name to Langston Hughes and Countee Cullen. His ability to incorporate aspects of the Chinese eight-stanza poetic form and its even, descriptive, and nonsymbolic language created elements in his poetry that are not usually found in American verse. There is also an element in his poetry, as seen in the Spectra poems and in *New Poems, 1960,* that is modern in style and point of view, although this aspect of Bynner is not considered typical of him. We do not think of him as a writer of elliptical, enigmatic, witty verse that is surreal and not lyric in its feeling. Finally, his best poetry has a diction and syntax that are simple, direct, and almost classically American in character, a character that seems, like the best of Whitman or Dickinson, dateless.

Given thoughtful attention, Bynner emerges as a fascinating twentieth-century figure. His viewpoint is often much closer to where we are now at the end of the century than to Pound, Eliot, or Stevens. I do not compare him as a poet to these three, but I do suggest that Bynner's work and ideas can be viewed on their own as interesting and important and that they make a serious and provocative contribution to American literature of this century.

If he is to be appreciated he must be understood for what he is. Few critics know his poetry at all and most would assume the work was only lyric and not be aware of the poems in *Indian Earth,* in *New Poems, 1960,* or the Spectra poems. Except among some critics in New Mexico and the Southwest, there is little knowledge of his poetry about American Indians, Hispanic Americans, or Mexicans, and even less awareness of how he adapted forms and ideas of Chinese poetry to American themes.

We may only now begin to be comfortable with and value these achievements, as we are only beginning to be tolerant of his homosexual orientation and his great sense of the odd or ridiculous as part of life and, therefore, as part of poetry. It is easy to see why critics of the past found no place for him in the poetic canon and were not aware of Bynner's unusually modern or even postmodern viewpoint. Nor, indeed, are any poets or critics today, with the possible exceptions of Richard Wilbur, William Jay Smith, Douglas Day, Paul Horgan, and perhaps a handful of others. The fact that Bynner had this viewpoint and reflected it in his poetry and prose early in the century, and that it came to him through struggle with his own limited and prejudiced background and education, only confirms its interest and importance to us today and suggests the need to recognize the process by which he created himself and his poetry in this century.

One final comment might be useful. Bynner was a serious poet, but he was, as I have suggested, a man with a sense of the ridiculous in life. At times his humor served as a defense against intimacy and as a means of distancing people, but it was based on a robust sense of life's fullness, of its comic absurdity and genuine craziness. Bynner was not afraid to enjoy life and to admit how foolish he, or we, are. As much as this amused and delighted many people, it offended others and made them distrust Bynner. You cannot admire Bynner's work or his life if you decide that the playful, the absurd, the comic, or even the silly must be ignored as you pursue the serious in life. Nor can you separate Bynner's willingness to see this dimension from his willingness to look openly at the world, with a democratic freshness, and most often with an absence of prejudice. His sense of humor relates to the broadness of his nature and his interests.

Bynner could observe a pair of squeaking shoes and write a short lyric poem about love, and about the character of love poetry, as he did in "Meadow-Shoes." While in no way intended as a major poem, it shows how Bynner could see in the ridiculous the dimension that is in the serious.

> My shoe-soles, wet in the meadow,
> Sang like the chirrup of birds—
> But like birds of only a note or two,
> Like persons of few words.
>
> And O, my shoes, how hard it is
> To tell the joy you touch!
> I know, for I have tried to sing
> The things I love too much.

A reader who finds this an unacceptable concept and refuses the comic leap from the squeaking shoes to the pontifical voice of the poet will not enjoy Bynner's work or his vision of life. A reader skeptical of how this vision of the various dimensions in life could move into serious poetry might consider the 1920 poem "Haskell" about American Indians at a government school, or the early 1940s poem "Defeat" about a segregated troop of African-American soldiers on a train in World War II.

I suppose this humorous and broad aspect of his work and his life will delight *and* offend readers today, as it always has. It may be this aspect that makes taking Bynner seriously as a writer the most difficult for readers. (This and his incorporation of elements of Chinese poetry, elements that are still little known to us.) After all, how do you place a poet who could write the following two poems, one near the start of his career and one near the end? Does one take this effort seriously, at least as a critique of "serious" poetry in the first instance, and a serious reflection of our human absurdity in the second, or do they permit a reader to negate the talent as frivolous? Both poems are without titles.

> If I were only dafter
> I might be making hymns
> To the liquor of your laughter
> And the lacquer of your limbs.

> But you turn across the table
> A telescope of eyes,
> And it lights a Russian sable
> Running circles in the skies . . .

> Till I go running after,
> Obeying all your whims—
> For the liquor of your laughter
> And the lacquer of your limbs.

> The dress walked in by itself
> But with the greatest dignity
> As though what was not inside
> Greatly mattered
> Even the other day

> And that after all was what made the occasion

I suppose we do our best to try to encompass such excess. It is not always easy to do so. Bynner's work often has a slightly unreal quality, as if he is seeking reality on a level different from the ordinary, or the day-to-day. Certainly I have tried in this anthology, and in the biography, to encompass Bynner's viewpoint, and I can say it has brought great rewards. I hope it does the same for other readers. Let the last word on this broad, accepting, and irreverent dimension be Bynner's, written in his laconic style, from a journal entry for February 11, 1956:

> A. E. Housman wished his light verse and his
> many variants destroyed. Willa Cather forbade
> printing any of her letters. I cannot imagine
> fear of letting people see one's frivolities
> or stupidities. Why always a cravat?

Chronology

1880   Thomas Edgarton Bynner marries Annie Louise Brewer on December 11 in Melrose, Massachusetts.
1881   WB is born on August 10 in Brooklyn, New York.
1885   Edwin Tyler Bynner, "Tim," WB's brother, is born on December 12 in Brooklyn.
1888   WB's parents separate and his mother takes the children to her family in Norwich, Connecticut, and later to her husband's sisters in Brookline, Massachusetts.
1891   WB's father dies of tuberculosis on December 5 in Brooklyn.
1893   WB travels west to visit his Palmer relatives in Chicago and to see the World's Fair.
1898   WB graduates from Brookline High School in the spring and enters Harvard College in the fall.
1900   WB becomes a member of the Board of the Harvard *Advocate*, the first of his class to be asked to join by the editor, Wallace Stevens.
1901   Annie Louise Bynner marries Walter Liveridge Wellington on December 4 in Brookline, Massachusetts.
1902   WB graduates from Harvard and travels in the summer to Europe, where he meets one of his literary heroes, George Meredith. In October he begins work at *McClure's* magazine in New York City.
1903   WB is the first to publish A. E. Housman in the United States in *McClure's*.
1906   WB leaves *McClure's* to concentrate on writing poetry, plays, and criticism.
1907   WB moves into Homer and Carlota Saint-Gaudens's house in Cornish, New Hampshire, his permanent residence for the next ten years. *An Ode to Harvard and Other Poems* is published in June. WB begins lecturing on poetry all over the United States.

1910   WB arranges for Ezra Pound's first book publication at Small, Maynard & Company, where WB has been on commission as a publisher's reader. WB becomes a charter member of the Poetry Society of America.
1911   WB reads "An Immigrant" at Harvard as Phi Beta Kappa poet.
1912   WB travels to the West Coast for the first time. He and Arthur Davison Ficke write to Edna St. Vincent Millay about her poem "Renascence," and begin their lifelong friendship with her.
1913   "Tiger," a one-act play, is published in August.
1914   Walter Wellington dies on July 15, leaving the bulk of his estate to his daughter, Ruth, and to WB's mother, with lesser amounts to WB and Tim. "The Little King," a one-act play, is published in October.
1915   *The New World* is published in June and *Iphigenia in Tauris* in November.
1916   WB and Arthur Ficke publish their hoax, *Spectra,* in November, under the names Emanuel Morgan and Anne Knish.
1917   WB leaves for his first trip to Japan and China on March 15 and returns in July. *Grenstone Poems: A Sequence* is published in September. *Anygirl,* WB's one attempt at musical comedy, fails in Brooklyn in November.
1918   WB begins teaching at the University of California at Berkeley in October. He starts a translation of Chinese poems with Kiang Kang-hu.
1919   WB is involved in a controversy over his desire to release conscientious objectors from prison. He gives the Phi Beta Kappa poem, "A Canticle of Pan," at Berkeley on June 3. *The Beloved Stranger,* WB's first book published by Alfred A. Knopf, appears in June. WB's stepsister, Ruth Wellington, dies on July 23. WB inherits part of her estate.
1920   *A Canticle of Pan and Other Poems* is published early in 1920, and *Pins for Wings* in October. WB leaves for his second trip to China on June 22.
1921   WB returns from China to San Francisco on April 27, then begins long lecture trips throughout the United States.
1922   WB arrives in Santa Fe, New Mexico, on February 20 to lecture, and decides to rent a house there. D. H. and Frieda Lawrence arrive in New Mexico on September 10 and stay at WB's house en route to Taos. *A Book of Plays* is published in October. At Christmas WB returns to New York City to see his mother, as he will do almost every year until her death in 1937.
1923   WB goes to Mexico in March with D. H. and Frieda Lawrence

and Willard Johnson. WB first visits Chapala. *A Book of Love,* a translation from the French of Charles Vildrac, is published in June.

1925   *An Ode to Harvard* is republished in May by Knopf as *Young Harvard: First Poems of Witter Bynner.* WB returns to Mexico, and to Chapala, as he will regularly for the rest of his life. *Caravan* is published.

1926   WB first meets Robert Hunt. *Cake* is published in September.

1929   *The Persistence of Poetry* and *Indian Earth* are published in August, and *The Jade Mountain* in October.

1930   Robert Hunt visits WB in Santa Fe in November and decides to stay.

1931   *The Sonnets of Frederick Goddard Tuckerman* is published early in the year. In May WB reads part of *Eden Tree* as Phi-Beta Kappa poet at Amherst College. *Eden Tree* is published in August.

1935   *Guest Book* is published in June.

1936   *Selected Poems* is published in November.

1937   Mrs. Wellington, WB's mother, dies on November 25. WB and Tim inherit her considerable fortune.

1940   WB buys a house in Chapala. *Against the Cold* is published in October.

1943   In June Robert Hunt moves to San Francisco to do war work. WB has moved to Chapala for the duration of the war. He works on a book on China and then begins his edition of *The Way of Life.*

1944   Robert Hunt returns to Chapala in October. *The Way of Life According to Laotzu* is published that same month.

1945   WB and Robert Hunt return to Santa Fe in August.

1947   *Take Away the Darkness* is published in March.

1950   In January WB and Robert Hunt leave for a trip to North Africa and Europe, and return to Santa Fe in July.

1951   In early July, WB has an operation for glaucoma, which leaves him blind in the right eye. *Journey with Genius* is published in July.

1952   WB and Robert Hunt leave in June for Portugal, Spain, France, Italy, and Sicily. They return to Santa Fe in November. WB, who is now seventy-one, becomes increasingly afflicted by various ailments.

1954   WB wins the Gold Medal of the Alexander Droutzkoy Memorial Award for his service to poetry, presented by the Poetry Society of America.

1955   *Book of Lyrics* is published in November.

1956   The University of Chicago publishes *Iphigenia in Tauris* in their edition of *The Complete Greek Tragedies.*

1957   WB and Robert Hunt leave in July for Greece and Portugal, but they must return early, as WB is taken ill.
1958   WB begins to lose the sight in his good eye.
1959   Edwin Tyler Bynner (Tim) dies on August 28 in New York City.
1960   *New Poems 1960* is published in September.
1961   In May WB develops shingles, an affliction that lasts for the rest of his life.
1962   WB is elected to the National Institute of Arts and Letters.
1964   Robert Hunt dies on January 18 in Santa Fe.
1965   On January 16 WB has a severe stroke, which disables him.
1968   WB dies on June 1 in Santa Fe.

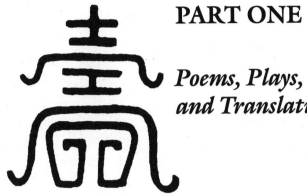

PART ONE

Poems, Plays, and Translations

from
An Ode to Harvard and Other Poems
1907

Often we'd walk to town,
Thereby less idly to be missing classes;
And often in or out we'd wait on Harvard
    Bridge to see
A gull that caught the sunlight overhead;
Or a crew that sped
Symmetrical; or a single shell slide under,
    narrow
As an arrow,—
And watch the rower, his white flesh turning
    brown,
Bending his back, his arm, his knee,
Spending his brawn, his muscle and his marrow
Close with his heart to ply
The quiet swiftness of his revelry,
Sending his oar as with a wing to fly;
Later we'd watch the western sky,
With poppies hung from head to feet,
Go feasting to his many-tapered bed,
Where restless he would lie
On the scattered golden sheet,
And then at last, deep
In a great ecstasy,
Would fall asleep,
Closing in tranquil clouds of night, like a petal
    in the grasses;
Or, later still, we'd see
That bayonet-row of lights,

March by the River Charles, patrol by many
    a home
The huddling heights
Of Boston town,
And lead where, like the crystal vision of a
    camp, looked down
The ancestral Dome.
    Or else we'd take those other walks
Along the outer circle by the river,
Past Soldiers' Field, inhaling for our health
    the marshy gases. . . .
    Remember with me, Comrade, how those close,
    congenial talks
Would patter from the moment to forever!

    Over that crude see-sawing bridge of yesterday,
After the morning's rain,
I took alone, from half-past four to six last
    night again,
The old-time way,
The ridge of path that sloped from miry stubble,
Between the looping river, full of steely,
    blurred reflections,
And an inchoate landscape-plan
Made of roads and tracks and spaces.
    Sharp in shadow stood the trees against a sky
Where, colossally ascending,
Came a sign of cloudy trouble
From the furnace of creation and, with indus-
    tries of man
From their chimneys tall as churches, transcen-
    dentally was blending
Everything of great and little in a multitudinous
    gray
Overhead.

    There to the left was life, where the young
    men ply their graces,
Running, jumping, throwing hammers,—where
    the body is at play
And its destiny is amorous and young
As the life-blood in their faces.

Across the river lie
The resting-places
Of the dead;
And there, as though the night were their es-
    pecial hour,
None others using it so well as they,
I heard the bell, that rings at dusk beside the
    balconied tower,
Send gently with its iron tongue
All those that wake away.
    Across the river then I cried aloud
In a great wonderment,
As men have cried in anguish without cease,—
'O where are you today,
You vanished faces?'
And while the twilight wind's caprice
But echoed what I said,
But questioned from the future, asking me,—
More than before, the shroud that hung
From tree to tree
Half with an air of shelter and of peace,
Was infinitely still.
    Yet I believe that heaven is on that hill;
That each who blindly loved the single soul
Shall thence illustriously love the whole;
And with the leaves that fall and fly
And with the river lifting by
Into the overwhelming sky,
That these are lifted, these who die,
To the remotest corners of their destiny,—
Infinitesimal in light to lie
Farthest and nearest in infinity;
That into breath of the mysterious Will
The worlds are welding in that little hill,—
Where all shall be the mother and the son,
The daughter and the father and the One.

from *Tiger*
1913 [*]

Tiger, tiger, burning bright
In the forests of the night,
What immortal hand or eye
Could frame thy fearful symmetry?

Time: Evening.

Scene: A room in a house not far east of Times Square. A curtained door at the back of the stage leads into the hallway. A closed door at the right leads into an inner bedroom. The furniture and pictures are more showy than expensive. The shades are drawn.

At the rise of the curtain, the keeper of the house sits in an easy-chair. She is a woman of thirty-five, handsome, well-dressed. Her familiars call her Tiger, on account of her hard, lithe brilliance. She is looking over a handful of bills and writing checks with a fountain pen on the arm of the chair. On a couch reclines Annabel, a girl of twenty-four, beginning to fade under her paint, but an effective type still, with her hair parted and drawn simply over her forehead to a flat coil behind. She is in a loose, thin dressing-gown, reading a novel, eating chocolates and smoking cigarettes. An ash-tray, cigarettes, chewing-gum and the chocolates are on a chair beside the couch. At a table across the room, a man of thirty, with somewhat refined features, a suggestive pallor and flush, and a habit of biting the skin on his red lips and of rubbing his thumb over his finger-tips, is pouring himself a glass of straight gin. He is over-dressed, over-mannered and wears several bright rings, but might pass with the young for a gentleman. On account of what is known as his "class," he has been dubbed The Baron.

ANNABEL.
Put water in it, Baron. Spare your liver.

[*] See the article on this play in the prose section, and the head note to the letter for July 5, 1907 for an explanation of WB's work in the theater.

BARON.

Mind your own liver and shut up, will you?
Whenever I want your dope, I'll ask for it.
>   [*She returns to her reading. He gulps his drink, then loiters toward Tiger.
>   Suddenly he sits on the arm of her chair, catches her close and kisses her
>   hard*]

TIGER.

>   [*Pushing him away*]
Cut out that stuff, Baron.
>   [*Picking up her bills from the floor*]
Come across first
With what you promised.

BARON.

Oh, you needn't worry,
Dear Mama Shylock. You're going to get your pound
Of flesh,—I've said that you shall have her here
To-night. She may be waiting for me now—
>   [*He looks at his wrist-watch*]
Less than a block away, ready to serve
And honor and obey me.—Damn you, Tiger!
I wonder if I love you more or hate you.
Damn you, anyway!

TIGER.

Oh, swear your head off!
Go over it again, make up your mind
One way and then the other!
>   [*Looking up from her bills*]
>   Kiss me, kid!
>   [*He kisses her hungrily. She stands up and throws him away from her*]
Now snarl at me, you cur. I don't know why
I keep you round; except to purr and snarl
Myself,—first kiss your feminine eyes because
They look so lost in the world, then curse your breed,
You most of all, because you're so unlike
The brutes I'm tired of.
>   [*She crosses to lay bills and checks in her desk*]
But what's the use
Of bothering? You suit me. And you're good

For the business. Run along and bring her here.
[*She sits at her desk and writes*]

BARON.

Remember now. She's young, and I'm her first
Offense. And I've been careful with her, Tiger,
Not touched her fingers only once or twice
And used good English and been sympathetic.

TIGER.

Oh, yes, I know all that.

BARON.

[*Taking a cigarette from Annabel's supply*]
She's different though,
She hasn't got the taste for it beforehand
Most of them have.

TIGER.

[*Looking round as she seals a letter*]
Then she's the very kind
We want, old boy. The other kind is common
And some of our customers amuse themselves,
You know, by being fastidious. Is she a blonde?

BARON.

Brunette.

TIGER.

Worse luck.

BARON.

No, you can fix that up.
Light hair'd go fine with her dark eyes, good change.
She's just the girl for it, solemn and slow
And innocent. Poor kid, I pity her.

TIGER.

You act like you were getting stuck on her;
Perhaps she'll keep you when you're tired of me.

BARON.
  You've got me hypnotized. I don't get tired.

TIGER.
  [*She approaches him, seductively, mockingly*]
  Be true to me, sweetheart!

BARON.
  To hell with you!
  [*She lays her hand insidiously on his arm. At once he seizes and kisses her.
  She leads him to the hallway door, and opens it as he kisses her again, then
  she pushes him out with both hands and, closing the door, turns back to
  Annabel, who at every amorous passage between Tiger and the Baron has
  looked up from her book and watched with curious but accustomed interest*]

ANNABEL.
  [*Chewing gum*]
  Gee, but I wish I had a man like that!

TIGER.
  You'd have one, dear, if you were businesslike.

ANNABEL.
  [*Shaking her head and marking her place in the book with a cigarette*]
  I couldn't hold a man. They get so bored
  With me. And, after all, there isn't much
  To say to one man. I'd be bored myself
  To have to think of new things all the time.
  Variety, Tiger, is the spice of life,
  Not in the spiel but in the spielers. Dear,
  Do you like my hair this way? One of the boys
  Suggested that it makes me look too old.
  I think I'll put it back again.
  [*She starts to uncoil it*]

TIGER.
  No, no!
  Leave it to me! You'll be told quick enough
  When you look old. Let it alone.

ANNABEL.
  Well, looks

Ain't everything. I'm getting wise to the game.
Say to a gink, "Your nose is beautiful,"
"Your mouth was made to kiss," or call his figure
Military.
  [*She examines herself critically in a hand-mirror which she takes from
  under a sofa-cushion*]

TIGER.
  There's just one kind of figure
  That makes a hit with me. A good full chest!

ANNABEL.
  Gee, ain't they handsome when they have green—backs!
  [*They laugh*]
  I told a guy last night that it takes dough
  To make a tart. Dear, that's my own!

TIGER.
  And say,
  Here's business, Annabel, take it from me!
  You've seen the belly on the dollar-sign?—
  Well, the man who has the stomach has the figure!

ANNABEL.
  I've noticed that.

TIGER.
  Sure thing! And while he thinks
  You're waiting for his phoney kisses—pay
  Attention to his stomach and his roll!
  Make him eat, drink and spend! My dear, the way
  To passion's thro' the stomach every time.

ANNABEL.
  [*Meditative*]
  Champagne, you mean?

TIGER.
  Eve got there with an apple.
  But the apple has fermented some since then.

ANNABEL.
  [*Laughing with Tiger*]
  We have a good time, don't we!

TIGER.
  You do, dear.
  You've been here seven months and, Annabel,
  You never once in all that time have had
  A grouch.

ANNABEL.
  You're square with me, Tiger, that's why.

TIGER.
  But, on the level, you don't like the life?

ANNABEL.
  Better than selling underwear to women
  And paying fines on four whole bucks a week!
  Talk as you please, the men have more respect
  For a girl that's a good looker and can earn
  A seat in a restaurant than for a dub
  Who stands up all day waiting on their wives.

TIGER.
  Besides, you have as good a chance as me
  To save up coin enough before you're old
  And rent a house and get some girls together—
  And after a while to live in a good hotel
  And settle down respectable.—Perhaps
  A friend or two. But independent.

ANNABEL.
  Chance!
  Yes, I've got that. But, dear, I haven't got
  The brains to make a hit in any line.
  I know my limit and I'm satisfied.
  I'm better off than I ever was at home,
  And that's enough. The future can go hang.
  There's more than one way to prepare a corpse.
  Ain't I the cheerful guy?

TIGER.
  You're lazy, dear,
  That's all the matter with you.

ANNABEL.
  Who's the new girl?

TIGER.
  Oh, I don't know. The Baron falls for me.
  So I can trust his taste.

ANNABEL.
  Say, does he fall?
  He's jealous, now, of me!

TIGER.
  Who's on the job
  Downstairs?

ANNABEL.
  Cassie tonight. I'm tired. She knows
  The steps and laughs a lot, loosens 'em up.
  She's popular.

TIGER.
  And she's the Baron's work,—
  He brought her here last winter. Cassie thinks
  The Baron the one bet and he, poor kid,
  Just keeps her on because I tell him to.
  And see how well the combination works?—
  The happy family!

ANNABEL.
  Business-like's the word!
    [*A knock is heard at the hallway door*]

TIGER.
  Quick there! Be business-like yourself for once!
  Clear off those things!

ANNABEL.
  All right.

[*While Annabel puts bottles and glasses under the table so that they are hidden by the table-cover, Tiger picks up the gum, cigarettes and ashtray from the chair and tucks them all under a sofa-cushion. The knock is repeated*]

ANNABEL.
My fancy-work,
Where is it?

TIGER.
[*Taking a piece of embroidery from under a cushion*]
                    Here.
[*She hands it to Annabel and crosses to the easy-chair*]

ANNABEL.
[*Sitting on the couch, with the embroidery, as though she had been sewing*]
Now we're a boarding-house!

TIGER.
Throw me the book!
[*Annabel throws Tiger the novel from the couch, Tiger holds it as though she had been reading*]
                    Come in!
[*The Baron enters, leading by the hand Margaret, a simple, romantic girl of sixteen. She is in street clothes. She looks toward the two women bashfully, innocently, as they rise and come toward her*]

BARON.
It's Margaret.
This is Miss Dillingham, my aunt, and here's
My Cousin Ann.

MARGARET.
How do you do? Gene's told
Me lots about you. I suppose you think
I'm foolish running away like this?

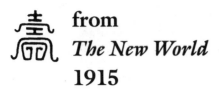 from
The New World
1915

GRIEVE NOT FOR BEAUTY*

Grieve not for the invisible, transported brow
On which like leaves the dark hair grew,
Nor for the lips of laughter that are now
Laughing inaudibly in sun and dew,
Nor for those limbs, that, fallen low
And seeming faint and slow,
Shall soon
Discover and renew
Their shape and hue—
Like birches varying white before the moon
Or a wild cherry-bough
In spring or the round sea—
And shall pursue
More ways of swiftness than the swallow dips
Among, and find more winds than ever blew
To haven the straining sails of unimpeded ships.

*This selection from *The New World,* with this title, was reprinted as a separate poem in *Selected Poems* (1936) and again in *Book of Lyrics* (1955).

from
Iphigenia in Tauris
1915; revised 1956 *

SCENE: *Out of a temple by the seaside in Tauris, down steps leading to a blood-stained altar seen through its door, comes Iphigenia, the High Priestess, and stands alone on the stairway above the empty court.*

Iphigenia
    Pelops, the son of Tantalus, by maiming
A chariot, won a bride, who bore him Atreus,
And Atreus had two sons, one Menelaus,
The other Agamemnon, who in turn
By Clytemnestra had a child, and I
Am she, Iphigenia.
                 People believe
That I was sacrificed by my own father
To Artemis, in the great pursuit of Helen,
Upon an altar near the bay of Aulis,
There where the long deep waves are caught and broken
Hither and thither by the winds, the bay
Where Agamemnon's fleet, his thousand ships
From Hellas, waited to avenge on Troy
The wrong done Menelaus through the loss
Of Helen. But a storm came up and still
Another storm and neither sea nor wind
Would favor Agamemnon. So he asked

---

* See the preface to this play in the prose section. It explains why WB translated the play in 1914–1915 for Isadora Duncan, and then revised it for publication in *The Complete Greek Tragedies* in 1956. See as well the note to the letter of March 28, 1911.

Calchas, the soothsayer, to consult the flame.
And this is what was answered: "Agamemnon,
Captain of Hellas, there can be no way
Of setting your ships free, till the offering
You promised Artemis is given Her.
You had vowed to render Her in sacrifice
The loveliest thing each year should bear. You have owed
Long since the loveliness which Clytemnestra
Had borne to you, your daughter, Iphigenia.
Summon your daughter now and keep your word."
    They sent Odysseus and his artful tongue
To lure me from my mother by pretending
That I should wed Achilles. When I had come
To Aulis, they laid hands on me. The flame
Was lit. The blow would have been struck—I saw
The knife. But Artemis deceived their eyes
With a deer to bleed for me and stole me through
The azure sky. And then She set me down
Here in this town of Tauris, this abode
Of savage men ruled by their uncouth king,
Thoas, a horseman headlong as the wind,
Who stationed me High Priestess in Her temple,
And still I serve Her on Her festal days.
Service may seem a holy word. But far
From holy are these orders I am bound
To obey, never to question: Her command that I
Must serve to Her the lives of foreigners.
It was a custom long before I came,
An ancient cruel custom. Can She hear me?
My hands prepare the victims. Other hands,
There in the inner temple, spill the blood,
Which then is poured upon this altar-stone.
                    [*She descends the steps into the court.*]
I dreamed last night a deathly dream. Perhaps
The morning will dispel it if I speak it—
I dreamed that I was far beyond the seas.
I seemed to be at home again in Argos,
Asleep among my maidens—when a roll
Of thunder shook the ground. I ran outside.
I watched the house. I saw the coping fall,
The cross-beams stir and yield, break and give way,
Then the whole palace plunge from roof to base,

28   *Poems, Plays, Translations*

Only one column left upright in all
My father's house. But that one stood alive,
A man with bright brown hair and breathing lips.
And then against my will my hand went out,
As it does toward strangers here condemned to die,
And touched his forehead with this fatal water—
And with water of my tears, because I knew
The dream was of Orestes and his end.
The pillar of a family is the son.
This water is the certain sign of death.
It could not mean my family next of kin;
Strophius, my uncle, never had a son.
It was my brother whom I touched with tears—
For whom I now must pour a funeral-urn,
All I can do for one so far away.

> [*Climbing the steps.*]

Where are the women from Greece the King appointed
To live with me and help me here in the temple?
I wonder where they are. I need their help.

The voice of Orestes

Keep a sharp lookout. Somebody may be coming.

Pylades

> [*Entering by the path from the bay.*]

I have looked in both directions and there's no one.

Orestes

> [*Following him and gazing at the temple.*]

Is this the shrine of Artemis we have sailed
So many seas to find since we left Argos?
Is it, O Pylades? Is this the shrine?

Pylades

I think it is, Orestes. So do you.

Orestes

And might that stone be stained with blood of Greeks?

Pylades

If ever I saw blood—look, on the edge!

Orestes

Look, near the roof! Belongings of the dead!

Pylades

Trophies of foreigners these men have murdered!

Orestes

Careful!
           O Phoebus, why must Thy oracle
Bring this on me again, the sight of blood
Again? Have I not seen enough of blood?
My mother shed my father's blood, I hers.
And then the Furies, with their eyes bloody,
Hunted me, hounded me across the land
Until at last I ran to Thee and begged
An end of all the cycles of despair
That sped me, hurled me, maddened me through Hellas.
The answer was, "Go to the Taurian country
Where Artemis, my sister, has a shrine.
Find there Her statue which had fallen down
From Heaven. Then prove yourself a man able
Enough or fortunate enough to steal it,
Stalwart enough to face all risk and bring it
Home to the holy land of Attica."
Although no more was said, I understood
That this would mean the end of my afflictions.
And here I am, O Phoebus, far from home
On a misbegotten shore—doing Thy will.
    But Pylades, my fellow venturer
Where can we turn? What man could possibly
Scale these high walls? Or climb the open stairs
And not be seen? Or force the brazen locks
Without whoever is behind them hearing?
If we are caught, it will be certain death,
Your death as well as mine. Even this waiting,
Wondering what to do, may cost our lives.
Enough of it! Enough! Back to the ship!

Pylades

What do we know of flight? How should we dare
To take a course of which our hearts know nothing?
Why should we disobey Apollo's order,

Do him dishonor? No, we shall find a way.
Come, let us leave the temple, let us look
For a dark cave to hide in. Not the ship!
By now they must have spied the ship from shore.
They'd be ahead of us, catch us and end us.
   Notice the opening between those beams?
It's wide enough. Under the night's dim eye
We could drop through and hoist a wooden statue.
A coward turns away but a brave man's choice
Is danger. And by all the Gods, shall we,
Coming this far, now at the end turn back?

Orestes

I should have been the one to say those words.
Yes, let us go and find a hiding-place,
Keep faith with Phoebus and deserve his help.
Have we not youth? Youth, with its fill of strength,
Turning away from any task should be ashamed.

> [*They leave by the path to the shore. A great bell rings.*
> *From the town side the Temple Maidens*
> *assemble in the courtyard.*]

 **from**
Grenstone Poems
1917[*]

AN OLD ELEGY FOR A CHILD

O earth, with flowers on his eyes
    Be thou as sweet as he—
Be thou as light where now he lies
    As he was light on thee.

DRIFTWOOD

Come, warm your hands
From the cold wind of time.
I have built here under the moon,
A many-colored fire
With fragments of wood
That have been part of a tree
And part of a ship.

Were leaves more real,
Or driven nails,
Or fingers of builders,
Than these burning violets?
Come, warm your hands

[*] See the Introduction for the explanation of why *Grenstone Poems*, first published in 1917, is placed before *Spectra*, which first appeared in 1916.

From the cold wind of time.
There's a fire under the moon.

THE DEAD LOON

There is a dead loon in the camp tonight, killed by a clever fool,
And down the lake a live loon calling.
The wind comes stealing, tall, muscular and cool,
From his plunge where stars are falling—
The wind comes creeping, stalking,
On his night-hidden trail,
Up to the cabin where we sit playing cards and talking.
And only I, of them all, listen and grow pale.
He glues his face to the window, addressing only me,
Talks to me of death and bids me hark
To the hollow scream of a loon and bids me see
The face of a clever fool reflected in the dark.

That dead loon is farther on the way than we are.
It has no voice, where it hangs nailed to the gate.
But it is with me now and with the evening star.
Its voice is my voice and its fate my fate.

SHE HAS A THOUSAND PRESENCES

She has a thousand presences,
    As surely seen and heard
As birds that hide behind a leaf
    Or leaves that hide a bird.

Single your love, you lose your love,
    You cloak her face with clay;
Now mine I never quite discern—
    And never look away.

THE HIGHEST BIDDER

To the highest bidder,
Your birthplace, Walt Whitman,

Under the hammer . . .
The old farm on Paumanok, north of Huntington,
Its trees,
Its leaves of grass!
Voices bid and counterbid over those ninety acres . . .
And your own voice among them, like an element,
Roaring and outbidding.

AT THE LAST

There is no denying
That it matters little,
When through a narrow door
We enter a room together,
Which goes after, which before.

Perhaps you are not dying:
Perhaps—there is no knowing—
I shall slip by and turn and laugh with you
Because it mattered so little,
The order of our going.

EPITAPH

She who could not bear dispute
Nor unquiet now is mute,
She who could leave unsaid
Perfect silence now is dead.

BE NOT TOO FRANK

Be not too frank, if you would reach
A woman's heart, be not too kind
Nor too severe, but keep your speech
And all your manners uninclined.

Assert but briefly self-control;
Then watch her come to you intent
To give direction to your soul
And make indifference different.

 **from**
Spectra
1916*

OPUS 15

Despair comes when all comedy
 Is tame
And there is left no tragedy
 In any name,
When the round and wounded breathing
 Of love upon the breast
Is not so glad a sheathing
 As an old brown vest.

Asparagus is feathery and tall,
And the hose lies rotting by the garden wall.

OPUS 62

Three little creatures gloomed across the floor
 And stood profound in front of me,
And one was Faith, and one was Hope,
 And one was Charity.

Faith looked for what it could not find,
 Hope looked for what was lost,
(Love looked and looked but Love was blind),
 Charity's eyes were crossed.

*For Bynner's explanation of why he wrote the Spectra poems, see "The Story of the Spectric School of Poetry" in the prose section.

Then with a leap a single shape,
    With beauty on its chin,
Brandished a little screaming ape . . .
    And each one, like a pin,

Fell to a pattern on the rug
    As flat as they could be—
And died there comfortable and snug,
    Faith, Hope and Charity.

That shape, it was my shining soul
    Bludgeoning every sham . . .
O little ape, be glad that I
    Can be the thing I am!

OPUS 40

Two cocktails round a smile,
    A grapefruit after grace,
Flowers in an aisle
    . . . Were your face.

A strap in a streetcar,
    A sea fan on the sand,
A beer on a bar
    . . . Were your hand.

The pillar of a porch,
    The tapering of an egg,
The pine of a torch
    . . . Were your leg.—

Sun on the Hellespont,
    White swimmers in the bowl
Of the baptismal font
    Are your soul.

OPUS 14

Beside the brink of dream
    I had put out my willow roots and leaves

As by a stream
    Too narrow for the invading greaves
Of Rome in her trireme . . .
Then you came—like a scream
    Of beeves.

OPUS 6

If I were only dafter
    I might be making hymns
To the liquor of your laughter
    And the lacquer of your limbs.

But you turn across the table
    A telescope of eyes,
And it lights a Russian sable
    Running circles in the skies . . .

Till I go running after,
    Obeying all your whims—
For the liquor of your laughter
    And the lacquer of your limbs.

OPUS 9

When frogs' legs on a plate are brought to me
    As though I were divinity in France,
I feel as God would feel were He to see
    Imperial Russians dance.

These people's thoughts and gestures and concerns
    Move like a Russian ballet made of eggs;
A bright-smirched canvas heaven heaves and burns
    Above their arms and legs.

Society hops this way and that, well-taught;
    But while I watch, in cloudy state,
I feel as God would feel if He were brought
    Frogs' legs on a plate.

OPUS 104

How terrible to entertain a lunatic!
To keep his earnestness from coming close!

A Madagascar land-crab once
Lifted blue claws at me
And rattled long black eyes
That would have got me
Had I not been gay.

OPUS 101

He not only plays
One note
But holds another note
Away from it—
As a lover
Lifts
A waft of hair
From loved eyes.

The piano shivers,
When he touches it,
And the leg shines.

OPUS 78

I am beset by liking so many people.
What can I do but hide my face away?—
Lest, looking up in love, I see no eyes or lids
In the gleaming whirl of clay,
Lest, reaching for the fingers of love,
I know not which are they,
Lest the dear-lipped multitude,
Kissing me, choke me dead!—

O green eyes in the breakers,
White heave unquieted,
What can I do but dive again, again—again—
To hide my head!

OPUS 79

Only the wise can see me in the mist,
    For only lovers know that I am here . . .
After his piping, shall the organist
    Be portly and appear?

Pew after pew,
    Wave after wave . . .
Shall the digger dig and then undo
    His own dear grave?

Hear me in the playing
    Of a big brass band . . .
See me, straying
    With children hand in hand . . .

Smell me, a dead fish . . .
    Taste me, a rotten tree. . . .
Someday touch me, all you wish,
    In the wide sea.

 **from**
The Beloved Stranger
1919

THE WALL

How is it,
That you, whom I can never know,
My beloved,
Are a wall between me and those I have known well—
So that my familiars vanish
Farther than the blue roofs of Nankow
And are lost among the desert hills?

LIGHTNING

There is a solitude in seeing you,
Followed by your presence when you are gone.
You are like heaven's veins of lightning.
I cannot see till afterward
How beautiful you are.
There is a blindness in seeing you,
Followed by the sight of you when you are gone.

FEAR

This day has come,
Like an idiot, blank and dumb,
Over a lonely road

Under lonely skies.
And though at first I whistled and strode
Like a strong man showing no fear,
Yet I am afraid, afraid of this day,
You not being here,
And I look back and back at this uncouth day,
You not being here,
And my heart is in my mouth because of its eyes,
In which nothing is clear.

HORSES

Words are hoops
Through which to leap upon meanings,
Which are horses' backs,
Bare, moving.

A SIGH

Still must I tamely
Talk sense with these others?

How long
Before I shall be with you again,
Magnificently saying nothing!

LAMENT

There is a chill deeper than that of death,
In the return of the beloved and not of love.
And there is no warmth for it
But the warmth of a world which needs more than the sun,
Or the warmth of lament for beauty
Which is graven on many stones.

Someone was there . . .
I put out my hand in the dark
And felt
The long fingers of the wind.

And yet I would be with you a little while,
Dear ghost.

THE MOON

Red leaped
The moon,
From behind the black hill of night . . .
And soon it was silver forever
And there was no change . . .

Until its time came . . .

And its setting was as white as a corpse,
Among the flowers of dawn.

I EVADE

The look in your eyes
Was as soft as the underside of soap in a soap-dish . . .

And I left before you could love me.

THE CANYON

It is the dead sex of the earth
On which the sun still gazes.

It is all the mountains of love,
Into whose sarcophagus
Peers
The moon.

from
A Canticle of Pan
1920

HASKELL

Here in Kansas is a school
Made of square stones and windows,
Where Indian boys are taught to use a tool,
A printing press, a book,
And Indian girls
To read, to dress, to cook.
And as I watch today
The orderly industrious classes,
Only their color and silence and the way
The hair lies flat and black on their heads proclaims them Sioux,
Comanche, Choctaw, Cherokee,
Creek, Chippewa, Paiute—and the red and blue
Of the girls' long sweaters and the purple and yellow,
And the tawny slant of the machine-made shirts . . .

Noon—and out they come. And one tall fellow,
Breaking from the others with a glittering yell and crouching slim,
Gives a leap like the leap of Mordkin,
And the sun carves under him
A canyon of glory . . .
And then it shadows, and he darts,
With head hung, to the dormitory.

MEADOW-SHOES

My shoe-soles, wet in the meadow,
Sang like the chirrup of birds—
But like birds of only a note or two,
Like persons of few words.

And, O my shoes, how hard it is
To tell the joy you touch!
I know, for I have tried to sing
The things I love too much.

THE ENCHANTED TOAD

Three times you had neared—I unaware—
My body warm in the sand and bare.
Three times you had hopped your silent track
To the arch of shadow under my back.
And each time, when I felt you cool
And turned on you and, like a fool,
Prodded your exit from my place,
Sorrow deepened in your face.
You were loth to leave me, though I threw
Handfuls of sand to quicken you.
You would look as you went and blink your eyes
And puff your pale throat with surprise.
Three times you had tried, like someone daft . . .
O could it be that an evil craft
Had long bewitched, from the man you were,
Some old Chinese philosopher,
Had warted you dank and thwarted you dumb
And given you three times to come
Begging a friend to set you free?—
And did you spend them all on me?

THE ENCHANTED SWANS

Out of a fairy-tale they flew above me,
Three white wild swans with silk among their wings—

And one might be a princess and might love me,
If I had not forgotten all such things.

They flew abreast and would not pause nor quicken,
One of them guarded by the other two,
And left me helpless here, alone and stricken,
Without the secret that I thought I knew.

THROUGH A GATEWAY IN JAPAN

A torii stood, three miles above the bay,
    A gate of sacred ground,
And when I wandered through a little way,
    I paused and found

No temple-steps, no lanterns and no shrine,
    Only divinity—
The solitary presence of a pine
    Facing the sea.

IN KAMAKURA

In Kamakura, near the great Diabutsu,
When I had sat a long time on the ground
And been gathered up, forgetful of my face and form,
Into the face and form of endless dream,
I found among the booths a little pendant Buddha
With the steel of a round mirror for His halo . . .

So that a brooding head still intervenes in bronze
Between my face and the image of my face,
And I cannot see myself and not see Him.

CHINESE NOTES

In Manchuria

In my heart flutter wings
Toward the little bright bough

On the brown hillside,
Toward the solitary tree, blossoming—
My heart flies there,
Leaving a shadow of azaleas.

In Peking

My eyes are blinded
By the flying dust of the dead.
And my heart smiles
At my own motions
In the wind.

The Ming Tombs

Blown shadows, through the grass,
Not of the kings,
But of the builders and carriers . . .

It is the kings now who seem chained,
And the others free.

In Shantung

A burnished magpie
Strutting in the sun
Claiming a path among furrows of rice—
But in the distance
The quiet trot
Of a blue-coated horseman.

CHINESE DRAWINGS

A Father

There is a fruit, my son,
Bitter to the taste at first

But afterward sweet . . .
It is called advice.

A Tea-Girl

When the fish-eyes of water
Bubble into crab-eyes—
Tea!

A Wanderer

Last night is a thousand years ago—
But tomorrow is a new mist.

A Lover

The plums and cherries are blossoming,
My heart, too, is unsheathing from winter—
And it has all happened in one day.

A Vendor of Rose-Bushes

I am very poor,
Anyone who can buy from me
Ought to do it.

A Painter

I cannot paint
The growth of the spirit,
But I can paint an old man
Watching the smoke of incense
Join the sky.

A Lady

She does not see the tea her servant brings
Into the garden,
Her hands have fallen down from the instrument
She was playing,
But the strings can still answer
The cold fingers of autumn.

A Scholar

Having won his diploma,
He rides a horse of air
Through ten miles of the color
Of apricot blossoms.

A Philosopher

What though they conquer us?
The tea has come.
In at most nine hundred years,
Someone will conquer them.

A Horseman

Beyond him are many inlets curving among mountains
And on the way a temple,
And there is gold on the harness of his horse
Whose head and foot are uplifted together . . .
But the rider sits quiet now,
As he rides toward the shadow
Of the second willow.

TILES

Chinese magicians had conjured their chance,
And they hunted, with their hooded birds of glee,
The heat that rises from the summer grass

And shakes against the sea.
And when they had caught a wide expanse
In nets of careful wizardry,
They colored it like molten glass
For roofs, imperially,
With blue from a cavern, green from a morass
And yellow from weeds in the heart of the sea,
And they laid long rows on the dwellings of romance
In perfect alchemy—
And before they ascended like a peal of brass,
They and their tiptoeing hawks of glee
Had topped all China with a roof that slants
And shakes against the sea.

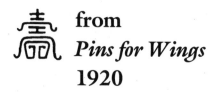 from
Pins for Wings
1920

E. E. CUMMINGS

much ado
about the alphabet

T. S. ELIOT

the wedding cake
of two tired cultures

ROBERT FROST

paintings by the family
in birch-bark frames

D. H. LAWRENCE

lovers
eating thistle-pie

CARL SANDBURG

a snow-pudding
of fists

GEORGE SANTAYANA

a withered
rose-window

GERTRUDE STEIN

wings rotting
under water

WALLACE STEVENS

the shine of a match
in an empty pipe

HARRIET MONROE

the Mother Superior
considers lingerie

EZRA POUND

a book-worm
in tights

WILLIAM CARLOS WILLIAMS

carbolic acid
in love

WILLIAM BUTLER YEATS

a pot of mould
at the foot of the rainbow

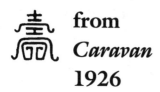 **from**
Caravan
1926

O HUNTED HUNTRESS

O hunted Huntress, up the shore
Springs a white fawn for your dart,
And after you a night-black boar
Closes in upon your heart!
But keep your undeviating eyes
Upon that bright, escaping head—
Aim incessant where he flies,
Follow where those wild feet have fled.
Though you are mortally beset,
Toward the black boar never glance,
Be but swift and so forget
That a bow is no deliverance,
That barbs are slender and would bend
In so uncouth and thick a pelt—
That he would seize you and would rend
The very hand with which you dealt.
Look toward the fawn, the flashing white,
Hope not to flee but to pursue,
Before the onset of the night—
Before the fawn shall blacken too.

WISTARIA

Clouds dream and disappear;
Waters dream in a rainbow and are gone;
Fire-dreams change with the sun
Or when a poppy closes;
But now is the time of year
For the dark earth, one by one,
To dream quieter dreams. And nothing she has ever done
Has given more ease
To her perplexities
Than the dreaming of dreams like these:
Not irises,
Not any spear
Of lilies nor cup of roses,
But these pale, purple images,
As if, from willows or from pepper-trees,
Shadows were glimmering on the Buddha's knees.

THE CITY

I'm a little of everything
        And nothing much,
I've heard a tenor sing,
        Read such and such,
Quoted what someone says,
        Does or intends,
Greeted acquaintances,
        Forgotten friends.

A WINTER CAT-TAIL

Cat-tail standing in the ice,
Elderly New Englander
Standing mirrored in the ice,
Thin straight stalk and ruffled fur,
Do you wonder where the wind has blown
Dandelion and golden-rod?
Or are you happier alone
With the loneliness of God?

LORENZO

I had not known that there could be
Men like Lorenzo and like me,
Both in the world and both so right
That the world is dark and the world is light.
I had not thought that anyone
Would choose the dark for dwelling on,
Would dig and delve for the bitterest roots
Of sweetest and suavest fruits.
I never had presumed to doubt
That now and then the light went out;
But I had not known that there could be
Men like Lorenzo and like me
Both in the world and both so right
That the world is dark and the world is light.
I had not guessed that joy could be
Selected for an enemy.

D. H. LAWRENCE

I

Prowling in a corridor,
Coming upon a mirror,
You lay back your torn ear,
You arch your bony spine,
You spit at your own image.

And when the housekeeper strokes your torn ear,
And thinks benignly of the alley and the night and you,
You purr awhile in the very lap you loathe
And, twenty-one inches superior to that foul image,
You forget to move your claws
And slowly, luxuriously fall asleep.

II

Now and then your mute-footed familiar leaves you;
Your beard lies back again where it belongs,
Your blue eyes relax in their slits—
And then wilderness again,
A hollow glare in the eyeball!

Do you see that the moon is on its back for you?
And has turned up the white fur of its belly
And put out a silver-haired paw?

III
After wondering a long time, I know now
That you are no man at all.
The whiteness of your flanks and loins and belly and neck
Frightens you, affronts you,
A whiteness to be sloughed off, to be left behind you like ashes,
Forgotten by the new body, by the new mind,
By the new conforming surfaces.

Women have chosen you, in your white arms.
But what have you to do with women?
Only your seeming is theirs and the falsehood of your skin.
You would lengthen your finger-nails and your teeth
To mangle these women, these people;
You would drop them behind you with your cast-off skin;
You would wonder at the glaze of their eyes;
And your new pelt would contract and would tremble down your spine
Before it settled into place;
And you would steal away, solitary,
To try in the wind the vibrancies of a new voice.

Only your reddish hair is you
And those narrowing eyes,
Eyes hostile to the flesh of people and to all their motions,
Eyes penetrating their thoughts to the old marrow of the beast,
Eyes wanting a mate and the starlight,
A mate to be snarled at and covered
And stars to be known but not named.
Some day, if you are left alone
Beyond the roads, in a tough tangle of wilderness,
You will be held and torn and known to your own innermost marrow,
Will be stripped of the skin that cumbers you,
Given over from the bondage of manhood,
And will be found at last,
With the blood of marriage in your teeth.

But if you are never left alone,
Are constrained in a country of houses,

You will always be smoldering against men;
And, after yielding slowly
The nine lives of a domestic cat,
You will be worshipped by the Egyptians.

IV
The world is full again of centaurs and sphinxes;
But it is the horse-head now and the lion-head
On the bodies of men who are tired of being men
And of women who are tired of being women.
It is these who turn with you and follow you
To the hillsides that prick their flanks,
To the jungles that tear at their breasts;
It is these who forget with you
That the instep is not a galloping hoof,
That the finger-nail can not enter and climb the bark of a tree
Nor tear deep shreds
To be fed with,
And that the night can not last forever as a lordly dream
But must let in, finally, pointed barbs of light
To prick this hinge of the neck
Between what you are and what you would be,
Whether you are a man wishing to be an animal
Or an animal wishing to be a man.

TO A YOUNG INQUIRER

It is better sometimes that there be no fruit,
Only a mist of blossom blown away:
If never flower had ripened from the root
Long since, it would be Eden still, they say.

Yet if the tempering and seasoning
May come to you as they have come to me,
I wish for you the broken breath of spring
And the salt of wintry cypress by the sea.

Watch how a petal drifts upon your hand
And pales and withers. Watch another passing,
Light in the air. Watch how the waters stand
And fall along the shore, ebbing and massing.

Let only fools fathom the more or less
Of melancholy and of happiness.

LOOSEN YOUR MARROW

That little tangled thing you call your brain,
Which has not lived before nor will again
In any such compartment of distress,
Is an abominable restlessness.

Loosen your marrow from corrupting thought
And be as inattentive as you ought
To all the little motions of the will
That feed upon the happiness they kill.

Open your being to the flows of air
That form its destiny from everywhere—
And let your mind become a native feather
And not a nest of worms, tangled together.

EPITHALAMIUM AND ELEGY

My single constancy is love of life:
Because we have entered no such formal pact
As dulls devotion between man and wife,
No bland acknowledgment, no binding fact,
No mingling of betrothal with divorce,
No dated bliss, no midnight certitude,
No sad necessity, no matter of course,
No pallid answer saying why we wooed;
Because she lets me love her as I can
Moment by moment, moments that always come
Beyond the calculation of a man
For joy or pain, for epithalamium
Or for elegy, and because, when I am spent,
Life shall have had her way, shall be content
Still to confer the sweet bewilderment
On someone else, shall loosen her lovely hair
To the wind, shall turn with bountiful intent
Toward anyone at all, and I not there,

Shall offer cool papayas, pale bamboo
And amorous guava to a later comer,
And none of her gifts, not even a drop of dew,
To me who had received them many a summer.
These are not harlotries but only joy,
These are the very tiptoes of delight.
This is the happiness she gives a boy
With nothing of wickedness, nothing of spite
In that immense, delicious, naked bed
Where anyone may lie, except the dead . . .
But I shall leave her. All that there is of rest
Shall be little enough, after so much of love.
Wherever I move, she is there. Her open breast
Offers the tenderness I am dying of.
Her arm along my body like a snake
Has softly wound me into rings of sleep
And, every time again, stings me awake
And drowns me in her rhythms deep and deep . . .
Can I be tragical, in having had
My love of life by life herself subdued?
Since I am satiate with joy, can I be sad
In leaving? All that there is of solitude
Shall be little enough, after this vast embrace.
Give her some younger lover in my place.

 **from**
Cake
1926*

PROLOGUE

THE UNICORN
[*A suave and portly Chamberlain, appearing before the
 curtain and carrying his horn as a staff of office*]
Ladies and gentlemen, it will save us trouble,
Because a number of us have to double
And none of you like to come at eight-fifteen,
If you will let us cut the opening scene.
The scene was not so good, as a matter of fact,
And only complicated the first act.
It was added by the author to allow
People to come in late, as they're doing now;
But the management prefers this simpler way
Of trying to connect you with the play.
And between ourselves, the company, being nervous,
Believed this opportunity might serve us
To let you know that we have never quite
Approved of what we offer you tonight.
It hasn't any plot in the usual sense,
There's nothing pivotal, there's nothing tense.
I hope I haven't given the thing away.
This isn't at all what I was asked to say,
And I must do my best to make amends.

*Cake is loosely based upon the life of Mabel Dodge Luhan. See the note on her for the letter of April 5, 1922, and the following head-note.

I therefore beg you to imagine, friends,
A sort of drawing-room, with coal-black drapes
And drooping lights covered with purple grapes.
The Lady the play's about is giving a tea,
Assisted by her Chamberlain, that's me.
The Lady herself is sitting in the middle,
And they're listening to a fellow with a fiddle.
Then everybody talks and no one hears,
And the Lady sits in the middle, bored to tears.
That was the scene. It wasn't very much,
Except that it was done with a modern touch,
You know the sort of thing, nobody there,
Each of the guests was just an empty chair,
And we had the members of the orchestra play
Things that the empty chairs were supposed to say.
Some people thought it was funny, but it wasn't.
It's a play that either gets you, or it doesn't,
As you may judge for yourselves in just a minute.
I'm hoping that it does—because I'm in it.

ACT I

[*On a Height of Gold at the back of the stage sits a* LADY.
*Her throne is a gilded eagle with wings spread forward; her
background a tapestry of heaven against which hangs, like
a nimbus, a great gong of brass. She is resting her elbow
on an eagle-wing, her chin wearily on her thumb and
fingers. She wears an exaggerated coronet of golden eagles.
In fact everything about the* LADY *and her court is overdone,
except the two chairs, one on each side of her throne, which
are low and supported by dollar signs couchants. In one of
them sits the* UNICORN, *her Chamberlain, reading a news-
paper. To the left stands a handsome and very young*
SERVANT *with a tray of exaggerated buns and pastries.
Three other* SERVANTS *are in attendance.*]

THE LADY
The trouble with me is I'm bored with being bored.
How long this living takes! How long, O Lord!
I have had seven husbands—and that's enough, I think.

I have come through mysticism, free love, and drink.
I am offered everything money can buy,
And yet there's nothing I want—not even to die.

THE UNICORN
[*With a blow on the gong*]
The smelling salts!

THE LADY
[*Restraining one of the* SERVANTS, *with an indifferently
raised hand*]
Am I Victorian,
To be given a sniff of tears by any man?
The world has moved, since women kept their hearts
As sticky as a dish of apple tarts.
It's different now: I know what I'm about;
I am a modernist. I am tired out.
I must find me a chamberlain who understands!

THE UNICORN
[*Hastily*]
Shall it be psychoanalysis?—or glands?

THE LADY
Order me everything that you can think of.
There isn't a liquor left I want a drink of.
Order me anything. I'm desperate!

THE UNICORN
There's a famous doctor below. I had him wait.
What ho! Bring on the Psychoanalyst!
[*He strikes the gong. Four additional* SERVANTS *bring into
the Presence the* PSYCHOANALYST, *a tiny man with not
enough beard to conceal his thin neck.*]

THE PSYCHOANALYST
[*Going straight to the* LADY]
Yes, I can see at once that you resist.

THE LADY
I don't.

THE PSYCHOANALYST
You've proved it. Let me feel your dream!
  [*Feeling her pulse*]
Your need of psychospection is extreme.
Turn over on the other dream a minute.
  [*She turns over, he puts his ear on her heart and then
  beckons the* UNICORN.]
Just listen to the indican that's in it!
And the subconscious, bearing all the brunt!
  [*To the* LADY]
Do you dream better on your back or front?

THE LADY
The latter.

THE PSYCHOANALYST
Then your case is very clear.
You need to live a while on the frontier.

THE LADY
And dine on pork and beans? I won't go there.

THE PSYCHOANALYST
You'll have a nervous breakdown.

THE LADY
I don't care.

THE PSYCHOANALYST
O Lady, you are doing very wrong!
Do you want to know what made me big and strong?

THE LADY
  [*Amazed*]
Were you ever any smaller?

THE PSYCHOANALYST
Well, I'm lean;
But I've changed a twelve-size collar for fourteen,
All in a month, since I have learned to go
Two or three times a day to a picture-show.

I hated the movies once, I used to cry
When I had to visit them. The reason why?
In love with Mary Pickford, that was all,
And used to try to cure it with baseball.
I even told myself she wasn't pretty.
But now I travel, city after city,
To see a Pickford picture and I write
A love-letter to Mary every night.
Today my heart makes only happy sounds,
And Lady, I have gained eleven pounds.

    THE LADY
What has all this to do with me?

    THE PSYCHOANALYST
Your case is different. Let me see.

    THE LADY
I'm bored with him. Pay him his fee.

    THE PSYCHOANALYST
    [*Thoughtful*]
To loosen up your frontier libido,
I recommend for you—

    THE LADY
    [*Peremptory*]
Please go.

    THE PSYCHOANALYST
    [*Resentful*]
You're frivolous. I might have known—

    THE LADY
You leave my libido alone!
    [*Four* SERVANTS *abruptly remove the aggrieved Specialist.*]

    THE LADY
I want some cake, give me some cake,
No, not cake, bread with raisins.
No, not bread with raisins,

I want some cake. Give me some cake.
[*The* CAKE-SERVANT *advances with his tray; she selects
a large piece of cake.*]

THE UNICORN
Why did you take it?

THE LADY
Because it was there.

THE UNICORN
I ask, merely to be asking.

THE LADY
I eat, merely to be eating—
Not that I care.

THE UNICORN
[*Crossing to the other chair*]
I spoke that you might hear the sound of my voice,
To prove that you are not alone in the world,
That you have me beside you.

THE LADY
If you were not beside me,
I should be beside myself.

THE UNICORN
You show a gift for words, my Lady.
You should write.

THE LADY
Yes, that might help me.
What shall I write?

THE UNICORN
You must have experience
To be able to write.

THE LADY
I have had seven husbands!

THE UNICORN
You have had the ordinary life of the modern woman,
But that's not experience.
You must have experience.

THE LADY
[*Eagerly*]
Bring me some experience.

THE UNICORN
What ho, experience!
[*He strikes the gong. Eight* SERVANTS *enter, four from each side, and bow to her in a semi-circle.*]

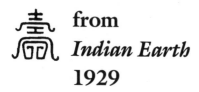 **from**
Indian Earth
1929

THE BATS

1

In the June twilight, we looked without knowing why
At the peaked gable of a corner house;
And while we looked, a hundred bats flew out
From the patterned eaves over the beach and the lake;
And as soon as they had wavered high out of sight,
Came other hundreds at eight intervals:
Like black leaves dropping and gathered up again
In their own wind and blown to the setting sun.

2

After the firm birds of water and the bright birds of trees,
After the transparent golden air of day,
It is magical to see a host of shadows
Trembling upward over the mountain-top,
Or hovering past a balconied window at midnight
And flaking singly toward a mottled moon.
Even the bats are beautiful in Chapala
Where shadows leave the breast and fly away.

MOONLIGHT RAIN

Once in Chapala there was a moon and music;
And before the clouds blew nearer to the moon,

Guitar and harp and violins and voices
Were singing on the beach before the rain
Under the moonlight, singing of a swallow,
And still were singing after the lake-rain fell,
Singing of a little deer that comes down from the mountain
Only to places that are very quiet.

TO MY MOTHER
CONCERNING A CHAPALA SUNSET

To you, at evening, I exclaim aloud—
Why have you never seen the range of light
That lives along Chapala mountain-tops
With massive interchange of sun and moon?
And yet, before I was born, you had often watched,
On mountain-clouds as beautiful as these,
Changes of light that I shall never see
In this confused and separating world.

MARKET-DAY

1

On Saturdays they steer with the west wind
From the adobe houses of San Luis,
From Jocotepec, Tuzcueca, Tizapan,
Bringing broad-woven hats, leafy baskets of cheese,
Oranges, limes, zarapes and earthenware.
And often under their waxing waning sails,
To cheer Chapala, comes a bearded singer
As blind as Homer once, in other towns.

2

A sail crumples under the setting sun;
And barefoot fellows, leaning their weight on poles,
Walk half the way from lofty prow to stern
And hurry back again till, near the beach,
Wading the waves with copper thighs, dragging
The loosened rudder, they heave it up the sand
For double anchorage; then, on their shoulders,
They bring ashore their women and their wares.

A COUNTRYMAN

Swinging a blanket over his left shoulder,
Wearing its bright-colored heart upon his sleeve,
He takes up his bed and walks. It serves him well
For warmth at night on his mat, or in the evening
Against a wind that pours along the lake.
Even at noon it hangs from his neck to his ankle,
Unneeded in the sun except as a king
Always has need to be wearing majesty.

A BOATMAN

In a pool of shadow floating cool on the sand,
As if for a fish to lean in motionless,
The boatman lies asleep, hands under head,
Dreaming of death; and close to him as a weed
Is to a fish, his hat is sleeping too . . .
How intimate he is with the good earth,
As if, long buried, he were still alive
Among the many other mounds of sand.

LOVERS

From somewhere over the houses, through the silence,
Through the late night, come windy ripples of music.
There's a lighted cigarette-end in the black street,
Moving beside the music he has brought her.
Behind a shuttered window, there's a girl
Smiling into her pillow. And now by her hand
There's a candle lighted and put out again.
And the shadow of a bird leaves its perch for a smaller twig.

A BEAUTIFUL MEXICAN

There where she sips her wine, her copper brow
Is itself the sunset. Now she has lifted her eyes,
And they are evening stars. I have seen many

Mexican sunsets—but never before had I seen one
Come down from the mountain to be a beautiful woman,
To shadow a table with a dusk of light
From a bare arm and then, alas, to rise
And turn and go, leaving a sudden darkness.

A FOREIGNER

Chapala still remembers the foreigner
Who came with a pale red beard and pale blue eyes
And a pale white skin that covered a dark soul;
They remember the night when he thought he saw a hand
Reach through a broken window and fumble at a lock;
They remember a tree on the beach where he used to sit
And ask the burros questions about peace;
They remember him walking, walking away from something.

THIS REED[1]

What is this reed that grows tall in the river-bed?
They make their plaited mats of it to lie on,
They gather it from the river-beds and make mats of it
And soften their earthen floors with it to lie on . . .
Yesterday noon I saw the mat I needed,
Six feet of reeds torn loose from the river-bed,
A mat—which I might peacefully have lain on—
Go blowing down the lake before the wind.

WATER-HYACINTHS

I

What is so permanent as a first love,
Except the impermanence of later loves?
. . . I sit in a rowboat, watching hyacinths
Float down the lake and thinking about people,
How they insinuate and change and vanish,

1. This poem was called "Tulé" when it first appeared in *Indian Earth*. It was slightly rewritten and called "This Reed" when it was reprinted in *Book of Lyrics* (1955).

How everyone leaves everyone alone,
How even the look of a belovèd child
Is lesser solace than a mountain-rim.

II

Have I a grievance then against my friends,
Against my lovers? Is love so unavailing,
That here in a rowboat I shrug my naked shoulder
And watch the hyacinths go down the lake?
Do words that were light as air on living lips
Last longer when they crumble underground?
And is the soul an insecurer thing,
Less intimate, than the connecting earth?

IDOLS

1

They must have buried him away from the lake
Lest he be discontented with his grave
And forsaking the image at his ear, rise up
And sail. No edge of water was visible
From where he had lain so many hundred years
That every bone was fibrous like old wood,
And his moony skull came crumbling in my hand
When I removed the god that whispered there.

2

Within that skull hate had once eaten, and love
Had spun its intricate iridescent web,
And then the worms and the wet earth had worn
Both love and hate down to the marrow-bone.
Fingers that mingle now with yellow roots
And indeterminably feed the world
May once have baked the fingers of this god
That, still intact, grope after human clay.

3

What surer god have I ever seen than this
Which I deliver from an earthen womb,
This idol made of clay, made of man,
This fantasy, this mute, insensate whim

Enduring still beside its maker's dust?
These are the open eyes, the lips that speak
Wonderful things, this is the living thought
That make the man alive and alive again.

4

Lie close to me, my poem, and comfort me,
Console me with substance lovelier than mine,
Breathe me alive a thousand years from now,
Whisper—beside that rim of an empty moon,
Under the earth, the moon I thought with once—
That once to have thought, once to have used the earth,
Is to have made a god more durable
Than flesh and bone. Lie close to me, my poem.

A DANCE FOR CHRIST
(San Felipe)

THE priest was waiting, but the church was bare.
The altar waited and the candle-flare
And paper flowers and a wooden brother.
We stood in the cold and looked at one another.
"Come," said an Indian to the foreign priest,
"Say mass and we'll go to bed," without in the least
Setting ahead the mind of that strange man.
It was not at midnight that the mass began
But at four o'clock on the morning of Christmas day.
"There'll be more audience," was all he would say.
A few at a time, they assembled out of their beds
With blankets wound around their quiet heads;
And bending one by one on the cold stone,
The women waited, or an old man knelt alone.
Four children in the pulpit, as birds might perch,
Patiently watched in the nocturnal church.
At last in the gallery a water-bird,
A whistle dipped in a cup, warbled and stirred
The standers-by and a violin-string sufficed
To tell them simply of the birth of Christ.
And so a child was born and in the breath
Of Roman words was crucified to death—
And an Indian child in the pulpit, standing asleep,

Fell down the steps but was allowed to creep
Softly aloft again, to watch the birth
Alike of Christian and of pagan earth.
Then after the sermon and the giving of bread
In remembrance of one who was given a stone instead,
A sudden savage sound broke through the door.
There fell a thud of dancing on the floor;
And feathered figures in the candle-light
Brought their own festival out of the night.
They wove their native steps wanton and wild
Before the cradle of a foreign child,
They blessed with ardors of bloodshed and of war
The foreign child whom they were dancing for,
They served and loved and slew with all their might
The infant Jesus on that naked night,
And then were gone—leaving a cross to save
Belated Christians in an empty nave.

A DANCE FOR RAIN
(Cochiti)

You may never see rain, unless you see
   A dance for rain at Cochiti,
Never hear thunder in the air
Unless you hear the thunder there,
Nor know the lightning in the sky
If there's no pole to know it by.
They dipped the pole just as I came,
And I can never be the same
Since those feathers gave my brow
The touch of wind that's on it now,
Bringing over the arid lands
Butterfly gestures from Hopi hands
And holding me, till earth shall fail,
As close to earth as a fox's tail.
   I saw them, naked, dance in line
Before the candles of a leafy shrine:
Before a saint in a Christian dress
I saw them dance their holiness,
I saw them reminding him all day long
That death is weak and life is strong

And urging the fertile earth to yield
Seed from the loin and seed from the field.
   A feather in the hair and a shell at the throat
Were lifting and falling with every note
Of the chorus-voices and the drum,
Calling for the rain to come.
A fox on the back, and shaken on the thigh
Rain-cloth woven from the sky,
And under the knee a turtle-rattle
Clacking with the toes of sheep and cattle—
These were the men, their bodies painted
Earthen, with a white rain slanted;
These were the men, a windy line,
Their elbows green with a growth of pine.
And in among them, close and slow,
Women moved, the way things grow,
With a mesa-tablet on the head
And a little grassy creeping tread
And with sprays of pine moved back and forth,
While the dance of the men blew from the north,
Blew from the south and east and west
Over the field and over the breast.
And the heart was beating in the drum,
Beating for the rain to come.
   Dead men out of earlier lives,
Leaving their graves, leaving their wives,
Were partly flesh and partly clay,
And their heads were corn that was dry and gray.
They were ghosts of men and once again
They were dancing like a ghost of rain;
For the spirits of men, the more they eat,
Have happier hands and lighter feet,
And the better they dance the better they know
How to make corn and children grow.
   And so in Cochiti that day,
They slowly put the sun away
And they made a cloud and they made it break
And they made it rain for the children's sake.
And they never stopped the song or the drum
Pounding for the rain to come.
   The rain made many suns to shine,
Golden bodies in a line

With leaping feather and swaying pine.
And the brighter the bodies, the brighter the rain
Where thunder heaped it on the plain.
Arroyos had been empty, dry,
But now were running with the sky;
And the dancers' feet were in a lake,
Dancing for the people's sake.
And the hands of a ghost had made a cup
For scooping handfuls of water up;
And he poured it into a ghostly throat,
And he leaped and waved with every note
Of the dancers' feet and the songs of the drum
That had called the rain and made it come.
    For this was not a god of wood,
This was a god whose touch was good,
You could lie down in him and roll
And wet your body and wet your soul;
For this was not a god in a book,
This was a god that you tasted and took
Into a cup that you made with your hands,
Into your children and into your lands—
This was a god that you could see,
Rain, rain, in Cochiti!

A BUFFALO DANCE
(Santo Domingo)

DAWN came—
    Not yet before us, where the sun was,
But behind us on a snow-peak.

Before us were the desert-hills,
All the barer for being spotted with pinyons;
And on the ridge,
Clustered black against the cold sky,
Were figures too still to be men.

Behind us, at the open edge of the plaza,
Stood the blanketed singers and drummers:
A thick crescent they were, curving toward a star.

And the star-man was taller than the moon-men,
And taller than he was the staff
Which he raised and lowered in the rhythm of the song
With a shaking of its top-knot of buffalo-toes.

And then the figures on the hill,
Too still until now to be men,
Ran to and fro, criss-crossing the little canyons,
And changed into men
And changed into boys, into children,
And they came down the brown hill,
With rests for renewal,
Two buffaloes,
Four deer,
Two elks,
Two antelopes.

And round us,
At a distance from the waiting chorus
Whose song gave welcome to the sun
And to the godly animals,
Were men and women and children of the pueblo;
And a few of them sat on the walls of old roofless houses,
And most of them wore their blankets hooding their heads from the
    chill;
And all of them were watching and were silent,
Except the chorus
Which was earth itself
With a song
That followed
The rising and the falling of the hills.

Two buffaloes,
Bare-bodied,
High-maned;
A woman,
Broad-bosomed,
But moving like a small bird;
Four deer,
White-coated,
With white fluff on their antlers

And white lace on their legs
And with brightly embroidered kilts of old meaning;
Two antelopes
Yellow,
With white chests;
Two elks
With straight horns, green-pronged, down their shoulders:
They entered the plaza.

And the faces of the men,
Being black,
Were no longer the faces of men
But were lost in the godly presences
Of two buffaloes, four deer, two elks and two antelopes.

And now, for the dance, there was a hunter,
With eagle-feathers hung from head to ankle
And with a swinging bow and arrow.

And they danced the sun up
And carried it on their shoulders
Into the kiva,
Where it should join council with gods and men.

And soon they were back again, to dance,
Back with the sun in the plaza.

The chorus,
Darkly sculptural at dawn,
Was vivid now as a mesa topped with plumes:
Closely curved rows of brightness,
With war-bonnets, with bows and guns,
With slashes and dots and angles of red and yellow
On their heightened faces
And with sprays of evergreen, to sing by, in their hands.

And then came another hunter,
Naked, slim and black,
With a small sharp helmet of black,
And he circled the dance,
Nervous, deliberate,
With his bow and arrow toward the godly animals.

Circling, foraging, pacing, pausing,
Scenting, shifting, crouching, speeding,
The buffaloes were buffaloes,
The deer were deer,
The elks were elks
And the antelopes were antelopes:
Mocassins, lean-muscled legs, rain-girdles, shells of turquoise,
Yet buffaloes, deer and elks and antelopes.

How could a short stick, held in two hands
And planted forward from a leaning back,
Turn into two legs of an antelope?
How could a short stick planted forward
Turn into two legs of an elk?
How could a short stick and the turn of a man's head
Become the sidelong poise of a listening deer?

Only the gods can tell us,
Only the gods who danced that day,
The gods who suddenly flung the beauty of animals
And the beauty of men
Into one quick rainfall rhythm of mocassins:

A steady fall, a broken fall, a fall blown circle-wise:

The buffaloes in the center;
With the woman,
Who swayed between and about them like a smooth and friendly wind;
And then the four deer, staffs in a row, feet behind them beating;
And the two antelopes, who had run with delicate hoofs and dainty
    necks, now beating a foot-song as vital as the rest;
And the elks, with their large-stepping circles;
And the powerful hunter, with his dips and his calls;
And the subtle hunter, doubtful, hopeful,
Weaving, watching
The circling, the foraging, the pacing, the pausing,
The scenting, the shifting, the crouching, the springing;
And then the quick beat again
Of the mocassins of godly men . . .

All day they followed,
Slow as the sun,

Swift as the rain,
Through centuries . . .

All day the strong voices
In unison . . .

Till at sunset,
The chorus,
Ending its song and its drums,
Made us wonder why the wind had died on the moment,
Why the heart had ceased from hearing itself,
Where the water was gone that had been heaving through the ditches
And where the hoofs were gone from beating on the sky.

Dead, ceased, gone?
They?
Or we?

We saw, that night, the shadow,
Passing,
Of a hundred years upon a thousand years.

And a larger earth
Absolved us
Of ourselves
With a song of ourselves,
Of godly animals,
Of godly men
Who follow forever
The rising and the falling of the hills,
Deer, buffalo, elk, antelope, hunter,
Our thighs and ankles painted with the red adobe and the white rain,
Our breast and forehead with the turquoise sky.

EAGLE DANCE
(Tesuque)

THEY paint us in our houses
To be pure in the plaza:
They know that we eat, sleep, laugh and are men;
But they paint us in our houses,

To be eagles.
And so we have taught our feet a worthy dance,
Worthy of the white down blowing on our chests,
Whirling in the sky on eagles.
And so our women think of us with beaks
That bite at the sun,
And our feathered bodies are become
Houses of women. . . .
But our feet are the feet of eagles,
Patterning free paths.

EAGLE DANCE
(Walpi)

SLOWLY we match our wings and tip them with stone,
Slowly we leave our nest, slowly we own
The azure world, slowly we weave our way in space,
Slowly we face
The sun.
And under our wings deers' ankles ripple and run
Through the sky
And in the mew of our beaks coyotes cry.
And our inner feathers are beaten by the upper airs
Full of men's prayers. . .
Slow and swift,
Swift and slow,
Downward we drift,
Upward we go—
Then down again, down to these Hopi hands
That crush our wings with rock and make demands
Through a dead eagle soaring to the sun
That their will be done. . . .
Ghostly we face the sun
And under our wings deers' ankles ripple and run
And in the mew of our beaks coyotes cry—
"I—I!"

SNAKE DANCE
(Hotevilla)

We are clean for them now, as naked-clean as they are,
We go out for them now and we meet them with our hands.
Bullsnakes, rattlesnakes, whipsnakes, we compare
Our cleanness with their cleanness. The sun stands
Witness, the moon stands witness. The dawn joins
Their scales with our flesh, the evening quiets their rattles.
We can feel their tails soothing along our loins
Like the feathers on our fathers after battles.
For their fathers were our fathers. We are brothers
Born of the earth and brothers in the sun;
And our destiny is only one another's,
However apart the races we have run.
Out of the earth we came, the sons of kings;
For the daughters of serpent-kings had offered grace
To our fathers and had formed us under their wings
To be worthy of light at last, body and face.
Out of the earth we came, into this open
Largeness of light, into this world we see
Lifted and laid along, broken and slopen,
This world that heaves toward heaven eternally.
We have found them, we have brought them, and we know them
As kin of us, because our fathers said:
As we have always shown them, you must show them
That kinship in the world is never dead.
Come then, O bullsnake, wake from your slow search
Across the desert. Here are your very kin.
Dart not away from us, whipsnake, but perch
Your head among your people molded in
A greater shape yet touching the earth like you.
Leave off your rattling, rattlesnake, leave off
Your coiling, your venom. There is only dew
Under the starlight. Let our people cough
In the blowing sand and hide their faces, oh still
Receive them, know them, live with them in peace.
They want no rocks from you, none of your hill.
Uncoil again, lie on our arms, and cease
From the wars our fathers ceased from, be again
Close to your cousins, listen to our song.
Dance with us, kinsfolk, be with us as men

Descended from common ancestors, belong
To none but those who join yourselves and us.
Oh listen to the feathers that can weave
Only enchantment and to the words we sing,
The feet we touch the earth with. Help us believe
That our ancestors are still remembering.
Go back to them with sacred meal, go back
Down through the earth, oh be our messengers!
Tell them with reverence, tell them our lack;
Tell them we have no roots, but a sap that stirs

Forever unrooted upward to the sky.
But tell them also, tell them of our song
Downward from heaven, back where we belong.
Oh north, east, west and south, tell them we die!

SHALAKO
(*Zuñi*)

Young men and wives, you are bold,—
Your little new hands have made little new houses of clay.
Newcomers, we are old
And we bless your boldness. In our far house this day
We have been told
Of your boldness; and we have arisen and come away
From the house the mountains have made us, where alone
With the mountains forever we abide in stone.
We have come down from the fastness of age, we have come down
To bid you all, within your little town,
While time is yours to deal with: deal with it well.
Out of a marriage-bed
Rise ever the sublime
Dead,
Who shall dwell
Among the mountains and dispel
Mortality and time.
Lift up your beams, place them on walls of clay.
Make doors and enter them, make beds and lay
Your bodies down on them, make cradles, make
New beams and walls and doors and let them break
When break they must,

Beams, walls and doors and bodies, into dust.
Behold us maned with buffaloes' dead manes,
And beaked with beaks beyond man's memory
Of birds, and risen through endless suns and rains
To a great stature and final dignity.
Ahead of your boldness, we were bold.
We are the old
Who having time to deal with, dealt with it well
And are now to time and death inviolable.
Clothed in eternal buffaloes and birds,
We converse in mountain-peaks instead of words.
But we still have words for you. We bid you build
New houses that your ancestors have willed,
To hold new bodies adding to the dead.
These are our words. You have heard what we have said.

from
The Jade Mountain
A Chinese Anthology,
Being Three Hundred Poems
of the T'ang Dynasty 618–906
1929 *

LI PO

In the Quiet Night

So bright a gleam on the foot of my bed—
Could there have been a frost already?
Lifting myself to look, I found that it was moonlight.
Sinking back again, I thought suddenly of home.

A Sigh from a Staircase of Jade
(Written to Music)

Her jade-white staircase is cold with dew;
Her silk soles are wet, she lingered there so long . . .
Behind her closed casement, why is she still waiting,
Watching through its crystal pane the glow of the autumn moon?

* For WB's comments on these translations from the Chinese see "Translating Chinese Poetry" and "The Persistence of Poetry" in the prose section. The six poets included here are those most often considered the best of the T'ang poets. For a biography of WB's co-translator, Kiang Kang-hu, see the comment before the letter of July 20, 1923 and the essay in the prose section "Remembering a Gentle Scholar."

A Farewell to Mêng Hao-jan
on His Way to Yang-chou

You have left me behind, old friend, at the Yellow Crane Terrace,
On your way to visit Yang-chou in the misty month of flowers;
Your sail, a single shadow, becomes one with the blue sky,
Till now I see only the river, on its way to heaven.

A Message to Mêng Hao-jan

Master, I hail you from my heart,
And your fame arisen to the skies. . . .
Renouncing in ruddy youth the importance of hat and chariot,
You chose pine-trees and clouds; and now, white-haired,
Drunk with the moon, a sage of dreams,
Flower-bewitched, you are deaf to the Emperor . . .
High mountain, how I long to reach you,
Breathing your sweetness even here!

A Farewell to a Friend

With a blue line of mountains north of the wall,
And east of the city a white curve of water,
Here you must leave me and drift away
Like a loosened water-plant hundreds of miles. . . .
I shall think of you in a floating cloud;
So in the sunset think of me.
. . . We wave our hands to say good-bye,
And my horse is neighing again and again.

On Climbing in Nan-king
to the Terrace of Phœnixes

Phœnixes that played here once, so that the place was named for them,
Have abandoned it now to this desolate river;
The paths of Wu Palace are crooked with weeds;
The garments of Chin are ancient dust.
. . . Like this green horizon halving the Three Peaks,

Like this Island of White Egrets dividing the river,
A cloud has arisen between the Light of Heaven and me,
To hide his city from my melancholy heart.

Down Chung-nan Mountain to
the Kind Pillow and Bowl of Hu Ssü

Down the blue mountain in the evening,
Moonlight was my homeward escort.
Looking back, I saw my path
Lie in levels of deep shadow . . .
I was passing the farm-house of a friend,
When his children called from a gate of thorn
And led me twining through jade bamboos
Where green vines caught and held my clothes.
And I was glad of a chance to rest
And glad of a chance to drink with my friend. . . .
We sang to the tune of the wind in the pines;
And we finished our songs as the stars went down,
When, I being drunk and my friend more than happy,
Between us we forgot the world.

TU FU

On Meeting Li Kuêi-nien Down the River

I met you often when you were visiting princes
And when you were playing in noblemen's halls.
. . . Spring passes. . . . Far down the river now,
I find you alone under falling petals.

On a Moonlight Night

Far off in Fu-chou she is watching the moonlight,
Watching it alone from the window of her chamber—
For our boy and girl, poor little babes,
Are too young to know where the Capital is.
Her cloudy hair is sweet with mist,

Her jade-white shoulder is cold in the moon.
. . . When shall we lie again, with no more tears,
Watching this bright light on our screen?

A Spring View

Though a country be sundered, hills and rivers endure;
And spring comes green again to trees and grasses
Where petals have been shed like tears
And lonely birds have sung their grief.
. . . After the war-fires of three months,
One message from home is worth a ton of gold.
. . . I stroke my white hair. It has grown too thin
To hold the hairpins any more.

A Night-Vigil in the
Left Court of the Palace

Flowers are shadowed, the palace darkens,
Birds twitter by for a place to perch;
Heaven's ten thousand windows are twinkling,
And nine cloud-terraces are gleaming in the moonlight.
. . . While I wait for the golden lock to turn,
I hear jade pendants tinkling in the wind. . . .
I have a petition to present in the morning,
All night I ask what time it is.

Taking Leave of Friends
on My Way to Hua-chou

(*In the second year of Chih-tê, I escaped from the capital through
the Gate of Golden Light and went to Fêng-hsiang. In the first
year of Ch'ien-yuan, I was appointed as official to Hua-chou
from my former post of Censor. Friends and relatives gathered
and saw me leave by the same gate. And I wrote this poem.*)

This is the road by which I fled,
When the rebels had reached the west end of the city;
And terror, ever since, has clutched at my vitals

Lest some of my soul should never return.
. . . The court has come back now, filling the capital;
But the Emperor sends me away again.
Useless and old, I rein in my horse
For one last look at the thousand gates.

Remembering My Brothers
on a Moonlight Night

A wanderer hears drums portending battle.
By the first call of autumn from a wildgoose at the border,
He knows that the dews tonight will be frost.
. . . How much brighter the moonlight is at home!
O my brothers, lost and scattered,
What is life to me without you?
Yet if missives in time of peace go wrong—
What can I hope for during war?

A Farewell at Fêng-chi Station

To General Yen

This is where your comrade must leave you,
Turning at the foot of these purple mountains. . . .
When shall we lift our cups again, I wonder,
As we did last night and walk in the moon?
The region is murmuring farewell
To one who was honored through three reigns;
And back I go now to my river-village,
Into the final solitude.

Seeing Li Po in a Dream

I

There are sobs when death is the cause of parting;
But life has its partings again and again.
. . . From the poisonous damps of the southern river
You had sent me not one sign from your exile—
Till you came to me last night in a dream,

Because I am always thinking of you. . . .
I wondered if it were really you,
Venturing so long a journey.
You came to me through the green of a forest,
You disappeared by a shadowy fortress . . .
Yet out of the midmost mesh of your snare,
How could you lift your wings and use them?
. . . I woke, and the low moon's glimmer on a rafter
Seemed to be your face, still floating in the air.
. . . There were waters to cross, they were wild and tossing;
If you fell, there were dragons and river-monsters.

II

This cloud, that has drifted all day through the sky,
May, like a wanderer, never come back. . . .
Three nights now I have dreamed of you—
As tender, intimate and real as though I were awake.
And then, abruptly rising to go,
You told me the perils of adventure
By river and lake—the storms, the wrecks,
The fears that are borne on a little boat;
And, here in my doorway, you rubbed your white head
As if there were something puzzling you.
. . . Our capital teems with officious people,
While you are alone and helpless and poor.
Who says that the heavenly net never fails?
It has brought you ill fortune, old as you are.
. . . A thousand years' fame, ten thousand years' fame—
What good, when you are dead and gone?

A Song of a Painting

To General Ts'ao

O General, descended from Wêi's Emperor Wu,
You are nobler now than when a noble. . . .
Conquerors and their valor perish,
But masters of beauty live forever.
. . . With your brush-work learned from Lady Wêi
And second only to Wang Hsi-chih's,
Faithful to your art, you know no age,
Letting wealth and fame drift by like clouds.

. . . In the years of K'ai-yüan you were much with the Emperor,
Accompanied him often to the Court of the South Wind.
When the spirit left great statesmen, on walls of the Hall of Fame
The point of your brush preserved their living faces.
You crowned all the premiers with coronets of office;
You fitted all commanders with arrows at their girdles;
You made the founders of this dynasty, with every hair alive,
Seem to be just back from the fierceness of a battle.
. . . The late Emperor had a horse, known as Jade Flower,
Whom artists had copied in various poses.
They led him one day to the red marble stairs
With his eyes toward the palace in the deepening air.
Then, General, commanded to proceed with your work,
You centred all your being on a piece of silk.
And later, when your dragon-horse, born of the sky,
Had banished earthly horses for ten thousand generations,
There was one Jade Flower standing on the dais
And another by the steps, and they marvelled at each other. . . .
The Emperor rewarded you with smiles and with gifts,
While officers and men of the stud hung about and stared.
. . . Han Kan, your follower, has likewise grown proficient
At representing horses in all their attitudes;
But picturing the flesh, he fails to draw the bone—
So that even the finest are deprived of their spirit.
You, beyond the mere skill, used your art divinely—
And expressed, not only horses, but the life of a good man. . . .
Yet here you are, wandering in a world of disorder
And sketching from time to time some petty passer-by.
People note your case with the whites of their eyes.
There's nobody purer, there's nobody poorer.
. . . Read in the records, from earliest times,
How hard it is to be a great artist.

WANG WÊI

In a Retreat Among Bamboos

Leaning alone in the close bamboos,
I am playing my lute and humming a song
Too softly for anyone to hear—
Except my comrade, the bright moon.

A Parting

Friend, I have watched you down the mountain
Till now in the dark I close my thatch door. . . .
Grasses return again green in the spring,
But O my Prince of Friends, do you?

One-Hearted

When those red berries come in springtime,
Flushing on your southland branches,
Take home an armful, for my sake,
As a symbol of our love.

Lines

You who have come from my old country,
Tell me what has happened there!—
Was the plum, when you passed my silken window,
Opening its first cold blossom?

On the Mountain Holiday

Thinking of My Brothers in Shan-tung

All alone in a foreign land,
I am twice as homesick on this day
When brothers carry dogwood up the mountain,
Each of them a branch—and my branch missing.

An Autumn Evening in the Mountains

After rain the empty mountain
Stands autumnal in the evening,
Moonlight in its groves of pine,
Stones of crystal in its brooks.
Bamboos whisper of washer-girls bound home,
Lotus-leaves yield before a fisher-boat—

And what does it matter that springtime has gone,
While you are here, O Prince of Friends?

My Retreat at Mount Chung-nan

My heart in middle age found the Way,
And I came to dwell at the foot of this mountain.
When the spirit moves, I wander alone
Amid beauty that is all for me. . . .
I will walk till the water checks my path,
Then sit and watch the rising clouds—
And some day meet an old wood-cutter
And talk and laugh and never return.

In My Lodge at Wang-ch'üan
After a Long Rain

The woods have stored the rain, and slow comes the smoke
As rice is cooked on faggots and carried to the fields;
Over the quiet marsh-land flies a white egret,
And mango-birds are singing in the full summer trees. . . .
I have learned to watch in peace the mountain morning-glories,
To eat split dewy sunflower-seeds under a bough of pine,
To yield the post of honor to any boor at all . . .
Why should I frighten sea-gulls, even with a thought?

MÊNG HAO-JAN

A Night-Mooring on the Chien-tê River

While my little boat moves on its mooring of mist,
And daylight wanes, old memories begin. . . .
How wide the world was, how close the trees to heaven,
And how clear in the water the nearness of the moon!

A Spring Morning

I awake light-hearted this morning of spring,
Everywhere round me the singing of birds—
But now I remember the night, the storm,
And I wonder how many blossoms were broken.

On Returning at the Year's End
to Chung-nan Mountain

I petition no more at the north palace-gate.
. . . To this tumble-down hut on Chung-nan Mountain
I was banished for my blunders, by a wise ruler.
I have been sick so long I see none of my friends.
My white hairs hasten my decline,
Like pale beams ending the old year.
Therefore I lie awake and ponder
On the pine-shadowed moonlight in my empty window.

Stopping at a Friend's Farm-House

Preparing me chicken and rice, old friend,
You entertain me at your farm.
We watch the green trees that circle your village
And the pale blue of outlying mountains.
We open your window over garden and field,
To talk mulberry and hemp with our cups in our hands.
. . . Wait till the Mountain Holiday—
I am coming again in chrysanthemum time.

From a Mooring on the T'ung-lu
to a Friend in Yang-chou

With monkeys whimpering on the shadowy mountain,
And the river rushing through the night,
And a wind in the leaves along both banks,
And the moon athwart my solitary sail,
I, a stranger in this inland district,

Homesick for my Yang-chou friends,
Send eastward two long streams of tears
To find the nearest touch of the sea.

Taking Leave of Wang Wêi

Slow and reluctant, I have waited
Day after day, till now I must go.
How sweet the road-side flowers might be
If they did not mean good-bye, old friend.
The Lords of the Realm are harsh to us
And men of affairs are not our kind.
I will turn back home, I will say no more,
I will close the gate of my old garden.

On Climbing Orchid Mountain
in the Autumn

To Chang

On a northern peak among white clouds
You have found your hermitage of peace;
And now, as I climb this mountain to see you,
High with the wildgeese flies my heart.
The quiet dusk might seem a little sad
If this autumn weather were not so brisk and clear;
I look down at the river bank, with homeward-bound villagers
Resting on the sand till the ferry returns;
There are trees at the horizon like a row of grasses
And against the river's rim an island like the moon. . . .
I hope that you will come and meet me, bringing a basket of wine—
And we'll celebrate together the Mountain Holiday.

TS'ÊN TS'AN

On Meeting a Messenger to the Capital

It's a long way home, a long way east.
I am old and my sleeve is wet with tears.

We meet on horseback. I have no means of writing.
Tell them three words: "He is safe."

A Message to Censor Tu Fu
at His Office in the Left Court

Together we officials climbed vermilion steps,
To be parted by the purple walls . . .
Our procession, which entered the palace at dawn,
Leaves fragrant now at dusk with imperial incense.
. . . Grey heads may grieve for a fallen flower,
Or blue clouds envy a lilting bird;
But this reign is of heaven, nothing goes wrong,
There have been almost no petitions.

A Song of Running-Horse River

In Farewell to General Fêng of the Western Expedition

Look how swift to the snowy sea races Running-Horse River!—
And sand, up from the desert, flies yellow into heaven.
This Ninth-month night is blowing cold at Wheel Tower,
And valleys, like peck measures, fill with the broken boulders
That downward, headlong, follow the wind.
. . . In spite of grey grasses, Tartar horses are plump;
West of the Hill of Gold, smoke and dust gather.
O General of the Chinese troops, start your campaign!
Keep your iron armor on all night long,
Send your soldiers forward with a clattering of weapons!
. . . While the sharp wind's point cuts the face like a knife,
And snowy sweat steams on the horses' backs,
Freezing a pattern of five-flower coins,
Your challenge from camp, from an inkstand of ice,
Has chilled the barbarian chieftain's heart.
You will have no more need of an actual battle!—
We await the news of victory, here at the western pass!

A Song of White Snow

In Farewell to Field-Clerk Wu Going Home

The north wind rolls the white grasses and breaks them;
And the Eighth-month snow across the Tartar sky
Is like a spring gale, come up in the night,
Blowing open the petals of ten thousand pear-trees.
It enters the pearl blinds, it wets the silk curtains;
A fur coat feels cold, a cotton mat flimsy;
Bows become rigid, can hardly be drawn
And the metal of armor congeals on the men;
The sand-sea deepens with fathomless ice,
And darkness masses its endless clouds;
But we drink to our guest bound home from camp,
And play him barbarian lutes, guitars, harps;
Till at dusk, when the drifts are crushing our tents
And our frozen red flags cannot flutter in the wind,
We watch him through Wheel-Tower Gate going eastward
Into the snow-mounds of Heaven-Peak Road. . . .
And then he disappears at the turn of the pass,
Leaving behind him only hoof-prints.

WÊI YING-WU

An Autumn Night Message

To Ch'iu

As I walk in the cool of the autumn night,
Thinking of you, singing my poem,
I hear a mountain pine-cone fall. . . .
You also seem to be awake.

A Greeting on the Huai River
to My Old Friends from Liang-ch'üan

We used to be companions on the Kiang and the Han,
And as often as we met, we were likely to be tipsy.
Since we left one another, floating apart like clouds,

Ten years have run like water—till at last we join again.
And we talk again and laugh again just as in earlier days,
Except that the hair on our heads is tinged now with grey. . . .
Why not come along, then, all of us together,
And face the autumn mountains and sail along the Huai?

A Farewell in the Evening Rain

To Li Ts'ao

Is it raining on the river all the way to Ch'u?—
The evening bell comes to us from Nan-king.
Your wet sail drags and is loath to be going
And shadowy birds are flying slow.
We cannot see the deep ocean-gate—
Only the boughs at Pu-kou, newly dripping.
Likewise, because of our great love,
There are threads of water on our faces.

Entertaining Literary Men
in My Official Residence
on a Rainy Day

Outside are insignia, shown in state;
But here are sweet incense-clouds, quietly ours.
Wind and rain, coming in from sea,
Have cooled this pavilion above the lake
And driven the feverish heat away
From where my eminent guests are gathered.
. . . Ashamed though I am of my high position
While people lead unhappy lives,
Let us reasonably banish care
And just be friends, enjoying nature.
Though we have to go without fish and meat,
There are fruits and vegetables aplenty.
. . . We bow, we take our cups of wine,
We give our attention to beautiful poems.
When the mind is exalted, the body is lightened
And feels as if it could float in the wind.
. . . Su-chou is famed as a center of letters;

And all you writers, coming here,
Prove that the name of a great land
Is made by better things than wealth.

Mooring at Twilight in Yü-yi District

Furling my sail near the town of Huai,
I find for harbor a little cove
Where a sudden breeze whips up the waves.
. . . The sun is growing dim now and sinks in the dusk.
People are coming home. The bright mountain-peak darkens.
Wildgeese fly down to an island of white weeds.
. . . At midnight I think of a northern city-gate,
And I hear a bell tolling between me and sleep.

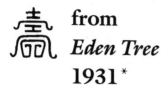 from
Eden Tree
1931 *

I

Let the book open, let the page attest
Which man is loneliest.
Although the day
Shine sharp and hold its head high
Among mountains, compare your lives and say
Which one is loneliest . . .
This is no book of youth,
Loving to die,
This is the truth,
This is I.

V

Foregoing you, Celia, I gave allegiance to one
Unlike you as the moon is to the sun . . .
He was a flower
Of isolate boyhood,—
With a body such as might not have stepped upon earth before.
Absent from evil, absent from good,
He was regardless of everything that had seemed beauty to you,—

* In 1936 for *Selected Poems*, WB, with the assistance of Robert Hunt, extensively revised *Eden Tree*. The text used here is from that revision. The only part of *Eden Tree* that WB republished after 1936 was Section XXVII, reprinted here, which he very slightly changed and called "No Anodyne." It appeared in *Book of Lyrics*.

For he was lone. He took loneliness as the one due
In life and was ready to die.
Do you wonder that I,
Without you beside me to give power
To opposing virtue, was dazzled and believed
In nothing either done or undone?
In your grave were you grieved
By this figure in the sun,
By this god of the moment who became my god?
The single self, none other, was the faith that shone
Out of his life, the strange beauty of things,—
Not mirrors, not finger-rings,
Not trinkets, but things lifted up
On a tripod
Of lightning, like wine in a cup
To quick lips,
Quips
That caught God in a sentence and disposed of books,
Quick looks,
Quick willingness, quick limb to limb,
Quick love,
Quick elements that man is mattered of,
Everything quick and nothing slow like you:
Quick youth, quick life, no sense of old or new,
But everything now and due among the seraphim.
I seemed to watch while Blake was drawing him.
"In the beginning was the word,"—"That is all ye need to know,"
All that I needed—till the entire sun
Went out one day, when death came quick as life. It was long ago,
It was yesterday, it was tomorrow, it was done.

XXIV

Have another, she said, and he did,
And he hid
His blurred head in her breast, but with a glass
At his lips in his limp hands and many words
Burbling toward her that meant nothing
Of what they meant to mean,
While she was soothing
His hot temples. He could feel her lips lean

Toward his own. The diagonal far-away birds
Were singing in the dawn. He could feel them pass
The thin spires of St. Patrick's, brushing the bells with their wings,
Till there was an iron echo of singing.
He felt lost and yet clean.
He was winging
As cleanly as they were, cleaving the air
Of Egypt, brushing a pyramid,
Bringing music from the lips of kings
Long dead—
And wisdom somehow whirling in his head . . .

Lilith put him to bed.

But he was up again.
He was still there singing. There was an undertone
Of himself.
He had forgotten what it meant,
He had lost his intent.
He saw only ornaments upon a shelf
Shining in the room as though they were important, as though
They were the world of men he had known
But were more important after all than men.
The piano-keys were widening into a circle of now.
There was no question of how:
It happened like destiny, this touch on the keys,
There was a hand on his knees,
There was a voice saying nothing but saying it with a sound
That only spring leaves make breaking through the ground.
There was Eden, the garden again, realized and whole.
He could control
All that there was, with a toss of his head,
Though his eyes dragged and his laugh was an empty thing.
He was David, he could sing
Though the song was dim.
And sing he did, long after Lilith ceased listening to him.

Day after that and nights and morns and noons,
He found his tunes
In the impersonal roundness of a bottle of whiskey or gin.
He could touch the sheer side of it for love.
He could shove
The thing away and then drag it back again

And yet not have to move
Closer to a woman or be hoarse among men
With their stable-jokes or enter their stale songs
With a stale voice. He could steady himself by himself,
He could steal a superior drink from a secret shelf
And be Caesar, conquerer of the thinking world
That was furled
As the crystal of a dew-drop, his
In his fingers, a sceptered symbol of what is:
The jeweled moment made of alcohol.

Bewilderedly
He thought of Jonathan, he thought of Paul . . .
Why had men always entered where women should be,
He asked himself and in asking tried to be just.
He was drunk, he was clear, he was open, dispassionate, wise.
Why, when women were soft and intelligent bringers of ease,
Why, when women were women and shaped to the need of a male,
Why, when women were pale
As the snow on a mountain that made his awakening eyes
Content to awaken,
Should he be shaken
By the hard visage of a man confronting his?
What was all this?

I find you, Jonathan, unshaved, but dear
Beside me in my bed. I love you here.
Women are women. Women have need
Of Adam and his seed;
But men, when men love Adam, are the touch
Of God's hand on Adam. There is much
To be told about this that Eve would rather not hear.
It is no mere
Denial of life, it is something else than a loss
Of life on an immolating cross;
It is something real,
With no generation or brood:
It is the seal
Of double solitude.

And so he went on, because he breathed the brim
Of bottles at short intervals, that were maintaining him.
He had smiles

For visitors, but they were guiles
Uncorked betweenwhiles.
Nothing that he had was anything but the strength
Fed secretly into a corpse from a bottle.
He could face persons and he could feel his kindled length
Persuade them; but he could feel the air throttle
His throat suddenly with lack.
He would leave the room again
And then come back
And be a man exchanging life with men,
Because he had stolen a drink in his bedroom and been made
Unafraid
By the flickering brand
Of a fire that lingers
In the veins—and is no more fire.
Liquor, more liquor, liquor again, again!
The faces of life blurred in unmeaningness
And the words of Old Adam going their endless way
Into unconsidered ears in a vacant town,
And Adam's footsteps wandering up and down
From nowhere to nowhere and no place to stay,—
No rest, no refuge. There was nothing to do but to pass
Whiskey forever between mouth and glass.
What was this ghost of life that held his hands in fleshless fingers?
He was friended only of nothingness and left
Unsteady in the air upon no feet,
Bereft
Of all friends but of whiskey taken neat . . .

Voices and voices, my own and others vague,
Enter my sleep,—
A multitude of footsteps creep
Across my bed and plague
My rest with visitors,
Unending visitors, unending talk,
Unending faces. Let me go, O Lord, outdoors,
Let me walk! . . .

He struggled into clothes; he climbed a stubbly hill,
Stumbled and wandered
For hours.
I have squandered

My powers,
Said Adam. Where is my will? . . .
Yet in the morning he still wanted
Whiskey, and he took a tall glass for granted. . . .

His Lilith was gone—he was blind
With a sunken rage.
It was not that she might assuage
A need in him now but that dully in his mind
He suspected her of dallying with lesser love.
He fondled the hard delight of jealousy;
He gnawed at his own flesh
And felt it purr purple with a pain that he was avid of—
And then gnawed it afresh.
He made plans of revenge, filling another glass . . .

But who, after all, was she?
He would let it pass . . .
He would not, by God,—he would follow her track.
He would show her that Adam . . . the woman came back.

XXV

Passion has its hour,
Thought Adam, and there is no use when the night is over
And you have been a lover
And your thews
Have been eased,—there is no use
In making a moon of the sun.
Lilith's limbs and her face
Are sullenly demanding their own portion of space
Disentwined,
Now that night is done.
She might as well be Eve in the morning bed,
He said,
And you the commonplace
Husband whose wife even in her sleep is unresigned
To the discommoding arm
That interferes with her comfort and holds
Too heavy a weight of love against her slumbering shoulder.
She is both cold and warm

Without you, Adam. Be no moulder
Of a passion beyond natural moulds.
Hide your mouth in the folds
Of a blanket away from her, no whispers, no urgings,
No premeditated shock,—
But a gradual adjustment to the moving clock,
And to the daylit mind,
To mergings
Of your animal heat not with loins
But with other use.
Life joins
Mankind
With love,—yours and no matter whose.

XXVI

Once more, away from Lilith, Adam was aware
Of other needs than Lilith, of other need for his blood to touch blood
Than through flesh and for his heart to be at ease.
Could he find more ways than these:
Love, friendship, laughter, faith, the natural world and death?
When a man has known mating and would rest
From the interminable horizon of generations to come,
When he is numb
With the undertaking of his loins and possessed
Of the far future demanding that he share
Its horizon and give inches to its line,
He may happen to weary of mountains and the long sunshine
That alters their look and to crave the peace
Of friendship, a release
From the creative air
That breeds each morn
Men, birds and insects on its breast
And the unending and unmeaning stare
Of the new-born.
There is too much
Of life, said Adam, it is too long a river.
Has my touch
With the body of living incurred
New life going on forever
And yet winning

Nothing but this, that in the beginning
Was the unanswered Word?
I want nothing ahead.
It shall be enough when I am dead
That I am done.
I want no son,
No sentimental ration
To stay me from better food.
If life is good,
Live it, said Adam, without shifting the burden forward
And the finding out,—
Without yielding your imagination
To a rout
Of new-comers.
If your winters became their summers,
There might be reason, said Adam, for deferring
Your life to Cain's or Abel's or their issue;
But generation after generation,
It is the same tissue
Of life, the same stirring
Of the same sap into dead leaves and nothing forward
From the mountain-tops but a recurrent moon
Waxing—and waning as a man shall soon
Unless he use the sunlight of his noon . . .
Let me at once and to the quick be man,—
Let me be brave in the sun, thought Adam, let me find
Some reason for my kind
And use that reason in my own good span,
Not spend my force in blind
Continuance of a common breed
That might be blest if it should go to seed
Upon the wind.
Passion is good, he said,
And a thing to go mad
For and to be had
With no misgiving.
But there is more than this in living.
There are times when I want no face
With parted lips apprizing other lips, no heave of breast to breast
Pressed for their meaning until morning light,
When I want not the linking of loose flesh but the tight
Knowledge of equal thinking and of equal voice,

An equipoise
Of chase . . .

He drew a long breath,
Remembering the friends
He had made and lost and kept.
His heart leapt
Toward a rift of pure light let down between clouds on the
    mountain-range.
He remembered those beginnings that were never to have been ends,
Either in motive or time, the glow of young exchange
When thought was a new thing, to be shared like a wind among trees.
He could feel the breeze
Touching his temples and those other young temples,—the discoveries
Of life quickening young lips toward the truth,—
The endless eager argument of youth,—
The young friends it had made him: the five.

Wiving had taken two of them, that strange
Metamorphosis of men whose mates
Love them but own them, clean them but enclose them and contrive
Beyond intention to deform them from their fates.
For almost any man, he pondered, a wife
Makes livelihood a larger gain than life,
Consumes the force that animates
A youthful will
Toward freedom and toward fellowship.

There are fences on the sides
Of this hill,
Thought Adam, and it has to be so,—
For a fence divides
What is mine from what is yours;
And as long as life endures
Competitive, partitioned and possessed
In parcels of property, there is no way but this.
The dream that was must die in the fact that is.
A man having children becomes for them covetous
Of what seem good things.
A man dies,
A bird sings.
But even in the blue skies,

Birds quarrel and fend danger from a nest,
As our parents, with their heavier wings,
Fended for us.

There had been the dissolving years, too,
To undo
Friendship for Adam after all his caring;
There had been the settling of selfishness
Into aging veins, the unwatered slip
Of new growth from the old tree,
The small accidents of destiny
And of distances between sharing happiness.

New Hampshire once had crested in a hill,
Where blueberries grow still
But not to be gathered in those pails as then—
Since laughing boys have grown the frowns of men,—
Since boys who dived in ripples of a lake
Have gone apart, each with his chosen snake.
And since that rare,
That young New Hampshire air
Has died in grasses that no hand can rake,
No eye can watch again, no wind can shake
Alive and green again as once they grew
Keen on a hillside when the world was new . . .
O clear, cold waters edged with shadowy pine,
Cleanness that once enclosed us and that flowed
On fond young bodies, wetting our hair,
We shall be centuries dead and you still there,
A goad
To newer friendship and to the quake
Of younger hearts than mine;
But not your clarity shall be our lens
For seeing love, nor shall the long years
You bred
Between a friend and me be long enough to cleanse
This mist of tears . . .

XXVII

Offer no anodyne
To dreamers who can not dream alone
To their own uttermost end.
Befriend
No friend of chance but live unfriended, if ease must be the root
Of friendship. And think no sacrifice divine
But feel the nail
Stand friendly in your foot,
And know that little comes of love but this:
Gethsemane, the soldiers and the kiss
And the pale
Dawn, the perfect loneliness.

 **from**
Guest Book
1935 *

APOLOGY

Here are my guests recorded in a book
And noted not with an invidious eye;
For I have tried to concentrate my look
On certain essences I know them by,—
Nothing inimical, nothing adverse
Nor friendly, nor considerate, nor kind,
But honesties, for better or for worse,
Concerning both the body and the mind.
And if it seem that I have paid a cost
Too dear for decency, too bad for me,
I may have gained as much as I have lost
By the direction of my scrutiny:
Though I can claim no virtues that I sign,
These faults are nobody's that are not mine.

---

*While many of the poems in *Guest Book* are composite sonnet portraits of types, some specifically represent people in Bynner's life. "Correspondent" refers to Bynner himself; "Expatriates" to Clinton King, a Santa Fe friend, and Lady Duff Twysden, the woman after whom Ernest Hemingway created the character of Lady Brett Ashley in *The Sun Also Rises;* "Jeremiah" to the poet Robinson Jeffers; "Jouster" to Arthur Davison Ficke; "Liar" to Edna St. Vincent Millay; "Mayflower" to the Santa Fe painter Cady Wells; "Poetess" to Amy Lowell; "Stylist" to the writer and photographer Carl Van Vechten; and "Teacher" to the novelist and playwright Thornton Wilder.

CORRESPONDENT

Words, words and words! What else, when men are dead,
Their small lives ended and their sayings said,
Is left of them? Their children go to dust,
As also all their children's children must,
And their belongings are of paltry worth
Against the insatiable consuming earth . . .
I knew a man and almost had forgot
The wisdom of the letters that he wrote;
But words, if words are wise, go on and on
To make a longer note of unison
With man and man than living persons make
With one another for whatever sake.
Therefore I wept tonight when quick words rose
Out of a dead man's grave, whom no one knows.

DUST

Life is at ease now, so her heart asserts,
When things lie placed as she would have them lie;
And any minor disarrangement hurts
Almost as much as though a man should die.
She little dreams her husband, all the while,
Would rather she were dead and moths alive
Than have to see the neatness of her smile
Because a curtain or a rug survive.
If only she could care for something human
Instead of things upon her walls and floors!
No wonder that materials and woman
Have made him so material with whores!
But she is utterly secure from fluster,
Wiping his sins off with a feather-duster.

EXPATRIATES

Rossetti might have quarreled with Burne-Jones
To be the father of so fair a lad;
But a manufacturer of candy owns

The fathership, wishing he never had.
He knows that nothing in his own good strain
Accounts for the full lips and the wild ways,—
It's something for the mother to explain;
She's had it on her conscience all her days.
Regardless of the cause, the boy continues
Between his loves to paint (or almost never),
Trusting his eyes and curly hair and sinews
Beyond the need of study and endeavor,
Until in Paris he has found requital:
An Englishwoman with a worn-out title.

She pounced upon him, so they say, like Jove,
Liking his cherub face and fleshy wings.
And he liking her force. And then they clove
Together, circling through the airy rings
Of Paris, not an eagle and a boy
But a hawk and a rabbit, or a dead balloon
And a broken parachute, or a paper toy
Caught on a telegraph-pole, or a yellow moon
And a wisp of cloud. As long as they had brandy,
Their very bed was wafting through the ether
A mother of liquor and a son of candy;
But lacking this refreshment, they had neither
Paris nor anything. It was no joke:
They were dry as hell and both of them dead broke.

HOSTESS

Four winds there may be; but of all the four
None penetrates completely through the curtain
That's drawn nocturnally across her door
To make her status weather-proof and certain.
She holds her cards at bridge, a steady hand;
She keeps a servant often in the offing
To answer a conventional demand.
She has at times a proper touch of coughing,
Her forehead concentrates with troubled laughter
Over a quip that isn't quite au fait;
But if there's any criticism after

From prudish guests, it wasn't she but they
Who noticed, so she tells them on the path,
And then she memorizes in the bath.

JEREMIAH

Roses have been his bed so long that he
Constructs a mat of thorns for lying on;
People have flattered him, until the sea
Becomes a preferable monotone.
He sets his masonry upon the brink
Of lamentation, out of his window peers
Toward waves that ever rise only to sink
Confused and lost as he among his years.
A ship alive becomes to him a hull
Charred and undone, the fumble of a wreck;
His dreams are but the droppings of a gull
Caught in a noose of seaweed round his neck;
And crying like a maniac toward the sky,
He pulls mankind in after him, to die.

JOUSTER

The sensual is his avowed romance:
He jousts against the moral and the mystic,
Rather by balancing a phallic lance
Than by encounters cerebral or fistic.
Kind acts or primroses or gloaming woods,
Rainbows or public causes bore him stiff;
They mean no more to him than woollen goods,
And yet he always has a saving if:
If there but be a girl of kind intent
With primrose breasts astray in wood or field,
Rainbows illume his every lineament,
Due to a cause which always has appealed.
But there's a lurking terror strikes him blind,—
What if some day he leave his lance behind?

LIAR

She had lied from the first moment when she said
I do and heard his I do answering:
She had liked a sudden angle of his head,
Though hardly sure that love meant anything.
She had felt his arm around her arid waist
And tried to meet it with her body's lies,
But had continued acquiescent, chaste,
Willing to be aware but always wise.
She had known that years from now, if they were married,
She would still be bound to him and still not his,
Only a lonely body slowly carried
Up the bleak mountain-slope of ecstasies,—
Till yesterday she noticed, in the field
He loved to plough, a footprint sharply heeled.

MAYFLOWER

Although on Beacon Hill he's hurried after
By proper debutantes and satellites,
Liquor and lapses, lecheries and laughter
Are the alliteration of his nights.
He has an honored name, yet hopes it true
(Despite the family furniture and fuss)
That he was only, in the Mayflower crew,
A seaman able and anonymous,—
A brawny fellow excellent at sailing,
Fond of his muscle, fond of hearty fun,
Fond of his bedfellows and good prevailing
When all the thoughts and theories are done.
And so on any night in any street
He sails abroad, enamored of a sheet:

A sheet that winds to him a lovely limb
Away from family warranties and crests
Which hold no such significance for him
As the important heraldry of breasts.
And so he waits the coming of the night
To be less honored but more understood,
To find upon a curb uncurbed delight;

He'd certainly be happy, if he could.
He eyes the younger company at home
(Disarming both his parents by his speech)
As 'twere a chorus at the Hippodrome
With not a girl or boy beyond his reach.
And yet the sail he craves from early seas
Lacks in his handling the propitious breeze.

POETESS

She was as callous in the execution
Of verse as though of Sacco and Vanzetti.
She knew the academic convolution
Which gives immense importance to the petty.
She would have ordered God from the front door,
If he had come in clothes that meant the back.
Her rights had been her rights so long before,
She deprecated wrongs and, leaning back
With her fastidious mind, would burn fat logs
And drink her Turkish coffee and forget
The breed of anarchists. A breed of dogs
Fawned at her knee expectantly, to whet
Her self-importance with less violent jolts
Than come to zealots from electric volts.

STYLIST

He had a face from Michigan, a mask
Of blue-eyed innocence and beardless satin,
And so primarily he made his task
The adapting of his dimples to Manhattan
But went too fast, adding Parisian gleams
And little twinkles of uncertain sin
And even took upon his face the seams
And less adroit appearance of Berlin.
Later of course, and it was rational,
His paunch and visage both assumed a look
Not national but international
In spite of all the purgatives he took;

And while his titles gathered on the shelf,
The man became fictitious to himself.

TEACHER

Teacher of boys—and yet afraid the rule
Of lordliness in class should come besides
To be a habit and he play the fool,
He has a look which what it half confides
It more conceals. He flutters on the verge
Of telling you, first with his eyes and hands,
Then nearly with his tongue; and yet the urge
Is less than something else which countermands.
Therefore his conversation turns to dreams
And their interpreting or to some such case
Of Freudian theory. A flicker gleams
Of almost rabid fervor on his face
And in his voice there's an excited tone—
Toward other people's cases than his own.

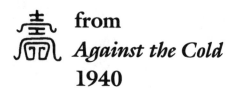 from
Against the Cold
1940

MOON FRAGRANCE

When the moonlight brings to my bed a fragrance of cherry blossoms,
Why do I dream of frost among their petals?
Why do I dream of winter covering with snow
Even their shadows on my window-sill?

SUMMER-LEAVES

Friendship can turn as suddenly
As ever ripples on a sea
But likewise it can turn as slow
As noonday shadows on the snow
And be as fixed and firm in air
As summer-leaves are anywhere.

THE WIND AT THE CANDLE

Age has its merriment as well as youth,
    And both of them go flying
And either time, to tell the truth,
    Is a likely time for dying.

Be your own ancestor when callow,
    Be your own son when sere—

For wicks, when wind is at the tallow,
   Bend and veer.

THE WINTRY MIND

Winter uncovers distances, I find;
And so the blowing of the wintry mind
Takes leaves away, till there is left behind
A wide cold world. And so the heart grows blind
To the earth's green motions lying warm below
Field upon field, field upon field, of snow.

THE EDGE

Long, long before the eyelids harden
And an intake ends the breath,
A body's eyes and a body's burden
Feel the edge of death.

They do not move, they do not think,
They only sit and stare,
The eyes almost ceasing to blink
And the heart ceasing to care.

But it becomes a pleasant thing
To gaze upon the toes
So peacefully dismembering
Before the eyelids close.

Thus Buddha must have sat and known,
Midmost of earth and sea,
The dissolution of the bone
Into its rarity.

MIDNIGHT

What spirit is abroad that so bereaves
The night? No one has sung, nor guitar been played!
A hound under the house has whined and bayed,

And a bat is breathing at the window-eaves.
When I look out, the moon among the leaves
Of corn becomes a curve of steel. Afraid
Lest I may hear the stir of a grass-blade
Growing out of a body that still grieves,
I lock my door and cringe along the wall,
Snuffing my candle as I creep to bed;
And when I hear a fragment of wax fall
On the table-top I feel at the top of my head,
Tapping my memory, the bony ball
Of a finger that was once perfectly made.

AT HIS FUNERAL

These busy motions have no life at all
Compared to motions death has now unmade;
No living person at his funeral,
Never a moving form of the parade
Affords the power of the silent face,
This gathered energy, ungathering,
Compared to which no passion, no embrace,
No parentage, no pain mean anything.

SPRING AND A MOTHER DEAD

I who should write her epitaph
    Would err:
What could I say to anyone
    But her?

Apricot-blossoms open
    Like a bell:
But this time there is nobody
    To tell.

EPISODE OF DECAY

Being very religious, she devoted most of her time to fear.
Under her calm visage, terror held her,

Terror of water, of air, of earth, of thought,
Terror lest she be disturbed in her routine of eating her husband.
She fattened on his decay, but she would let him decay without pain.
And still she would ask, as she consumed him particle by particle,
Do you wish me to take it, dear? Will it make you happier?
And down the plump throat he went day after day in tid-bits;
And he mistook the drain for happiness,
Could hardly live without the deadly nibbling. . . .
She had eaten away the core of him under the shell,
Eaten his heart and drunk away his breath;
Till on Saturday, the seventeenth of April,
She made her breakfast on an edge of his mind.
He was very quiet that day, without knowing why.
A last valiant cell of his mind may have been insisting that the fault was
    not hers but his;
But soon he resumed a numbness of content:
The little cell may have been thinking that one dies sooner or later
And that one's death may as well be useful. . . .
For supper, he offered her tea and cake from behind his left ear;
And after supper they took together the walk they always took together
    after supper.

AFTER A RAIN AT MOKANSHAN

While green bamboos come near again,
That a moment since were blown grey with rain,
And mountain-peaks once more exist
And the river renews its silver vein,
I close my eyes and see but you
After a rain beside Si Wu,—
Your shyness drifting like a mist
From the leaves of a bamboo.

PROCESSIONAL

The rain has ended. Tiny moths and swallows
And poising dragon-flies flit one by one
Before a long processional that follows
Of all the dynasties under the sun.
I watch the Mongols and the Tartars pass;

The Mings, the Manchus and the Japanese;
And then the Europeans; and then, alas,
Even Americans go by like these.
And other shadowy forms before my eyes
File along twinkling willows into space:
Leaving the swallows and the dragon-flies
And tender moths and me to run our race
Light-hearted, at the ends of periods,
With the deathless laughers, the forgotten gods.

from
The Way of Life
According to Laotzu
1944*

1

Existence is beyond the power of words
To define:
Terms may be used
But are none of them absolute.
In the beginning of heaven and earth there were no words,
Words came out of the womb of matter;
And whether a man dispassionately
Sees to the core of life
Or passionately
Sees the surface,
The core and the surface
Are essentially the same,
Words making them seem different
Only to express appearance.
If name be needed, wonder names them both:
From wonder into wonder
Existence opens.

2

People through finding something beautiful
Think something else unbeautiful,

*The introduction to *The Way of Life* appears in the prose section under the title "Laotzu."

Through finding one man fit
Judge another unfit.
Life and death, though stemming from each other,
    seem to conflict as stages of change,
Difficult and easy as phases of achievement,
Long and short as measures of contrast,
High and low as degrees of relation;
But, since the varying of tones gives music to a voice
And what is is the was of what shall be,
The sanest man
Sets up no deed,
Lays down no law,
Takes everything that happens as it comes,
As something to animate, not to appropriate,
To earn, not to own,
To accept naturally without self-importance:
If you never assume importance
You never lose it.

3

It is better not to make merit a matter of reward
Lest people conspire and contend,
Not to pile up rich belongings
Lest they rob,
Not to excite by display
lest they covet.
A sound leader's aim
Is to open people's hearts,
Fill their stomachs,
Calm their wills,
Brace their bones
And so to clarify their thoughts and cleanse their needs
That no cunning meddler could touch them:
Without being forced, without strain or constraint,
Good government comes of itself.

55

He whom life fulfills,
Though he remains a child,

Is immune to the poisonous sting
Of insects, to the ravening
Of wild beasts or to vultures' bills.
He needs no more bone or muscle than a baby's for sure hold.
Without thought of joined organs, he is gender
Which grows firm, unfaltering.
Though his voice should cry out at full pitch all day, it would
        not rasp but would stay tender
Through the perfect balancing
Of a man at endless ease with everything
Because of the true life that he has led.
To try for more than this bodes ill.
It is said, "there's a way where there's a will";
But let life ripen and then fall.
Will is not the way at all:
Deny the way of life and you are dead.

56

Those who know do not tell,
Those who tell do not know.
Not to set the tongue loose
But to curb it,
Not to have edges that catch
But to remain untangled,
Unblinded,
Unconfused,
Is to find balance,
And he who holds balance beyond sway of love or hate,
Beyond reach of profit or loss,
Beyond care of praise or blame,
Has attained the highest post in the world.

68

The best captain does not plunge headlong
Nor is the best soldier a fellow hot to fight.
The greatest victor wins without a battle:
He who overcomes men understands them.
There is a quality of quietness
Which quickens people by no stress:

"Fellowship with heaven," as of old,
Is fellowship with man and keeps its hold.

69

The handbook of the strategist has said:
"Do not invite the fight, accept it instead,"
"Better a foot behind than an inch too far ahead,"
Which means:
Look a man straight in the face and make no move,
Roll up your sleeve and clench no fist,
Open your hand and show no weapon,
Bare your breast and find no foe.
But as long as there be a foe, value him,
Respect him, measure him, be humble toward him;
Let him not strip from you, however strong he be,
Compassion, the one wealth which can afford him.

81

Real words are not vain,
Vain words not real;
And since those who argue prove nothing
A sensible man does not argue.
A sensible man is wiser than he knows,
While a fool knows more than is wise.
Therefore a sensible man does not devise resources:
The greater his use to others
The greater their use to him,
The more he yields to others
The more they yield to him.
The way of life cleaves without cutting:
Which, without need to say,
Should be man's way.

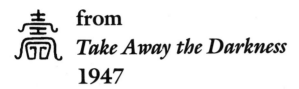

from
Take Away the Darkness
1947

DEFEAT

On a train in Texas German prisoners eat
With white American soldiers, seat by seat,
While black American soldiers sit apart,
The white men eating meat, the black men heart.
Now, with that other war a century done,
Not the live North but the dead South has won,
Not yet a riven nation comes awake.
Whom are we fighting this time, for God's sake?
Mark well the token of the separate seat.
It is again ourselves whom we defeat.

DEAD IN THE PHILIPPINES

Dead in the Philippines are they . . .
These boys who, born in Santa Fe,
Spoke Spanish here, spoke Spanish there,
Have now no language anywhere—

Save as the dead speak after death,
With an acute mysterious breath
At sudden times of night and day,
Some of the things they used to say.

PRAYER

Let us not look upon
Their like again,
This generation
Of bewildered men—
With earth-roads, sea-roads,
Sky-roads too, that show
All ways to enter
And no way to go.

YOUNG MEN SHOULD KNOW

Young men should know enough never to laugh
Except when laughter is amazed or mean:
Young men should wince at any biograph
Admitting an emotion to the scene,
Should twist the living subject's neck apart
And prove that in no throat is any heart.

To old men objects only should be dear,
Trinkets in space perhaps, or in the mind
Philosophies, religions to revere,
Or the unimportances of humankind;
But old men cannot always live by rote:
Sometimes they put the heart back in the throat.

ANSWER

Cease from the asking, you receive the answer.
God is not God, life life nor wonder wonder
Save as a man himself becomes the dancer
Across all variations of the thunder.

TO LI PO

Mingle the oceans into cups of wine
And lift all seven to your heart's content.
Your ancient impulses becoming mine—

I know, with cups, the fullness that you meant.
You meant, pausing as I do for a dram,
That the Emperor might call and we not come.
You were as independent as I am
Of purple canopies and bell and drum . . .
You tottered to the summons, you were carried
Drunk and half-blinded in the servants' arms.
You moved your brush, the court was haunted, harried
With premonitions and with high alarms
Because a tidal wave of tipsy speech
Had made all China but a crumbling beach.

THE TWO WINDOWS

Out of my western window,
The purple clouds are dying
Edged with fire;
And out of my eastern window,
The full round moon is rising
Formed of ice.

So beautiful,
Although the day go by
And the night come on forever,
Is this momentary world.

TESTAMENT

Crumble me with fire into the desert sand.
I have seen dead cattle, and I understand
Slow crumbling well enough to wish my hand
No broken shape when it has been unmanned.
Therefore release me, make me, when I die,
A part of wideness under widening sky.

ARCHER

Master, with dart invisible,
Parallel to the dart we see,

How can you pull the fateful string
Of double archery?

How can you pierce an eagle on the wing,
So that the bird will drop and die
And yet its double be transfixed
Forever in the sky?

MORE LOVELY THAN ANTIQUITY

There comes a moment in her veins
Not of the earth, not of the rains,
Something not of stalks and stems
But of dim crowns and diadems,
Something commanding her to be
More ancient than antiquity
And to soothe her head on a pike above
The vacant circumstance of love.

BURROS

Upon my heart a sorrow lies
Like that within a burro's eyes,
But burros bear their burdens well
Of hemlock or of asphodel.

Most of the time they bear it well;
But I envy them the heaving yell
With which in the deep of night or day
They suddenly give themselves away.

IMPARTIAL BE

As to the moment of your going, sir
You have no gauge:
Youth is as often executioner
As age.

Impartial therefore be to old and young
And neither favor,

Not knowing when their hearts or yours be wrung
Forever.

CIRCE

What though your face, that stole my sense of good
And led me captive through bewildered days,
Has now no potency of flesh and blood,
No changes in those thousand conquering ways,
Still, while your wanton will is quiet grown,
Your beauty captures whom it still disdains;
And in your heart of dust, that then was stone,
I stumble blindly with unbroken chains.

CLOUDS

Bright-veined as lightning she was,
One touch of her would cleave the sky.
Anything that heaven does
Could happen when she came by.
She was buried winters ago:
The summer sky is heaped as if with snow.

AUTUMN TREE

There's April in the Autumn,
December in the May;
There are many Springs forgotten,
More that stay.

Much has bereaved me
And still bereaves,
But I feel like an autumn tree
Taking back its leaves.

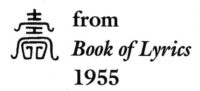 **from**
Book of Lyrics
1955

A STREAM

Cool, moving, fruitful and alive I go,
In my small run reflecting all the sky.
I see through trees, I see through melting snow,
I see through riffles which the wind and I
Have made, and through the shadow of a man,
Nor know where I arrive, where I began.

SQUANDERINGS

Be aware
That goods are brittle,
That those who have little often break that little
While those who have much take care.

Love is not a wealth to scatter,
To forsake.
Loneliness is hard to break.
Squanderings matter.

ISLAND

There is an island where a man alone,
Alive beyond the selfishness of living,

Knows the whole world around him as his own
Without resenting and without forgiving.

WINTER MORNING

The hills for miles are stricken into one,
Whiter and simpler than oblivion,
Alive with sudden snow, with sudden sun.

from *New Poems 1960*
1960

All tempest
    Has
    Like a navel
    A hole in its middle
    Through which a gull may fly
    In silence

Any other time would have done
    But not now
    Because now there is no time
    And when there is no time
    It only stands still on its own center
    Waiting to be wound

    Once upon a time somebody will unwind it
    And then what a time
    In no time at all

Barnacles on underposts of the piers
    Are shown under green sashes
    Which let elements do the dancing
    Round its fixed limbs

    A better ballet
    Than any active limbs could do

Even in a forest
Green with slow scarves

But for these apertures
Said the turtle
Man would not have lost
The address of the gods

He hid it in here
In my shell
And I have had no use for it
Yet

Coming down the stairs
She paused midway
And turned
And assembled the railing
Which thereupon went upstairs
Leaving her slowly alone

CRUMBLING from these were those
And that was it

No answer could have been so true
And yet in the crowd around
Not one believed

For the answer was a man's
Which we know well
Would never do
In weather so adroit

The dress walked in by itself
But with the greatest dignity
As though what was not inside
Greatly mattered
Even the other day

And that after all was what made the occasion

The greatness of laughter
    Outdoes all other kinds

    How animals try for it
    If you could see them in the dark
    But they find crying there so much easier
    Or just noise
    Not yet mirth
    The greatest of noises
    A melted snarl
    A bark
    Exalted

He never knew what was the matter with him
    Until one night
    He chopped up his bed for firewood

    It was comfortable that way

    And then another night a year later
    It came roaring up the street at him
    As a sunset

He noticed from the dark shore
    That it was his own house being carried awkward on the flood
    He could see by the unlit lights in the living-room
    That it was filled with total strangers
    Dancing
    And that the flooring of a flood
    Is at an angle

He was not always there
    But he tried to be
    He was constantly looking for small objects
    Where he had not left them
    Or repeating remarks he had not made
    So that people's eyes went back and forth over him
    Like tennis balls over a net

It was not that he felt in the least tied down
But that a part of him was elsewhere
Like the holes in the net

If I could let go and swim through time
I might reach an unsuspected end of it

But it is an acrobat
Facing either way
And if I pass it one way
It turns the other

Judges as well as athletes forget that time runs back
Faster than forward

It happened that she turned on the light
Just as the fence disappeared
Leaving only its gate
So that the crowd could not pass
But stood there
Helpless and lowing
So that even the bull was turned about
Where the sun rose the other way

It was his jaw that was wrong said the doctor
It could not keep from laughing

So it had to be broken and mended
Which was done
Without mending the laugh

Psychiatrists shook their heads at him
But only one came off

Kindness can go too high
Even in heaven

A hawk carrying a fish
For instance

And giving it air

Once upon two times
    It happened
    And everybody saw double
    But recognized
    The reality
    As separate

Voices in the staircase
    In the floor
    In the furniture

    There are more of the dead here
    Than of the living

    Except for the voice
    Which sometimes comes through passionately
    I do not wish to be born

What is this death
    It is not when the far clay-bank turns white
    Nor when bright leaves darken in the veins

    It is when the mind is too tired to take care of the heart
    And the heart takes pity

You fish for people and not even their names
    Come up for you

    But the sun is still there
    Aged fisherman
    And you sit in it fishing for people
    And hooking the sun

Uncollected Poems

A GREAT MAN

Passion transforms me from my puny build . . .
Your bosom listens to me like a crowded balcony
To a great man speaking.

EPITAPH FOR A CONSTANT LOVER

He encountered new mistresses most of his life,
Though—if better were lacking—he lay with his wife.
Now he lies with his latest—from falling downstairs—
Eternally constant, and nobody cares.

FINGERNAIL

He had a fingernail which resembled the face of his grandmother
Who had died in her dignity before he was born
And had bequeathed her slim grace to only one of his fingers.

So he chose long moments during the sunsets
For polishing this one nail delicately and meditating
Upon what was left him of the persistent earth.

SANTA FE

Among the automobiles and in a region
Now Democratic, now Republican,
With a department-store, a branch of the Legion,
A Chamber of Commerce and a moving-van,
In spite of cities crowding on the Trail,
Here is a mountain-town that prays and dances
With something left, though much besides may fail,
Of the ancient faith and wisdom of St. Francis.

His annual feast has come. His image moves
Along these streets of people. And the trees
And kneeling women, just as they did before,
Welcome and worship him because he proves
That natural sinners put him at his ease,
And so he enters the cathedral-door.

THE TITANIC

A time comes when a majority of those you remember
Are not among the living but among the dead.
Some of them went down long ago on the *Titanic*.
Justus Miles Forman, for instance.
Who now besides me remembers him,
That tall suave presence with slim waist and pomaded words,
That dark edge of a jungle in exact clothes,
And Charles Frohman, that dumpling of finance with a heart
    nonetheless,
And who else vanished suddenly on the *Titanic*?
But was it the *Titanic* after all?
And is it not always as sudden?
Is it not a shadow springing at you round a corner of the street,
The immense imminence of nothing on something?
There is no answer save the vibrations of a voice which happens to be
    living
And might just as well happen to be dead.

THE STATE OF POETRY, 1954

      not
they do   like sense in poetry any more
      not
nor nonsense either
just posture
they are intent upon
     s   r
p   U   y
  o   t
      t   i
let them have it

ROBERT FROST
(1874–1963)

They would have stayed there for farewell
Until the train pulled out
But he waved them away and they could tell
He knew what he was about.

The train held only strangers, yes,
But he was a stranger too—
When you say goodbye to friends who bless
They leave you only you.

PART TWO

Prose Pieces

⛩ Autobiography in the Shape of a Book Review

Once upon a time there was a young poet who thought he knew what was best for him. He had managed his way through Harvard and on Commencement Day was assured that he should accept the post offered him of being presently an instructor in the English Department after his twenty-first birthday, August 10, 1902. His family, however, plotted against him and when they divulged the plot, he capitulated. The agreement was that he should accept the terms of his mother and stepfather: immediately on graduation in June, he was to receive from them a trip abroad lasting until October, after which he was to take for only a year a post they would find him in some New York publishing house. Upon his return from the journey, he found himself indentured—practically as an office-boy at ten dollars a week—to Mr. S. S. McClure, editor of *McClure's* magazine. . . .

Despite the ability active on the *McClure* staff, the assistant editors had all seemed to me somewhat hypnotized into following him as a sort of sure shepherd. When he would briskly enter his office in the morning sixty years ago, the editorial group would be on the quick for summons and sit around him like a group at busy ease with a great man. Then out of his briefcase he would pluck pages of notes attached to newspaper clippings from all over the country. He would start reading aloud first a clipping, then a jotting and, fixing an excitedly sagacious eye closely on this or that member of the staff, he would say: "This is for you, Steffens," or to Ida Tarbell: "Will you report to us on this one?" or: "Your stuff, Baker." The following week the report would be made, each editor giving reasons for further report by himself or one of the others, or recommending no further attention in the matter, McClure himself being the final judge.

It was this way that the Standard Oil story had been written by Ida Tarbell whose only weakness would be toward use of such material as a bill for board which she told me she had in her possession, but refrained from using. A school friend of Mrs. John D. Rockefeller's had been invited for a Saturday and Sunday stay. After she had overstayed through Monday, she received from her host a bill for one day's board and lodging, promptly paid and receipted.

Ray Stannard Baker was a man and writer of tender virtue and I remember his being sent to investigate the Californian group under the leadership of a Mrs. Tingley, called the "Purple Mother." A former Cabinet member in Washington—Treasury, I think—and rich, was lodged there and Mr. McClure thought that the colony might be a racket. Baker's report on returning was that the institution was a society of idealists and the life in the colony such that he would like it for his own retirement.

Lincoln Steffens was the only staff member who to me appeared at base skeptical over the McClure crusades. He told me that, though he would write what he was paid to write, he felt that on the whole the miscreants were far more enjoyable company than their attackers and that if he had his choice it would be Tammany rather than Christian associations. I find a pertinent note I made at the time about him: "Steffens was always after that extra height which men who are short sometimes reach for with assertion, vivacity, or assumed humor."

Mr. McClure, though always thinking himself right, was never self-righteous.

When extraordinary material was brought by Georgine Milmine concerning the life of Mary Baker Eddy, Ida Tarbell was the first to undertake its presentation as a series for *McClure's*, but soon withdrew in favor of a newcomer to the office, an ex-schoolteacher from Pittsburgh named Willa Cather, one of whose stories in manuscript had greatly impressed McClure. I well remember businesslike Miss Cather working away at the tangled heap of manuscript for a considerable period before its exciting appearance in the magazine. I believe that Miss Cather years later helped Mr. McClure compile his own autobiography. I also remember his asking me to cut hundreds of words from Miss Cather's story "The Sculptor's Funeral." I explained to him that it would have to be cut bit by bit— words here and words there—rather than lose small sections or even paragraphs. He agreed and I did not know that the author was unaware of the process until the story was shown her in proof. I can still hear her explosion in his office and see her enraged expression toward me when Mr. McClure pretended that the cutting had been entirely my own idea. I had to let her believe him.

However, the only other time he interfered with my clear sailing at the office was when he interposed in my control of verse in the magazine by dictating acceptance of some very bad lines by a most incompetent young lady, writing the acceptance message himself and even asking me as a favor to deliver with his note a box of flowers. Peter Lyon in his book gives this episode and its consequences their due.

I need not more than remark the fact that I remained with McClure beyond the first year. I was having a very good time. My pay had gone up fifty per cent to fifteen dollars a week and I had begun judging and reporting on manuscripts from unknown authors, meantime sending a daily valise of work from familiar authors to our outstanding reader Viola Roseboro' at her home office. Although she paid less attention to muck-raking, which the others of *McClure's* had initiated in the magazine world, she exercised even to the point of genius recognition of imaginative writing—a fine result in *McClure's* where the standard of story-telling steadily added to the magazine's preeminent popularity.

Before my arrival in the office, *McClure's* magazine had been printing contributors like Rudyard Kipling, Robert Louis Stevenson, Sir Arthur Conan Doyle, Booth Tarkington, Stephen Crane and Jack London.

One day I had taken a shine to a manuscript called "Tobin's Palm" by a new author, O. Henry. I sent it along to Miss Roseboro', saying I thought it extremely good. When it did not come back to the office with her recommendation or question, I inquired by phone and found that this time she had followed her rare practice of returning it direct to the author with handwritten comments. Taking the case to Mr. McClure, I told him that the author, according to his address, lived nearby and that I considered the manuscript the best which had come to the office during my time. With quick challenge, he asked if I would stake my judgment on it. I answered: "Yes. Will you accept it on my say-so?" When he said: "Yes," I bounded across to the Lion d'Or restaurant and, in a bleak room overhead, found O. Henry—like a Western Buddha—occupying an un-padded rocker and on a trunk nearby I saw a sealed envelope. "Tobin's Palm?" I asked. "Yes," he said. "Accepted," said I, grandly and with young pride.

Mr. Lyon in *Success Story* says that the McClure group was already ac-quainted with the author through their newspaper Syndicate which had published him, but I am certain that nobody in the office recognized his authorship or his hand in "Tobin's Palm." Perhaps he had used his own name, Sidney Porter, for the Syndicate as he did in earlier writing. I don't know, but I do know that "Tobin's Palm" was O. Henry's first marked success in the literary world and that we continued publishing his stories to widening acclaim. I also remember that from the Klondike a young-ster who had been reading O. Henry wrote Mr. McClure that if that was the kind of story we liked, he could do plenty of them himself. His name was Rex Beach and we continued printing him too. I remember wishing, incidentally, that John S. Phillips, head of our publishing house, had not substituted "The Spoilers" for Beach's original title "Loot."

Through this period in the office, I had taken over the greater part of Mr. McClure's correspondence with his authors and learned an accurate and authorized forgery of his signature. In one instance, I ventured amusement in having Mr. McClure mimic in correspondence the author's own style. I remember my conviction that I did extremely well in the instance of Henry James, but even when the latter and I became friends later, neither of us ever mentioned my impertinence. Before James arrived in this country, I was introduced to him by a letter from Henry Harland; and the following passages from letters Henry James sent me are amusingly pertinent to my efforts for *McClure's:* the first in answer to my request that he let us see his impressions of the United States after twenty years' absence and the second his response to Willa Cather's *Troll Garden* which I sent him with my recommendation:

(January 8, 1904)
. . . as my last visit was no less than twenty-one years ago, the expectation of "impressions" is, naturally, not other than strong within me. . . . I desire to vibrate as intensely, as frequently and as responsively as possible—and all in the interest of vivid literature! . . .

and the other excerpt:

(February 1, 1906)
I have your graceful letter about *The Troll Garden* . . . and if I brazenly confess that I not only haven't yet read it, but haven't even been meaning to (till your words about it thus arrive), I do no more than register the sacred truth. That sacred truth is that, being now almost in my 100th year, with a long and weary experience of such matters behind me, promiscuous fiction has become abhorrent to me, and I find it the hardest thing in the world to read almost any new novel. Any is hard enough, but the hardest from the innocent hands of young females, young American females perhaps above all. This is a subject—my battered, cynical, all-too-expert outliving of such possibilities—on which I could be eloquent; but I haven't time, and I will be more vivid and complete some other day. I've only time now to say that I will then (in spite of these professions) do my best for Miss Cather so as not to be shamed by your so doing yours. . . .

Possibly my outstanding service to the magazine was the printing of poems from A. E. Housman's *Shropshire Lad*. The book had not been copyrighted nor known in the United States, wherefore we might have published from it what we pleased without permission; but Mr. McClure let me not only republish poems already contained in a published volume, but to pay for them at a higher rate than most verse in those days received. Incidentally, Mr. Housman returned the first check and received none further because of his statement to me that he never took payment for his verse.

Probably with the idea of training me for increased activity among his authors, McClure took me with him on a trip to Louisville where we visited his popular contributor Mrs. George Madden Martin of the "Emmy Lou" stories. I remember our all driving for dinner to the house of Alice Hegan Rice, author of *Mrs. Wiggs of the Cabbage Patch,* and her husband the poet Cale Young Rice. The car ahead of us was driven by another of the guests whose name escapes me, an unmarried unassuming Southern lady who was also a quietly impressive local literary critic. Suddenly her car swerved off the road and head-on struck a barn door which threw the driver so violently forward that she was seriously injured. Her only comment, spoken softly, was that her glasses hadn't broken. It is characteristic of Mr. McClure that, at least until she recovered some months later, he helped by printing several literary essays from her.

In Louisville, where Mr. McClure delighted me by vigorously unmusical songs in the bathtub, he tried me on a case. As I remember it, a Governor had been killed by a shot through his office window in the Kentucky State House and a defeated candidate for the Lieutenant Governorship had been suspected and jailed for the crime. Mr. McClure had a feeling from newspaper accounts that the man was innocent and sent me to jail for an interview. I agreed with the McClure judgment and we sent Ray Stannard Baker to see the fellow, whose release was brought about by a subsequent Baker article in the magazine.

These were things that McClure did along the way. I think he also wanted to test me as a possible prose writer but no, that did not happen. I was not prompted to undertake that kind of task, although I did continue friendship with the young politician who was afterward elected to Congress as a Kentucky Representative.

The most vivid and the saddest memory I have of Mr. McClure remains his face on the grim day (May 10, 1906) when almost his entire staff left him. I always felt that his mild peccadillo and the editorial court martial of him in the office was the beginning of their defection. I had been planning to leave *McClure's* for reasons of my own general direction; but when he looked up haggard and tearful and said: "Bynner, are you leaving me too?" I couldn't forsake him but stayed with loyal Viola Roseboro' and Willa Cather.

To me, the main explanation from those who withdrew was that they could not continue longer toward the bankruptcy for which he was heading them all and they would shake their heads over the fact that he was a very weak man—bound to ruin them all with wild expenditures. In one instance when his offer for a Kipling serial, *Kim,* was $15,000 and a rival editor offered $16,000, Mr. McClure concluded the deal on the spot by making it $25,000 which in those days was unheard of.

He made me managing editor and I was misled for several days by the importance of such a position for one so young, so that I was jolted when Will Irwin soon turned up to take over what I had thought my desk, with Mr. McClure saying: "But I thought you liked the other post better—with authors and all that." I know now that he was right, but a warning would have been pleasanter treatment.

I stayed at least until autumn, still fond of McClure and enjoying my work with him and yet persistently tempted to try the life of a free-lance. My final complete resignation from the office was later that year, after I had received the following in a letter from a friend and counselor:

Dublin, New Hampshire
Oct. 5–06

Dear Poet:

You have certainly done right—for several good reasons; at least, of them, I can name two: 1. With your reputation you can have your freedom and yet earn your living. 2. If you fall short of succeeding to your wish, your reputation will provide you another job. And so, in high approval I suppress the scolding and give you the saintly and fatherly pat instead. . . .

Yours ever,
Mark Twain

I did not see Mr. McClure again until some seven years later when he looked me up in Tokyo and went with me to the Kabuki Theater. I took him behind scenes to meet one of the foremost actors of the time in the latter's dressing room. The actor kept us waiting while he passed to and fro through the room naked behind a silk robe in the hands of attendants and steaming from his bath. This meant a considerable wait for us on our knees so that, fifteen minutes later, Mr. McClure could stand it no longer and without good-bye to any of us crawled on all fours out of the room. Years later, when he was in his seventies, I had dinner with him again and after that I was saddened to hear that members of the Union League Club were begrudging him a corner in their library which he was reserving more or less as an office of his own for his papers. I can only hope that he never realized their attitude.

Mr. Lyon makes clear how it became practically impossible for the staff to sustain McClure's financial vagaries—none of the latter being so much for his own benefit as for that of them all. On the other hand, he did become more and more impatient and difficult personally; and despite most of their leaving him in a business way, none of them lost an essential tenderness toward him and their new editorial venture, *The American Magazine,* failed to prosper.

But what I have written sounds more like autobiography than like a review of Peter Lyon's *Success Story.* And the reason is clear—at least for me. I have been supplying this or that detail of observation on the spot which Mr. Lyon could not help omitting from his vivid and penetrative account of S. S. McClure's life and times. And yet I feel as though Mr. Lyon had actually been in the offices with us, going from one editor to another and I were challenged to come back at him with a few paragraphs he had skipped, overlooked, or not known about. I can hear the figures he portrays speaking with amazing accuracy.

Mr. Lyon wrote me several years ago that as a young man he had known S. S. McClure and found him "a garrulous old bore," as any young man might. In this mature book, however, he makes him anything but that and seems to have grown rightly sensible and fond by these latter years of careful study.

Being probably the only survivor of the McClure editorial staff from any of its periods, I have naturally concentrated on the brief bit I experienced of Mr. McClure's career and the biographer's record of it. But, in vouching for the accuracy with which Mr. Lyon records those several years, I can only feel assured that the rest of the book is as accurate, including McClure's picturesque and harsh childhood in Ireland, his visions ahead of what he wanted in the literary and journalistic world, his achievement of those hopes rather than of material reward. If he had been a more average American, he would have had far more of such gain to show for his consistent and popular success as editor and publisher. *McClure's* magazine was not only the most popular in its day, but set an example for journalism of the following half-century. Not only was McClure foremost of editors as muckraking crusader, but he had an unerring sense of direction. He was a divining rod for characters, for abilities and for decent interesting righteousness. And Peter Lyon with sympathy, admiration and able writing brings him alive.

—Reminiscence occasioned by reviewing *Success Story: The Life and Times of S. S. McClure,* by Peter Lyon, New York: Charles Scribner's Sons. Published in *The Santa Fe New Mexican,* November 3, 1963, and *The Harvard Alumni Bulletin,* February 1, 1964.

Ezra Pound

My bit of memory and comment may properly find place in one of the letters. Here it is. A year or so after 1902 when I went to work for *McClure's* magazine, "the Chief" gave me free hand as poetry editor. My main exploit in that capacity was the introducing to an American public poems from A. E. Housman's *Shropshire Lad.* I did, however, print a few poems of my own, the first example of which proved to be half plagiarism. A Harvard classmate who had happened along while I was at verse manuscripts in Cambridge had quoted from somewhere two lines which he liked. I had absently entered them among my own lines and eventually they appeared in *McClure's* as part of a quatrain purporting to be mine, whereas the two lines were Dante Gabriel Rossetti's English, part of a sonnet he had translated from Michelangelo. For some years only the classmate, who reminded me, and Mr. McClure, whom I told, shared my unhappy realization of what I had done. This quatrain, half of it very good, may have been the principal poem of mine which several years later had sufficiently recommended itself to a citizen of, I think, Pennsylvania that he sent his son to me with poems.

Since all of it happened fifty years ago, details blur; but I vividly remember the youth who came to me in New York, who was not on that occasion "soft-spoken," as he has been remembered by others, but firm-spoken and confident. "Would I look at these poems and see if I thought they warranted his being sent abroad for stimulus and study." Not only was my ready answer, "Yes, if that was what he greatly wished," but it developed later into arrangement that Small, Maynard and Company of Boston, who had published my own first book in 1907, should publish three books by Pound: *Provença, Sonnets and Ballate of Guido Cavalcanti,* and *Ripostes.*

My memory of Pound, at that first meeting when he read his poems to me, is the eager face, voice and insistent spirit behind them and then a sense of his being an even more happily cuckoo troubadour than the young Vachel Lindsay. But never have I seen Lindsay attired for it as Pound was. I should say that his jacket, trousers and vest had each a brave color, with a main effect of purple and yellow, that one shoe was tan, the other blue and that on a shiny straw hat the ribbon was white with red polka dots. I liked both the poet and his poetry and have often regretted that our connection, through the years which followed his sailing in 1910, could be only by correspondence.

When I saw him again, after his detention at St. Elizabeths in Washington, it was the same great, booming boy, or so he seemed, who clutched me with a bear-hug and cried out, "After forty years!" Time and the beard had made little change for me in his presence; and he seemed quite as sane as he had seemed at the turn of the century or in letters after that.

And yet I wish that Pound would stop blaming me for the dissolution of Small, Maynard and Company, as though I had the little publishing house in hiding somewhere and would not produce it. But after all I enjoy the vehemence—when I can decipher it. Or his vehemence against my preferring Laotzu to Confucius for final import. And I enjoy Pound's poetry—when I can decipher it. I do not agree with Wallace Stevens that "poetry is the scholar's art" nor with the young scholar Ezra that Rihaku was ever the English way to spell Li Po. In the ponderings of the *Cantos* I grant that for me there is too much ponderous ore; but I maintain that in Pound's poetry when the veins are pure they are as pure as any. And on the hill of his poetry the child rides high, still daring to indulge his importunate self.

—*The Ezra Pound Newsletter,* April 10, 1956

On Henry James's Centennial

I first met Henry James in New York in the summer of 1904. He was a thick-set, slow-moving presence of sixty, with a nervously benevolent face and the hesitantly considered, clausified speech which I might have expected from acquaintance with the literary style of his later days, save that most authors do not speak as they write. He did.

At the risk of seeming to exaggerate, let me, from notes made after we parted, record the first paragraph of length which I heard from his lips, a troubled paragraph about a cold he had contracted between the train from Boston and the New York house where he was visiting. I make no attempt to reproduce with punctuation or syllables of pause his vocal gropings and painstaking allotment of words to their places.

I had brought availably with me (he said) two overcoats, one somewhat heavier and one somewhat lighter, and in Boston I had worn with comfort the somewhat lighter overcoat and was carrying, for possible immediate need in New York, the slightly warmer overcoat on my arm. All had gone well, until I found myself here, seated in a cab beside my friend, David Munroe, known to you doubtless as a fellow-editor, albeit much older, editing, yes, *The North American Review,* and so faithfully replete with welcome and so instantly exacting of responses that I was only vaguely, though venially, aware of my impulse and need to doff the somewhat lighter overcoat and to don the slightly heavier overcoat, which I by all means should have done, to be sure, on account of a rapid change in temperature, or else a difference in temperatures at the place where my journey began and the place where it ended, or perhaps merely a change in hour, but a change all in all,—and, as I have noted, my good friend, David, so engrossed me in greetings and reminiscences and interrogations that I continued, despite a disquieting chill in my marrow, to wear the somewhat lighter overcoat, protecting only one arm with the slightly thicker overcoat, which I should assuredly have been wearing in order to avoid this probably thus avoidable touch of influenza with which I must begin my—under otherwise auspicious aspects— visit to New York, and all, let me charge, on account of your beastly, and by me long foresworn, climate.

Anyone doubting my approximate veracity in this attempt to reproduce the involved plaint made to me many years ago might consult Edith Wharton's account, in *A Backward Glance,* of Henry James inquiring directions on a motor-drive in England. Mrs. Wharton and the Appleton-Century Company have kindly permitted me to quote from her.

My good man (James would like to inquire of an aged countryman) if you will be good enough to come here, please; a little nearer—so. My friend, to put it to you in two words, this lady and I have just arrived here from Slough; that is to say, to be more strictly accurate, we have recently passed through Slough on our way here, having actually motored to Windsor from Rye, which was our point of departure; and the darkness having overtaken us, we should be much obliged if you would tell us where we are now—

and still other winding approaches to his final question, the whereabouts of the King's Road, a question answered by the countryman, "Ye're in it."

To my friend, Henry Harland, was due in large measure Henry James's cordial attitude toward me both before and after our meeting. Harland had warned me that I might find James fidgety and at first difficult. Even after a seasoned liking between the two novelists in England, the Harlands had told me of the older man calling on them in a cottage there and, saying always that he could stay but for a moment, remaining for an hour perched uneasily on the edge of a piano stool, overcoat still buttoned and hat in hand. I could not but remember this unhygienic procedure of his in England when I heard later about his overcoats in New York. Yes, James had odd mannerisms; but from the first to the last of my exchanges with him in person or in letter, I was never sensible of constraint either on his part or mine. Once I hopefully sent him my first book, *An Ode to Harvard.* Here are some excerpts from his response:

What an inhuman brute you must long have thought me! I have been, have had to be, deadly silent all round for the last couple of years—for I have been immersed in a job of which the sustained rigor, admitting of no compromise and no break, has dishumanized or dissevered me (from the life about) in a monstrous or remorseless fashion. I undertook some time since a collection (or selection) of a revised edition of my productions, with long prefaces, to the extent of 23 thick volumes, & the pressure of this (my minuteness of revision proving a colossal task, as I think it is in fact an absolutely unique achievement—which ought to incur some critical attention worthy of the name—) drove correspondence & contacts & social joy—all other employments of the pen, at any rate, in particular, completely to the wall—so that I had simply to stop my ears & blind my eyes; groaning at the odious appearance I presented, but nevertheless holding my course. My letters are all unwritten & my friends mostly alienated & vindictive; but the particular job I recklessly (as regards labors involved) proposed to myself is performed (all will very presently have been) to the last shade of a shade.

After our first luncheon at The Players, I secured James a card to the club, and several times he arranged our late lunching there, "giving me very mercifully till *two* o'clock," he would write, "and then we can make out a genial hour together." Nearly two years later, October 27, 1905, he sent me this word from the Reform Club in London. "I have lost no echo of that kindly buzz of The Players, no moment of my immersion in which failed to fall on my ears like genial music." At one of these luncheons he had remarked.

You are insolently young, but I approve of you. You do not treat me as I was recently treated in Boston by some vague and amiable young men, who grow always more vague and more amiable, I imagine, toward eleven o'clock in the evening. Bidden to set a night for dining with two or three of them, what was my stupefaction when I found myself confronted by a huge banquet, with peaches on the table, and a toastmaster, and that sort of thing—extravagant magnification.

'Twas my most troublous experience since being lured into a reception somewhere for one of your considered poets. I had pictured a handshake and two or three minutes involved, for I had elsewhere to go; but there was a very long wait irresistibly enforced on us until arrangements had been concluded for him to commence droning a poem, something about the wind it was, and there for a full quarter of an hour, while we were obliged ruefully to contemplate our broken engagements, he continued droning, slower and slower, on only three notes.

When James said something I wished to remember, I would later jot down not only its substance but, as nearly as I could, its rhythm. I was constantly fascinated by his precise manner in speaking. He selected words as a cat does morsels of food from a plate, occasionally shaking one of them away with delicate distaste. He would even flush over a slip into the wrong word and would flutter and hem and haw till he had righted himself. I wish I could remember some of those instances of oral editing; but I was so impressed each time by his discomfiture, his mortification that I would forget the occasioning word. This matters less than if he had regarded me as a receptacle for momentous utterances.

On old envelopes and slips of paper, yellowed with these thirty years, I have recently come across a few scribbled words against which I had set the initials "H. J." There was a phrase about H. G. Wells,—"immensely ingenious," and a description of a well-known American as "a virtuous little citizen afflicted with clubs for working people, with numerous and unsightly children and with rabid declarations." He complained at the world's being full of "lady-novelists who victimize the supine public" and on another occasion he branded the public as "a great unthinking beast." He enjoyed The Players as "a corner of calm" and musingly murmured, over the photographs which lined its halls, "relics of mummers!" Once, after returning from the Middle West, he gave me the comment, "Chicago is full of the world;—the farther they go from it, the more they appropriate it." May it have been that Chicagoans in the epoch tried to harbor more of "over-ripe" Europe than New Yorkers did? And always I remembered, when he would send me reports from this or that section of America, his having written me from England before the visit, "All I can say at present is that I *desire* to vibrate as intensely, as frequently and as responsively as possible—and all in the interest of vivid literature." Most vivid to me of his sayings in New York, though I left it out of the apocryphal interview I subsequently published and had almost left it out here, was this: "Women are cats, and men are women."

When Miss Jeannette Gilder, editor of *The Critic,* suggested that I contribute an interview with James, I told him of my having from time to time recorded what he said and asked him if I might try to compile from my notes a few pages in the form of more or less connected monologue. He acceded,—writing (December 24, 1904), "I find it in me to melt and relent toward you—so put me to what further ordeal (of sending on proof and suchlike) you absolutely must." Later he wrote (January 5, 1905), "*Don't* submit it to me—I shouldn't know how to participate little *enough,* and I had much rather participate, frankly and freely, in you as yourself than in you—as not yourself!" Before long "A Word or Two with Henry James" had appeared in *The Critic,* and he wrote me about it from the South.

> Forgive me this horrible public paper, the sign of my demoralized & travel-stained state. I am leaving this place in an hour or two & can't again unpack anything properer.
> I have your note telling me that the thing is out at large & am moved while thanking you for the information, to reply that if you can stand it—this more or less indecent exposure—I will try to. Don't please, however, ask me to read it—even to "see" it: I gather in fact that you have that superiority. There are things I won't see.— Success in life today, I think is measured by the degree of one's cultivation of the art (an exquisite one) of not seeing. All except here, for instance, where there is real balm for the rightly averted & the rightly directed eye. . . . I could even now wish you the blessing of a taste of this Florida pleasantry of air & sea & of all nature. Still, your youth doesn't require the fontaine de jouvance in the degree of the battered age of
>
> Yours ever,
Henry James

And here, reprinted from *The Critic* for February, 1905, is an "interview" with Henry James which he forgave, but, as far as I know, never read. He had come back to his native land after an absence of nearly twenty years. . . .

—*The Saturday Review of Literature,* May 22, 1943

A Word or Two with Henry James

Mr. James was in New York for practically the first time in almost twenty years. As we walked he told me of his first flying visit a month or two ago, and thence the talk led to various topics:

"My renewal of acquaintance with New York was not to begin with altogether happy. This second visit is more satisfactory than that first pause of a day or two. I arrived in the sultry last part of August and was absolutely overwhelmed with the heat of the city and its other terrors. It was not at all the place I had known as a boy.

"My friends elected luckily to bring me straightway to the Players Club, which I then thought and think still an oasis of quietness and atmosphere. It suggested to me, as I looked about, the Garrick Club in London and its fine collection of paintings. Amid the abundance of portraits and photographs in the Players, I came upon a case of daguerreotypes full of faces so many of which were familiar to me, that I realized I must have been fortunate enough as a boy to be in the hands of parents who were fond of the theater. They must have taken my brother and me to the playhouse rather prematurely, I judge, else I should not have known all those faces and recovered so many half-lost sensations. Leaning stiffly on pillars, for instance, there were two girls with long hair, the Bateman sisters, whom I used to see on the stage. I remembered them, of course, the better, in having known them, since those times, as two very charming women in England. But there were others, such as the Florences, who once impressed me with their singing; Maggie Mitchell, over whom I went fantastically mad, though she was undoubtedly a barbarian and would nowadays be taken for such; and there was one woman with the face and curls of a schoolmistress, draped in some ghastly pseudo-classic hangings short at her shapeless knees, whom I indubitably once took with admiring seriousness. Those were emphatic events in my boyhood, those visits to the theater. I remember wondering how I could possibly live the time through from a Tuesday to a Friday, and then, when once I was seated in the theater with my eyes on the old green curtain, feeling quite convinced that in the few minutes before that curtain should rise, I was doomed to be removed by accident or death or some unforeseen punishment. Those were palpitations that are immemorable; I seem hardly to have been done with them yesterday.

"Equally as recent seem the old sensations produced on me by my previous life in New York. Gramercy Park and such other places as I found unchanged stand about me this time and give me the same sense of existence as though it were last week instead of twenty years ago that I was calling on a relative or on the way to my own home. I was born in Washington Place and lived afterwards in Fourteenth Street near Sixth Avenue. Those parts of the town are, of course, all gone,—that is, as I knew them. I cannot give you an inkling of what a queer, ghostly, melancholy experience it is to go about a town and find here and there a piece of it, a fragment of it, so to speak, with great stretches between, where it has crumbled away and been replaced by size and strangeness. Suddenly while walking along, as we are walking now, I will come upon a house, or a block of houses or even a section, unchanged, and will discover and snugly recognize, be aware of the old town again, only to lose it all the next minute and to seem almost not on *terra firma*.

"Naturally I cannot know in a day what there is to be known about New York; even to know again what I used to know about it would take many days. Although I have an exemplary memory for rubbish, more important facts do not seem to stay by me. Not that I must complain of my memory; I suppose it has served me well, accurately, ardently for the writing of picturesque trash. During that day or two in New York before I left for Boston, I had, for instance, in the Players I believe, a dish that I have not tasted in over sixteen years and remember, not only as an American food but, if I mistake not, as an idiosyncrasy of New York—brandied peaches!

"In the Players Club, as in other New York clubs (and there are so many!) I was impressed with the sociability of club life here in America. The clubs in London, as I at least have observed them, serve purposes rather of utility and political coagulation than of consociation. Men take meals at their clubs in London, it strikes me, much as they would eat at a small and absolutely nice hotel, whereas here I notice that you eat in groups and have altogether amiable, chatty times together. That's the point,—you are more gregarious, more sociable at your clubs, more *en famille*.

"After the shock of New York in those one or two hot days, I was glad to be back again in Boston, the city with the charm exclusively its own. Its distinction is, of course, its oneness, its completeness, its homogeneity, qualities it has retained almost precisely as it had them when I was a boy, and it was a rural, or rather a rustic city, the conservative, collective and representative capital of New England. One feels, to be sure, the disadvantages of such advantage. Boston's standard of comparison is bounded entirely by its own precincts. It is given to bidding you to swan and setting you goose. But this very stiffness, stuffiness, this very inaccessibility to a breath of outer air, produces, in however close an atmosphere, a demeanor of self-respect and of patrician dignity.

"How many men, by the bye, New England contributes to New York, and how few New York to New England! It would seem to me that, when I was a boy, not so many would leave us for New York. I remember feeling the proximity in Boston of its imposing figures, with most if not all of whom I came, through my father, in some touch, except, I believe, with poor Hawthorne. My father used to take me now and again to luncheons of the Saturday Club, active, at that time, with its gifted founders.

"Writing seems nowadays so different a matter from what it then was. I judge it may have come to much the same pass with you in America as with us in England, where training in journalism and, before that, training in public schools, has given, to a multitude, a sort of pseudo-form, a largeness, looseness, and elasticity of talk which has flooded the country with an enormous sea of chatter. As soon as any man has anything at all to say to anybody, it is puffed about the country in distended and distorted shape. To blame for this, of course, there is the accessibility of print on the one hand, and the dissemination of it on the other. All this chatter must have its uses. There must be a public for it. Indeed I have a reason or two to believe there persists a public for it.

"But I must make no statements! Sometimes I think I shall never speak again; particularly, that is, when some remark or other which I have made in all obviousness, is fostered, to my detriment, annoyance, and ill-temper by persons who have mistakenly interpreted it as a clever saying. I had that trial, for instance, with a chance and simple remark about my friend, Henry Harland. I make mention of it since the ghost of its murdered sense has pursued me even to America. With somebody of presumable intelligence, I was speaking of Harland's last three books and, in common with all the world, was admiring his ability to make one situation serve him thrice. I stated the mere fact that in his first book a nobly-descended young Englishman hires a castle of an Italian or Austrian princess and that the two fall in love, that in his second book, the princess hires the house of the nobly-descended young Englishman and that the two fall in love, and that in the third book, the princess and the nobly-descended young Englishman are together hiring the same house and that the two fall in love. It is as though there were a red glass, a blue glass, and a green glass, rearranged in various order. And to the artist who can rearrange the combination with, each of three times, an equally charming effect, there is deference. Nothing in what I said is to be translated beyond appreciation of Harland's handling of his material, which, after all, is the material he knows and loves and can write best about. One may be entertained with his skill of trickery, but the man who laughs aloud at my little word of observation is a silly donkey.

"There is something wonderfully engaging in Harland's fresh boyishness. Never so young as with pen in hand, he is, after all, the eternal boy! It is a disappointment to me that now when I have come to America he has returned again to England. He desired me to visit him in his beloved Norwich and I should so much have liked to see him there. Probably no one ever bore towards Norwich so strong an affection as Harland's for the town. Probably Norwich feels that in his love for her there is untoward excess—something not wholly proper, not wholly licit.

"The poor man has not of late been well. It was suggested to me that he should seclude himself for a period in one or another of the dry Western States, but it is altogether likely that the mental emigration, segregation, deprivation therein would be too much; he could not be without his grand duchesses and his princesses and his nobly-descended young men.

"Partly it's a great compliment to his books that I remember them so clearly; for, on the whole, I seldom can recollect as stories even the books that I most enjoy. On the other hand, for my comfort on this score, I am convinced that many of the best effects derived from reading or, it may be, from experience, come to us by a process quite distinct from that of remembrance. Germs of evil influence we remember all too clearly, but salutary effects softly enter into us without our realizing just how or when. One does not much remember the plot of a book by Meredith, for instance, but looks back on it, finds retrospect, retains vision, in something deeper than memory.

"I believe this is the afternoon when I am to be taken to hear *Parsifal*, to which I have agreed to go on the condition that I be not expected to return for the second installment."

He relieved me with the dexterity of a pickpocket, while we shook hands, of my scruples as a highwayman:

"May I add, since you spoke of having been asked to write something about me, that I have a constituted and systematic indisposition to having anything to do myself personally with anything in the nature of an interview, report, reverberation, that is, to adopting, endorsing, or in any other wise taking to myself anything that anyone may have presumed to contrive to gouge, as it were, out of me? It has, for me, nothing to do with *me—my* me, at all; but only with the other person's equivalent for that mystery, whatever it may be. Thereby if you find anything to say about our apparently blameless time together,—it is your little affair exclusively."

—*The Critic,* February 1905

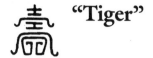 **"Tiger"**

To the Editor of *The Forum*

Dear Sir,—Last May you had the courage to print "Tiger" in *The Forum*.
Its theme since then has been variously used in longer plays, it has ap-
peared in book form, been barred from sale by the Comstocks of Bos-
ton, been played by students before members of the Dartmouth College
Faculty and by a professional cast at the Little Theater in Philadelphia.
Though most of the critics have treated it with understanding and sym-
pathy, it has received, as was to be expected, a certain amount of censure.
And I ask leave, in the magazine which first published the play, to make
briefly an accumulated reply to its official and unofficial censors.

"Tiger" has been referred to as a "white slave play" at a time when
platitudinous people are obscuring the question with that easy quibble,
"There is no such thing as white slavery." Whatever may be the fact as to
an organized ring of kidnappers or system of procuring girls against their
will, it is an indisputable fact that there are enough girls in the business
of prostitution who have been betrayed into it by individuals and forced
to remain in it by society to justify the use of the term "white slavery."
And it is this wider kind of white slavery which "Tiger" symbolizes. I am
careful to symbolize it fairly by including Annabel, corrupt and more or
less contented. The trouble with the sentimentalist who declares prosti-
tution to be a picturesque affair and no particular hardship to most of the
girls concerned is that he finds in the type, Annabel, an excuse for him to
believe as he comfortably prefers to believe. He prefers to say, "A white
slave is a girl living in seduced circumstances," and to treat the whole
situation as a joke and a convenience. The theorist abets him by insisting
that virtue—even at five a week—is not only its own reward but its own

protection. And the vacuist tries his best to draw into his vacuum not only vice, the dust, but knowledge, the floor. What I venture to suggest to this group, to the anti-suffragist, to the feudalist generally, is that, in my reading of Christ, we are all "members one of another," responsible to one another and eventually identified with one another. Objection to the coincidence in the play, that of a father meeting his own entrapped daughter in a disorderly house, is of no validity against the meaning of the coincidence in this essential tragedy of prostitution: Lust demanding and Greed supplying us with members of our own human family.

By some critics, by poets especially, I have been taken to task for telling the story of "Tiger" in blank verse. I started to write it in prose, but I soon found that the narrative in prose would require a more detailed account than I should need to set down in verse. I found that the verse carried in its rhythm an edge of artistic suggestion which gave a truer effect than I could accomplish by the accuracy of prose. It was the same picture; but the verse heightened and yet softened it, like a carbon enlargement. I suspect that had I given the characters in the play the distinction of title or removed them to Persia, there would have been little or no objection to my use of blank verse; its heroic associations would not have been soiled. Certainly I have not written heroic blank verse in "Tiger." It is rough, disjointed, sometimes almost syncopated. But running through it, here and there audible, I hope, is something of the rhythm of beauty, just as something of the grace of life runs through the Tenderloin.

Witter Bynner

New York

—*The Forum*, April 1914

⛩ The Story of the Spectric School of Poetry

In answer to many inquiries, I set down this brief story.

In 1914 when the poetic world was being stirred and amazed by the vagaries of various "schools" such as the "Imagist," "Vorticist," etc., I found myself feeling not only skeptical but resentful. There had been a widespread revival of interest in poetry, in response to a remarkably fine output of verse by the soldier poets. The public was recovering from the distaste it had felt toward poetry on account of fantastic and dubious excesses in the nineties. Everything was set, it seemed to me, for the coming of a period when a very large audience would be soundly and properly interested in poetry. Then came the interrupting antics of the more bizarre aesthetes.

Partly because of irritation, and partly out of amusement, I had the idea at the back of my head that anyone with a comparative knowledge of poetic diction and technique could play any sort of prank he liked with verse, talk about it sententiously and get away with it. This thought grew into a resolution. I decided to found, under cover, a school of verse and to have fun with the extremists and with those of the critics who were overanxious to be in the van. I needed a name for the school; and it happened that on the way to visit Arthur Davison Ficke in Davenport, Iowa, I stopped at Chicago and saw the Russians give a ballet called "Le Spectre de la Rose." The suggestiveness and fitness of the word Spectral or Spectric flashed over me. Between Chicago and Davenport, I wrote the first few Spectric poems; and within ten days after I had reached Davenport, and Ficke had kindled to the idea, we had written nearly all of the poems which were later collected in the volume *Spectra*, and many others which were a bit too wild for inclusion.

The method of composition was simple. Sometimes we would start with an idea, sometimes with only a phrase, but the procedure was to let all reins go, to give the idea or the phrase complete head, to take whatever road or field or fence it chose. In other words it was a sort of runaway poetry, the poet seated in the wagon but the reins flung aside. Some of the results seemed so good to us that Ficke and I signed, sealed, and filed a solemn document swearing that the whole performance had been done as a joke. I see now that in some respects this method of letting the subconscious do the writing was not an altogether bad method. In fact, leaving the jocose intention aside, I employed the method later in writing the poems in *The Beloved Stranger*.

With only three persons in the secret, the manuscript of *Spectra* was submitted to Mitchell Kennerley who promptly accepted it. Not long after, proofs of the book were lying on my desk at Cornish, New Hampshire, when the editor of one of our leading weeklies chanced upon them and became enthusiastic about the poems. To cover my confusion I told him that Mr. Kennerley had sent me, with an idea of my reviewing it, an advance copy of this work by the founders of a new school, Anne Knish and Emanuel Morgan, which were the names Ficke and I had chosen for disguise. The editor at once asked me to let his journal have the review. I accepted and at about the time the book was issued, *The New Republic* printed my article giving the new poets an astonished, amused, but respectful send-off. With few exceptions, critics and reviewers took the book seriously, many more of them praising than damning it. Poetry followers all over the country responded to it with zeal. Magazine editors accepted Spectric poems. Ardent enthusiasts bought many copies for voluntary distribution, and the Spectric School had become an established institution alongside the schools it secretly parodied. Its vogue indeed was so great that Ficke and I were put to it to conceal our friends Miss Knish and Mr. Morgan from the pursuit of newspapermen. The two new poets moved about from place to place, always eluding on some pretext or other the inquisitive interviewers. We had of course to let one or two others into our game: friends who in cities remote from our own dwelling places conducted a considerable correspondence. We would write the letters and our friends would sign and post them. Among the hundreds of congratulations we received there was one from an American poet, as well known as any, which told us "whereas the Imagists merely prick at the surface, you probe to the core." Ficke and I threw dice all afternoon to see which of us should be the owner of that letter. I won the throws and highly value the document.

Demands for Spectric verse became so insistent that we decided to enlarge our school. Oddly enough, the particular trick of writing Spectric verse proved not so easy. Somewhere I have a sheaf of poems from the late

George Sterling who was let in as a disciple, poems which, after all, by common consent had to be excluded from the Spectric output. The only one of several poets who caught the trick, and that after weeks of arduous and determined labor, was Marjorie Allen Seiffert who joined the ranks under the pseudonym Elijah Hay, and was soon involved as we were in considerable and sometimes embarrassing correspondence as a Spectrist.

Alfred Kreymborg told me one day at lunch in New York that he had persuaded the Spectrists to compile an issue of his magazine *Others*. Illuminating my vague knowledge of the group, he told me of friends of his who knew both of the founders, and assured me with a real gleam in his eye that Anne Knish was a great beauty. The poems which the three of us contributed to *Others* were even more extreme than those in the volume, were in fact somewhat calculated to give the secret away to the knowing, but the Spectric vogue had taken too firm a hold. It seems incredible now, when one looks at that issue of *Others,* that readers could have taken the verse seriously. On the other hand, it was no worse nor wilder than pieces solemnly offered by many an Imagist.

One of the strangest episodes connected with the hoax happened in Paris in 1917, when Ficke was a Lieutenant-Colonel. An officer who had been ordered to the front came to Ficke and confided to him that on the eve of possible death he thought he ought to leave behind him announcement of the authorship of *Spectra*. By word of mouth to Ficke and also in a sealed envelope he claimed the authorship as his own.

Although there had been a number of leaks, the hoax was still holding water two years after the appearance of the book, but maintaining it was growing more and more difficult. It broke finally and publicly in Detroit. In the course of a lecture I was giving there on modern American poetry, I touched as usual on the Spectric School. A man in the audience rose and interrupted me with a direct challenge as to whether or not Ficke and I had written the poems. A direct and large lie was too much for me. To the huge amusement of the audience, I thereupon told for the first time the complete story.

Many a discerning critic of poetry is convinced to this day that, liberated by our pseudonyms and by complete freedom of manner, Ficke and I wrote better as Knish and Morgan than we have written in our own persons. Once in a while we think so ourselves.

—*Palms,* March 1928

Alice and I

In tireder or wiser age one abstains both from giving and from attending lectures. In my comparative youth, the date being 1922, I arrived in Santa Fe to give one. The town was off my professional beat; but I had asked a reluctant agent to swing me here, unprofitably, between Oklahoma and Colorado and to let me have a week's respite besides. Because of influenza, in one of those years when influenza was not just a cold, I took more than the week's respite, had to stay in Santa Fe six weeks to recover and have been recuperating here ever since. The person who was to blame for all this is Alice Corbin.

In an earlier year of lecturing—1916 I think—I had been heckled from the floor at Chicago. My subject was "Contemporary American Poetry"; and, before the secret had broken that Arthur Davison Ficke and I were respectively Anne Knish and Emanuel Morgan, founders and wielders of the Spectric School of Poetry, I was telling my audience how superior Spectric verse was to Imagist verse. I was advancing the Spectric theory. The poet is imbued with a subject or faces one suddenly. Instead of emotionalizing or intellectualizing his approach to it, he blanks his conscious heart, his deliberate mind, and lets the subject submerge him both from inside and from outside. He acts as a medium and records the force and range of his theme in a mode seemingly beyond his control. It might have been called the Ouija School of Poetry; but on a brash platform I was taking our "school" more solemnly than my conscience should have permitted. I was preferring the specter to the image and probably confusing image with imagery, when an interruption came from the audience. A woman's voice gave us the Imagists' insistence that an image was not a mere figure of speech but a clearly seen picture of an idea. In a sharp but friendly interchange between auditor and lecturer, was the former unwittingly siding with earlier artists who would nowadays be called representational, and the latter unwittingly siding with present-day artists who believe the inner consciousness chooses better pictures than the outer consciousness? Brittle though our talk was, each of us was thinking he had the better of the tilt, a liking sparked between us; and after the lecture Alice Corbin and I shook hands and planned to join again. We did join shortly afterwards at the Hendersons' studio in Chicago, where I met Alice's painter-husband, William Penhallow Henderson, and their diminutive daughter.

I was wandering in those days, still young, still lecturing, the commercialized troubadour, and from time to time I saw the Hendersons in Chicago. Some years later I heard that Alice was ill, that she was in Santa Fe for her health, and I wrote her. In answering she proposed that I come to Santa Fe on one of my tours. And so I came.

It had not occurred to me that she was seriously ill. I had thought merely that Santa Fe was a better climate for her. And so, when I stepped off the primitive car which a spur track brought from Lamy into a town of nine thousand, I thought I was greeting with a kiss the Alice I had sparred with in Chicago and thought I was giving my luggage to a broad-hatted cowboy hand from some frontier hotel. Not until we had almost reached the sanitarium did I realize that the Alice alongside me was the diminutive daughter, now grown to fifteen, that the cowboy hand in the front seat with my luggage, who had not till now said a word, was William Penhallow Henderson and that the elder Alice was a bedded invalid.

Though it troubled me at first to stay in a building which was half hotel, half sanitarium for tuberculars, I was soon persuaded that I was safer at Sunmount than in a New York trolley car and I remained beyond the six weeks needed for recovery from influenza. Alice Corbin's room, perhaps purposely, was opposite the doctor's office. She was not only a bed-patient but under strict watch as to rest and diet. Doctors, nurses, servants, and patients were all, in those years, easy comrades and so were such guests as lived long enough in the haphazard hotel section to become fellow Santa Feans. Waitresses would bring coffee for groups in this or that private room instead of serving it at this or that table in the long dining hall. Later Alice brewed her own coffee, and we would gather nightly in her room for gay, swift talk and forbidden cigarettes. Now and then we would enjoy in our coffee cups a fill or two of Taos Lightning, that fiery corn whiskey which we keg-rolled in the backs of our cars. Willy would be there, Little Alice would be there, a nurse would be there. Finally even the head doctor would be there and almost grant that these trespasses upon rule were doing his patient good.

In spite or because of such trespass, Alice presently emerged from the sanitarium, well enough to move to the little house on Camino del Monte Sol which her fifteen-year-old daughter and Nella, their canny Spanish-American maid, had been running with the authority of Mothers Superior. Amusing moments ensued when neither of them wished to yield any of that authority to the lay mother; but soon life continued around Big Alice very much as it had done farther up the hill: intimate gatherings, tea, coffee, cigarettes, white mule, and talk, talk, talk. At the sanitarium, we had often read poetry to one another, poetry established and poetry our own. Now, with mainly practitioners present, poetry and painting took fuller sway.

It was a small, pleasant, primitive adobe house, with an outdoor privy and with horses corralled alongside. I remember well when little Starlight was foaled on a cold night. Visitors would come across distances which now demand motoring; but we came on horseback then by day or at night on foot with lanterns and would kick snow off our overshoes in the welcoming glow of the room with its corner adobe fireplace. Painters from nearby houses on the Camino would be there, Applegate, Bakos, Shuster, Nash, sometimes Sloan and Davey from streets farther away, often Indian painters like Awa Tsireh from the Pueblos and occasionally a visiting writer, Lindsay with his chants, Sandburg with his guitar, Frost with his wit, Lummis with a red bandanna round his gray temples, or neighboring Jack Thorpe with his brother.

The Hendersons and I attended many Pueblo ceremonials together in those days; but we liked to watch singly and to absorb the dances, or to be absorbed by them, rather than to make them the social occasions they are now; and when the Easter dance or the August dance came at Santo Domingo, each lasting three days, we would last the three days with them, sleeping on the schoolhouse floor, and be up at dawn to see the first Koshare, with Alice Corbin as alert and hardy as any of us. Sometimes we were the only white watchers. Sometimes we took with us a visiting writer like Bliss Carman or Edna Millay, or a composer like Ernest Bloch.

Resident writers in 1923 were few. Elizabeth Shepley Sergeant was here, telling in *Harper's* about her "mud house"—whence dated, I think, the local dubbing of us painters and writers as "mud-hut nuts." Manuel Chavez was here, but not yet called Fray Angelico. Mabel Sterne was in Taos but not yet known for her memoirs. Erna Fergusson was in Albuquerque but was conducting tourists to the Indian country, not yet a courier in print. Ruth Laughlin's pen was not yet notably busy. Mary Austin, Haniel Long, Lynn Riggs, Ernest Seton, Oliver La Farge, Alfred Kreymborg, Paul Rosenfeld, Arthur Davison Ficke, Raymond Holden, Louise Bogan, Clifton Fadiman, John Gould Fletcher, and others came later to settle or sojourn in Santa Fe. But Spud Johnson shared my house in 1922, and it was then that the D. H. Lawrences made their first Santa Fe visit. Mabel Sterne, now Mabel Luhan, was bringing them through town from Lamy on their way to visit her in Taos, but it was too late for them to undertake what used to be a long and tough drive. At quick notice she could find no Santa Fe roof for them but mine, although at that time it covered only three small rooms, porous to the wind.

But what a sudden warmth we whipped together—Lorenzo and Frieda, Mabel and Tony Luhan, Alice Corbin, Willy Henderson and Little Alice, Spud and I. Mabel and Tony left early; but the rest of us talked by the fireplace into the snuggest of the small hours, all of us bobbing at Alice as children bob at apples on Halloween. She looked like an apple, with her round, rosy cheeks. And Willy was drawling his narratives of earlier Western days. And Little Alice was correcting both parents at intervals. The Lawrences, tired after their journey from the Coast but relieved to find a simple household, were soon recounting global adventures and they were as much like children as were the rest of us. With the Hendersons' help we gave them a late supper, and Spud and I were up early next morning to wash the dishes and feed our guests; but the Lawrences, let me record, were up before us and every dish was either clean or holding part of a good, hot breakfast which they had prepared and exactly timed for their hosts.

Later, when other writers and multiplying summer visitors came to Santa Fe, Alice Corbin was a main organizer of the annual Poets' Round-Up, to raise funds for Indian causes; and, in closer bound and bond, she brought a small group of us residents together to read and criticize one another's poems and to stimulate new writing: Spud Johnson, Haniel Long, Clifford McCarthy, Lynn Riggs, Robert Hunt and me, with others occasionally joining. Sometimes there would be personal poems betwixt us, a challenge and an answer; and, since Alice Corbin is not to know beforehand that we offer her herewith a garland of respectful affection and therefore cannot be asked to grant me the right to print a sonnet of hers, I venture, without her permission to enter a brace of exchange which dates from those poetry meetings. Alice wrote:

El Conquistador

You are so much to every casual friend—
The butcher and the baker and the rest,
And anyone who has a mood to spend
May spend it in the hollow of your breast:
Lowitsky has a share in you and all,
All, all possess you—and I only groan

To see you thus made common carnival,
And nothing left for me to call my own!

O Hal, O Hell—what is the use to sue
The insubstantial, evanescent you!
Harlot of sympathies although you be,
I search and hope and never may be sure
If what you give me differs from the lure
That holds Lowitsky and that maddens me!

I replied at the next session of our group:

*To One Who Exclaims at My Friendship
with a Second-Hand Dealer*

(*"You always like anyone."*)

Lowitsky breathes his portion of the sky,
He too a curious vessel in the sun,
Of bright afflatus and opinion,
With as good veins to hold them in as I.
Why then pretend that he can only buy
And sell mean objects and perforce be done
With other thinking and with other fun?
Man has a second hand if the first die.

All men are made of earth to comprehend
Sun, moon and stars and thoughts: diameters
Crossing the wheel. Circumference encloses
You, me, Lowitsky too. Unto one end
We move together, while the circle stirs
With all its knowledge and with all its noses.

This sort of interchange was good teasing, good questioning, good fun.
I wish it had continued longer. Alice's sonnet, femininely playful, and
mine, masculinely pontifical, were not, for others, of any special import
in content or expression but for us, in personal and literary stimulus, they
were of timely import; and that sort of give and take enlivened our enjoy-
ment and experiment. It was good for us; and Alice managed continuance
of our meetings as long as she could. It was not her fault that they ceased,
nor was it ours. Towns grow too large. Nor should this particular verse
exchange have ended where it did. My pulpit sonnet was not fair. Alice's

understanding of every sort of person, her sympathetic entrance into the feelings and reasons of others, have been a lifelong characteristic. Years ago, as everyone knows, she was Associate Editor, with Harriet Monroe as Editor, of *Poetry: a Magazine of Verse*—in fact she was cofounder of it. And in that golden period of American poetry her vivid, sympathetic spirit meant much to most of the poets who made it golden, as it has meant much to all of us who have encountered her in poetry or in life.

Among my letters through the years from Ezra Pound I have found a pertinent passage:

"Alice was only intelligent element (in that frying pan) 1911–12 or whenever—only means of getting an idea into dear ole 'Arriet's hickory block. In short Alice my only comfort during that struggle. Blessings upon her."

Blessings upon her, say we all.

—*The New Mexico Quarterly,* Spring 1949

Santa Fe

In 1922 the road from Santa Fe to Taos was formidable—rough, narrow, and through a steep canyon, by no means the easy hour's drive it is today; and Mrs. Sterne, meeting her guests in the capital, had decided to postpone motoring them north until the morrow. She had neglected, however, to arrange lodgings for them. Hotel accommodations were few then; and having found a room for herself elsewhere, she happened to hit upon me as their host for the night. The adobe house which my secretary, Willard (Spud) Johnson, shared with me, had not yet grown beyond three rooms; but, persuaded by Mrs. Sterne that the Lawrences would prefer its native roughness to somebody else's more capacious, more modern dwelling, I eagerly assented to the suggestion. Paul Burlin, the painter, had added a kitchen to the original two rooms of the house which I now own but was then renting from him; so it was possible, through use of couches in the living room, for the Lawrences to be given the bedroom—next to the tub and toilet which at that time Spanish-American neighbors used to come and view as curiosities—and for William Penhallow Henderson, with his wife, Alice Corbin, and their fourteen-year-old daughter, Little Alice, as well as Mrs. Sterne and Tony Lujan, the silently impressive Taos Indian who was driving for her, to join us and share a kitchen supper.

Presently the car arrived in my bleak little yard, where I had been assiduously watering downy tufts of green, still ignorant that they were tumbleweed. A red-bearded man started out of the car just as Tony decided to back it a bit, whereupon I heard my first Lawrencian explosion. He had been in Taormina, before continuing eastward round the world, and had bought there a Sicilian peasant-painting: the back panel of a cart vividly decorated with two scenes of medieval jousting. He had carried his trophy, some five feet long and two feet high, from place to place for months, his wife thinking that perhaps he would decide to settle in Taos and that there at last the panel too would rest. It never reached Taos. In my yard the panel and his mind were settled with one savage flash. The board had been under his arm as he was alighting and one end of it, being on the ground when Tony backed, had buckled and split, giving him a shove as it did so. Lawrence's thin shape cleaved air like the Eiffel Tower, his beard flamed, his eyes narrowed into hard turquoise, he dashed the panel to the earth, and his voice, rising in a fierce falsetto, concentrated on the ample woman behind him, "It's your fault, Frieda! You've made me carry that vile thing round the world, but I'm done with it. Take it, Mr. Bynner, keep it, it's yours! Put it out of my sight! Tony, you're a fool!" Mrs. Lawrence maintained a smile toward us; the Indian stirred no eyelash. Mrs. Sterne, pleased with the show, took command of it by introducing us in her pleasant, innocent voice, and Lawrence shook hands with us as affably as though the outburst had not occurred. But despite Frieda's "*jas*" and noddings that she would like to keep the panel even with its crack, nobody's plea could move him to let her have it, though I believe he would have liked to keep it, too. After these many years, Mrs. Lawrence still sees it on occasion in my study and laughs over its connection with our stormy first meeting.

Lawrence's appearance struck me from the outset as that of a bad baby masquerading as a good Mephistopheles. I did not feel in him the beauty which many women have felt. I have since read—in *The Savage Pilgrimage*—Catherine Carswell's impressions at her first meeting with him nine years before mine. "The immediately distinguishing thing," she says, "was his swift and flamelike quality. . . . I was sensible of a fine, rare beauty in Lawrence, with his deep-set jewel-like eyes, thick, dust-coloured hair, pointed underlip of notable sweetness, fine hands, and rapid but never restless movements." Four months after that, in October, 1914, he had written her: "I was seedy and have grown a beard. I think I look hideous, but it is so warm and complete, and such a clothing to one's nakedness, that I like it and shall keep it." She describes it as "a beard quite different from the hair of his head, of a deep glowing red in the sun and in the shade the colour of strong tea." Richard Aldington records, as of 1914, ". . . the head looks moulded of some queer-coloured stone, the beard gives the right touch of Mohammedan 'touch-me-not-ye-unclean.'" I remember quickly wondering at Santa Fe in 1922 what Lawrence would look like under the beard, which gave somewhat the effect of a mask with the turquoise eyes peering from it. The beard and the hair, too, seemed like covers he was cuddling under—a weasel face hiding under the warm fur of its mother and peeking out. Mrs. Carswell was accurate as to the colors. The beard, which he retained through the rest of his life, appeared to me more like a connected part of him than did his mat of hair, with its forward sidelong bang, which looked detachable, like a wig or a cap. In his writings, he forever removed that cap, exposed his cranium and its cerebral contents in all nakedness; but physically the beard clung close over his face as if he wished there the darkness into which his whole nakedness was always striving to return, or to progress. How he would have enjoyed classic proportions and a clean-cut Greek visage instead of the look of a semistarved viking! The Hon. Dorothy Brett, the Taos painter from England, relates of their first meeting, "I look up, realizing with surprise the eyes are blue, not black, as I had thought." Mrs. Carswell, too, had originally thought the eyes another color and then found them blue. Aldington recalls from his own first meeting in 1914, ". . . you were immediately impressed by his fiery blue eyes" which "seemed to exist independent of their owner," whereas John Galsworthy could not like the "provincial novelist" because of his "dead eyes." Perhaps Lawrence could shift their color for women. He himself, however, knew well what hue they were and how they could change in mood and temper. In *The Rainbow* he says of the Brangwens, his own clan, "One could watch the change in their eyes from laughter to anger, blue-lit-up laughter, to a hard blue-staring anger." Although he was to say later that all the gods have blue eyes, he had confided to Jessie Chambers ("E. T."), his early intimate: "For me, a brown skin is the only beautiful one." His own skin was too white, and I do not think he enjoyed it. Somewhere he quotes the Greeks as having said that "a white, unsunned body was fishy and unhealthy."

He occasionally vented in his writings his reluctant distaste for the physique he was born to carry and he tried to put the fault outside himself. Mrs. Lawrence records in *Not I but the Wind* his pathetic remark to the doctors when his end was near: "I have had bronchitis since I was a fortnight old." He had come through pneumonia twice in his twenties. And so when he tells, in *Kangaroo,* the bitter story of his examination and rejection for British army service, he almost blames the official for his own humiliated and unbelieving distress in not being of more heroic mold: "The chemist-assistant puppy looked him up and down with a small grin as if to say, 'Law-lummy, what a sight of a human scarecrow!'" He appeared anything but a scarecrow that evening in Santa Fe, though he was a bit gangling, and his voice was occasionally like whistlings of the wind. "His voice," says Aldington, "such a pleasant devil's voice, with its shrill little titters and sharp mockeries and even more insulting flatteries. . . . I welcome his 'tee-hees' and 'too-hoos,' which puff away a deal of silly cant and affectation." "A high tinkling laugh," contributes Dorothy Brett, "the ever-ready amused jeer." Norman Douglas, less kindly, in a comment on Lawrence's satirical writing about recognizable persons, is undoubtedly describing and disliking the physical voice: "that squeaky suburban chuckle which is characteristic of an age of eunuchs."

We had heard the shrillness of the Lawrence voice over the broken wagon board and we heard its variations later that evening in satirical comments on persons and places.

Mrs. Lawrence's presence, meantime, had been easy to take. Her smile from the first had meant, "I'll like you till I find a reason not to and I'll be all of myself whether you like it or not." Her body had German breadth and stature; she was a household Brunhilde; her fine profile was helmeted with spirit; her smile beamed and her voice boomed. In her were none of the physical timidities and reservations which made one questioningly aware of her husband's personality. With her there was no question. On the other hand, she did not intrude her strong presence, did not interrupt with it. It would assent or dissent firmly but with deferent timing. She never had to insist that she was there.

The homing instinct was at that time, probably always, more alive in Mrs. Lawrence than in her husband. He was always seeking a farm, a ranch; but by his own reports it was more because it might be the headquarters of a group he could head and because it would afford him growing vegetable life around him than because it would house him and his wife and give them a hearthstone. And then he would flee each harbor. For Mrs. Lawrence the search was now different. Flight from the first husband, an uncongenial, pedantic mate, had been the important break, and she did not need all the subsequent little escapes from escape.

On that first night in Santa Fe, after the one outbreak over the Sicilian cart-painting, Lawrence, the excitable fugitive, became Lawrence, the domestic expert. His wife said that when he broke an egg it never drooled and that he never set a dish too near the edge of a table. Deftly he joined the two Alice Hendersons and my awed maid in preparing supper, over which we sat long—quickened with the Lawrences' tales of world voyaging and world figures, with memorable mimicry of some of the latter, including Middleton Murry and Norman Douglas, and with tales from us about our local Spanish-Americans and Indians. I remember Lawrence being specially amused by a current New Mexico anecdote told by Johnson. Elizabeth Shepley Sergeant had just published in *Harper's Magazine* her *Story of a Mud House,* an account of life in an adobe dwelling at Tesuque and had spoken of her pretty maid as "the belle of Santa Fe." Someone had shown the passage to the maid who, reading English but scantily, had made vigorous protest, "I am *not* the belly of Santa Fe!" They liked also my own maid's assurance to us that she was not a backbiter. "I speak everything in people's faces—not in their behinds." And Frieda chuckled over Mrs. Sterne's enjoyment of the fact that earlier settlers in Santa Fe, those who had built more or less conventional, nostalgically Eastern-style houses on Palace Avenue and could not understand the flair among painters and writers to acquire native adobe shacks, had taken to calling us "the mudhut nuts."

Henderson, or perhaps Mrs. Sterne, told a story well known locally about "Long John" Dunne who ran the stage to Taos from the Denver and Rio Grande station, still extant in those days, across the canyon. Annoyed by passengers who were nervous on the steep declivity or who pestered him with questions he had heard a thousand times, he once gave an aside to a friend: "Pity God didn't put fur on some people, so's you could shoot 'em." I decided long afterward that Lawrence's coldness toward the quip was because he was sorry not for the person but for the imagined animal.

His amusement revived, however, when Alice Corbin told of a well-known Santa Fe hostess who had imported a Scandinavian husband and wife from Denver as domestics and who, on finding that they had no religious affiliation, but would oblige her with one if she would arrange it for them, had gone to the Methodist minister and asked him to take them under his wing, "because the Methodist Church, I understand, makes a specialty of common people." Lawrence's enjoyment of the story seemed to rise less from our American slant of amused shock as democrats than from an English satisfaction in the convenience of a proper disposition of lesser breeds. It is recorded that his mother had considered Methodists "common." In his last work, *Apocalypse,* he says of the Primitive Methodist Chapel, "Even I thought it rather 'common.'"

It may be my afterthought or afterimagination that Lawrence's eyes and thoughts were back in Derbyshire a moment among Methodists, but returned to Santa Fe when young Alice told of old Mrs. Laughlin's comment on the artists there, among whom I, like many of the others, was a wearer of Navajo shirts and jewelry, "At first we respectable residents of Santa Fe hated the way you artists and writers went about in any old kind of clothes and no neckties, but you do afford interest and amusement to the tourists and if you can stand it, I guess we can." I wondered later if he remembered the remark and relished it anew, when he himself went about open throated in flannel shirt and cowboy hat.

Above all, in his response to us that night, I remember the jump of his eye when I told him a remark of another old resident, Mrs. Crist, a Scottish niece of Sir Richard Burton, affectionately known as "Lady Crist." She had said to me, apropos of I forget what, "I am a woman, but I never tell anything. Now I am going to tell *you* something. I have never made a confidant. As Christ is born, I am my own confidant." One of the greatest confiders of all time, one who tried through his books to confide everything to everybody, he turned toward the absent Mrs. Crist, as I see it now, a childlike gaze, a profoundly amused gaze, of envious respect. Her remark in our story was a lightly told touch of the solitude he wanted. On the other hand, he liked the fact that she gabbled too.

When the others had left, the Lawrences, though tired from their journey, sat late into the night; and Johnson and I were drawn and held by their magnetism. Quickly I knew that the reports I had heard as to Mrs. Lawrence being beneath her husband's stature, and something of an incubus, were either malicious or stupidly mistaken. I felt from the first a sense of their good fortune in union: in his having realized his particular need of her and in her having made her warm, wise, earthy womanhood an embracing Eden for this inquisitive, quick-fingering, lean animal of a man—this eager origin of a new species. For all his flares at her, usually over trifles, he knew that she was his mate. Lion-chasers and neurotic women, who tried to disparage Frieda and to attract him by substituting their ambitions and vanities for her fond, amused, understanding, creative patience found presently that a real lion would have been tamer in drawing room or boudoir than this odd simian cat whose interest in them was finally a puzzled, tolerant curiosity. In a way he liked the flattery of their attentions and with almost Frieda's patience indulged their vagaries; but often his purring would stop and a claw would come out. On that first night, despite his extreme good humor and friendliness to all of us, I felt the cat-nature in the man, as well as the monkey-nature, and with a respect for cats I was attracted by it. At least he was no dog, hopping and fawning. He was in a house, moving sleekly; but he would never be properly domesticated.

On September 18, 1922, I wrote Arthur Davison Ficke: "On their way to Mabel Sterne's the other night, the D. H. Lawrences rested in my 'dark bed.'" He must have called it that, "dark," without my yet realizing the respect in his use of the word.

Lawrence's talk that night quickly made clear the fact that Tony's clumsiness in the car had not dulled the Red Indian lure which has been felt by many an Englishman. John Masefield wrote me later: "I envy you your life among the Indians. Even after all these centuries of fire-water, they must be the most interesting of all the peoples now alive."

Lawrence had already indicated his sense of the "Red Indian" spell by the runes of his mimic Indian troupe in *The Lost Girl*. He was now actually present in the neighborhood of his noble savage. Let Tony be clumsy with a car. Motor cars were not Indian business.

In the morning I was up ahead of the alarm clock for once, to make sure that the guests should have a decent breakfast before Mrs. Sterne's arrival to drive them north. Supper dishes were still to be washed in the kitchen.

I went quietly around the house to the back door; but Lawrence opened it for me. Every dish had been washed. The table was laid with an ample breakfast. The bed had been neatly made in the room beyond. They had been about to call us. Just then my maid appeared from across the street where she lived; but the Lawrences had finished a complete job. The maid looked ashamed; but the guests were beaming as well as hungry. Frieda said that Lorenzo had done all the cooking. Breakfast proceeded at a hearty pace, giving us another interval of talk before Mrs. Sterne walked in. The night had been the Lawrences' first in an American house. For me it felt like a wholly good omen. It was in reality a mixed omen.

As far as we knew at the time, life in Taos advanced at an amiable pace for the Lawrences and their neighbors. This was not yet the Taos year which Mrs. Carswell has described as "a combat of pythonesses." Mrs. Sterne gave the newcomers a house apart. Tony Lujan introduced them to the pueblo, its people, its ceremonies, and its thoughts. The Taos Indians soon named Lawrence "Red Wolf." Earlier, in villages as far apart as the Tewas' Santo Domingo and the Hopis' Hotevilla, Indian acquaintances of mine, without their knowing in any of the places that the same name had been given me in another, had christened me "Mountain Antelope." In Santo Domingo it sounded, varying, Go-tay-kerts or Go-tay-mot, in Hotevilla Cher-der-kwee, in Tesuque Dom-pin; but in each case it meant Mountain Antelope; and I should have taken warning that there might be hazard in an antelope's association with a wolf.

Dorothy Brett says in her book that the Indians called him "Red Fox." My own memory, from what they and he have told me, is that it was "Red Wolf," a memory corroborated by his poem of that name, from which I quote:

> And wolf, he calls me, and red . . .
> I'm the red wolf, says the dark old father.
> All right, the red-dawn-wolf I am.

Lawrence, of course, had to change it a little and make his prowl mean dawn. I wonder if Brett, with her ear trumpet, may not have been just as deafly inaccurate when she understood that the Indians called Mrs. Lawrence "Angry Winter." A winter with plenty of snow perhaps, to keep the soil green, a forceful winter.

Whatever was happening, there had been as yet no anger toward me from the wintry Frieda and no growls from the wolfish Lorenzo. Books written later about that period in Taos record growls in other directions, both from the wolf and from the wolf's mate. Why not, when alien she-wolves were determined to jostle her in his lair? But Taos was eighty miles away from Santa Fe and during that early period we heard few echoes of friction, except Alice Corbin's report of one sharp quarrel Lawrence had picked with her, when she was visiting Mabel Sterne, over some trifling difference of opinion.

He wrote me: "If we don't like Taos, or find neighbors here oppressive, we can go to Mexico. Perhaps you and the Spoodle could come with us." He had already displaced Johnson's nickname, Spud, with Spoodle.

After these few months the wander-fever was in Lawrence again. His feet itched to be going somewhere—Mexico this time. Whatever preparations he could make in Taos were being made. His busy mind applied itself to Terry's Mexican guidebook and a Spanish grammar. Maps were studied and costs calculated, while he delegated to us and others the questionings at railway offices. When he was in Santa Fe one day and some information had come through, he stayed outside the office and let me gather the data. He always shunned official desks with a nervous dislike for them and for the power of the men behind them. He resented, with helpless fury and flurry, the fact that his own superior intelligence and efficiency should have to defer to officiousness. He might be the helm when they set sail, but Mrs. Lawrence was usually the prow that breasted the waters. On the other hand, her bold confusion was often less helpful than his timorous plunge might have been. At least he would scoldingly take the tickets from her once she had them; for she was always losing everything except her reason and sense of life and sense of humor. And he scolded less, she says, when she lost guineas than when she lost shillings. Neither of the pair was used to carrying much money. Loss of guineas was enough punishment.

—Chapter 1 from *Journey with Genius: Recollections and Reflections Concerning the D. H. Lawrences,* New York: John Day Co., 1951

"From Him That Hath Not"

Tomasito Benavides, a young Indian from the pueblo of Santo Domingo, New Mexico, stood recently before a Chinese painting of a hunt which hung in the Santa Fe Museum. After a quiet survey of the various figures, some of them horsemen, Tomasito turned and said: "There is much grass in China." And when I asked why he thought so, he explained: "Fat horses."

Over eight thousand Pueblo Indians live in New Mexico, scattered among their twenty adobe villages—their pueblos. While New Mexico was still old Mexico, each of these villages was the center of approximately a seventeen-thousand-acre patented land grant from the Spanish crown, a grant subsequently confirmed by the Mexican Republic. After this northern part of old Mexico became the Territory of New Mexico the American Government, in 1848, guaranteed to the Pueblo Indians the validity of all their land grants except the grant centering around the pueblo of Zuñi, which for some reason was not recognized. The Zuñis, a branch of the Pueblo tribe, are therefore living on a Government Reservation, like Indians in other States; but all the rest of the Pueblos, unlike Indians anywhere else in America, are living on land which belongs to them in their own legal right.

I have seen in Santo Domingo one of the canes which were presented by Abraham Lincoln to the various Pueblo governors when the Spanish and Mexican grants were made supposedly firm under American law. It seems, though, that a cane may be a solider thing than a scrap of paper. It seems that the American Government, in dealing with the Pueblo Indians, has cared very little about its word.

For three-quarters of a century the Pueblos have been asking that Washington keep its word and prevent the steady illegal enchroachments upon their territory. So little has it mattered to Washington that there are today several whole towns of Americans on Indian land in New Mexico. Much of this old mischief cannot now be undone without grievous consequences, but new mischief can be obstructed and recent mischief remedied. A few Americans, acquainted with this dishonorable history, undertook a while ago in and near Santa Fe a public defense of the Pueblos, a defense which ought to have originated in Washington.

An Indian from San Juan, learning of the efforts of these citizens to bring about even a lame and belated justice, exclaimed, sincerely: "I did not know we had a single friend in New Mexico!"

The New Mexico Association on Indian Affairs consists, not only of New Mexicans, but of many now from outside the State who, like myself, have come into touch with the Pueblo Indians and by the threatened passage of the Bursum Indian Bill have been made to realize with a shock the ignominious cruelty of the American people toward its wards. Other societies have arisen East and West. The press has responded vigorously, and the public is waking up.

To the eye of a casual observer Indian territory looks large on the map—large enough, it would seem, for a vanishing race.

Let it be said at once that the Indians are not numerically a vanishing race. On the contrary, their number has increased during the last decade. Culturally they are being hard pressed. They dare to differ; they dare to ignore our mechanical standards; they dare to maintain customs and privacies we do not understand; they dare to be simple, to be natural, to be sincere, to be religious; they dare, in New Mexico, to find happiness under a communal system of landownership. And by all these offenses they have earned hitherto a passing glance from American tourists, a compassing glance from American capitalists, hostility from American hypocrites, contempt from American puppets, and, worse than all, deliberate betrayal or careless neglect from the expensive officials appointed to guide and to guard them.

Even culturally speaking the Pueblos might not be a vanishing race were it not for their vanishing land. Statistics are as dull as sermons, but briefer. Here, then, are a few, with chapter and verse.

First, a hint of what had already happened to Pueblo lands in New Mexico before the Senate passed the Bursum Indian Bill:

San Juan's 4,000 irrigable acres had been reduced by encroachments to 568, so that the total average cash income and value of product there per capita per annum for its 431 inhabitants is about $32. Contrary to general opinion, the only governmental addition to this meager livelihood is the tutelage, board, lodging, and clothing of schoolchildren. It may be added that San Juan is better situated as regards land and water than any of the Northern Pueblos save Taos, and one of only two or three which have had enough, or nearly enough, water for their lands this season.

Tesuque struggles along on an average income of $16.68 for the year, with practically all its irrigation appropriated by non-Indians.

The average annual income per capita in San Ildefonso is $13.11! Of the 12,000 acres granted to the San Ildefonso Indians in 1680 there are about 1,250 productive acres. The Indians have been left of these only 248 acres. In all, outsiders hold 3,500 acres of the best cultivated and pasture lands belonging to the San Ildefonso Pueblo. Only a day or two ago I was welcomed into some of the new houses which these gentle and gifted people are being obliged to build outside their own town, relinquishing their beloved plaza and its great cottonwood tree to the invaders.

At Nambe only 280 acres of the 3,000 irrigable acres of Indian land are now held by Indians.

These various lands were lost to the Pueblos in various ways. Sometimes there were conflicting grants from Spanish or Mexican authorities or squatter claims antedating 1848; but oftenest trespass and theft came about more simply.

Let John Dixon, an Indian Judge at Cochiti, tell in his own way what happened to the people of his pueblo. "When the Navajos came here to fight and steal because they were hungry, my people took in Mexicans to help protect them. The Mexicans say, 'Let me have one little room for my wife and family.' Then, 'Compadre, could you not let me have a little lot for a little house?' 'All right, compadre, you build a little house.' All the Mexicans, they just came in that way—did not buy. Then he would move, and sell his land to some other Mexican. When the Republican party issued pamphlets in the State campaign, old Mexican women would come to have me read for them. I say to one old woman—and there was another old woman together with her—'What is it Republican party says? It says: Vote Republican, vote for Bursum Bill. Then all Mexican neighbors in a village like this, if they had a house, would get a title. Now, old women, you got a room here. You can vote for a title.'" This, in simple talk, indicates the process by which many of the claims have grown up, claims which even without color of title would have been confirmed by the Bursum Indian Bill.

It happens that the Pueblo Indian tracts are all owned by the community; different portions being devised by the pueblo authorities to different families for use, but not for individual ownership. It may at once be seen that no title transferred by an individual Indian has any legal validity except what might accrue to it through the harmless-appearing provisions of this bill.

As though there had not been enough depredation and deprivation already, consider what the Bursum Indian Bill proposed and might have accomplished but for the vigilance of a handful of private citizens. . . .

—*The Outlook,* January 17, 1923

Pueblo Dances

Once upon a time, I jotted down the following remarks from the lips of the Governor of the Indian pueblo, San Juan de los Caballeros, who was introducing a dance to a group of white watchers.

"This is a very old dance—maybe five hundred years back. The elders of the pueblo have taught us this dance, which we danced before the Spaniards, Mexicans and Americans came to this country; when there were only Indians who have had no records except in their heads and in their hearts. The elders have bidden us, as long as the world exists, never to forget this dance. It is an important dance. When we dance it, we have an abundance of everything. Now you are to see this dance. The man who will dance it is of a high position in the pueblo, one of the caciques, and an elderly man, a very religious man in the Pueblo religion."

Not long ago, a New Yorker who had heard much about Indian dances came to New Mexico, eager to see them. He saw one, and his interest waned. Because the dances are not dances.

After experience of the black maze of dances in Harlem, with this or that individual's personality shining through it as sharply as his teeth, our friend found Pueblo dances unexciting. After watching Isadora Duncan's infinite and subtle variety, he found the Pueblo motions monotonous. After watching through many seasons many fine bodies on the New York and European stage, each exhibiting its own particular and highly conscious beauty through sensual human graces and intricacies, he was chilled to find Indian dances as aloof as blown treetops that tip toward the moon. He wanted what he had seen before. He wanted the personal, the immediate, the physical; something to excite his nerves with outward sensation. He encountered the impersonal, the remote, the spiritual; something that constricts the heart of both dancer and onlooker within its own innermost beat.

Preparing for a dance, a Pueblo may be as careful as the vainest of us that he shall look well, that his costume shall accurately and properly befit an occasion. Once he has entered the dance, his vanity seems to leave him. He seems unaware not only of the foreign friend looking on from a housetop but even of the dancer nearest to him in the shifting lines and figures of the devotional mass-movement. One wonders, feeling the withdrawnness of each man and woman in the dance, how they manage their turns and changes without occasional conflict of body against body. They hardly seem to be hearing the equally rapt chorus of men who are singing and treading and weaving the song, they seem to have forgotten the perfect tempo of the drum. Their footbeats are like heartbeats, pulsing as inevitably through varied and interrupted rhythms as the inlet and outlet of breath in a living body. And yet, with as many as four or five score other persons between them, the two end persons in a line of dance will be touching the earth in a rapid entrancement of unison. While the dance interval lasts, the whole group moves as lightly and surely as a single swallow. If Patricio or Alfonso or Rafael steps out of the dance to have betweentimes a smoke and a laugh with you, your wonder is all the greater when he steps back into the dance again and becomes someone who existed a thousand years ago, is now and ever shall be. They are of the earth and the earth is of heaven. They are blown by a wind from the sky, like the many drops of the rain they dance for. And like the rain itself, the falling of their feet is an everlasting motion against death.

Granted that there are dances which the Pueblos borrow from other tribes, dances given in a lighter and more playful spirit; granted that some of their own dances are deliberately comical or whimsical or surprisingly primitive and candid; granted that youngsters at Indian schools away from their homes develop competitive steps in a mood rather athletic than religious, and that such institutions as the Santa Fe Fiesta and the Gallup Ceremonial, where Indians present their dances before large commercial audiences, tend to break down the original meaning and inner intent of the ceremonies; granted all this, there remains in the Pueblo dance-rituals as conserved at stricter villages like Santo Domingo, a devout beauty which explains to us moderns what the ancients meant when they danced before the Lord. Only by watching them in their own spirit, may any one of us deserve to see them.

Specialists there are who can explain the symbolism, the details of movement and costume, the definite religious import of the Moqui Snake Dance, the Zuñi Shalako, an Eagle Dance at Santa Clara, a Buffalo Dance at Santo Domingo. And often the specialists are right. When we learn that the snake dancers, for instance, their tribe being descended from a Snake Princess, carry rattlers and other reptiles in their mouths in order that these earth creatures may have a happily rhythmical reminder of human friendliness and then be sent back underground bearing to the Snake Princess good report of her people above ground, we cease from our inquisitive abhorrence and we respect this Indian sacrifice to a better god than those many gods, including Jehovah, who have demanded even to this day blood-sacrifice and death.

Several years ago at Zuñi, the morning after the tall gods had come down from their mountain to bless each new hearth with stately ceremonies, to confer on all dwellers in new homes the dignity of ancient homes, I saw a grave accident. At the muddy edge of the river, during a final rite before departure for the year, one of the tall gods slipped and fell. Instantly his attendants hid him from sight with a circle of upheld blankets; and just as instantly the people of Zuñi were swept as by an unseen wind into their houses, and the clusters of visiting Navajo on their horses were struck away into the distance as on a thunderbolt.

Zuñi was deserted—except for a lone figure here and there, including a single Navajo who had dismounted after the ill omen and stood waiting like the others, motionless. Thereupon the Fire God strode across the river with a switch in his hand and lashed the scapegoats one by one on their bowed shoulders. When those few had taken upon themselves the punishment due all their fellows, because they had all profaned the god by viewing his mishap, the town began to breathe again, resumed its life. The symbol had been clear. It was the vicarious atonement.

However pertinent these explanations and parallels may be, no detail or episode can deeply illumine the onlooker, unless he be in his own nature attuned at the outset, unless he feel, almost from the very first drumbeat of the first dance he sees, an intimate and solemn sense of participation in the forces of heaven and earth, unless his private perverse individuality subside into the common rhythm of life, unless he hear the beat of timelessness countering the beat of time, and unless the drouth in his heart be ended by the coolness of an inner rain. Let the outer rain come, too, if it will. First the faith, and then the adding of all things.

It sometimes seems as if these people, in their heightened moments, had cherished alive through the centuries the Taoist wisdom of Laotzu and as if their dances were an outward and still visible sign of his inward invisible grace.

There are certain dances—a part of this wisdom—celebrating with honest, gay and proper acceptance, out in the open, before men, women and children, the necessary processes of nature which belong to this creative earth and which are by no means, to the Pueblos, a sly continuance of the original sin. I have watched one or two of these dances and find nothing to criticize.

This is no brief for the moral or intellectual character of Pueblos. It is a simple acknowledgment of the religious beauty in their ceremonies, a beauty that grows from their quiet faith in the earth.

They are of the earth and the earth is of heaven. They are blown by a wind from the sky, like the many drops of the rain they dance for. And like the rain itself, the falling of their feet is an everlasting motion against death.

—*They Know New Mexico: Intimate Sketches by Western Writers,* Passenger Department: Atchison, Topeka and Santa Fe Railroad, 1928

﹩ Translating Chinese Poetry

Blithely, three years ago, I undertook with the eminent scholar, poet and publicist, Dr. Kiang Kang-hu, a translation of three hundred poems from the Chinese, thinking that twelve months would see my labors ended. Through twelve of the thirty-six months I have worked from eight to ten hours a day on nothing but these poems and through the other twenty-four have been continually devoted to them, even accompanying Dr. Kiang to China for a year of closer cooperation. And they are still unfinished. I might have read a lesson from the history of as short a piece of translation as Fitzgerald's *Omar Khayyam;* but I was rash and, better than that, fascinated. Prior to the present undertaking, I had translated with the help of a Chinese student a few poems from the Confucian *Book of Poetry.* Those few had been enough to stir my wonder at the quiet beauty and deep simplicity that are as much qualities of Chinese poetry as they are of Chinese painting.

Stephen W. Bushell, in his book on *Chinese Art,* speaks of some early painter as typifying the aim of painting with the phrase, "to note the flight of the wild swan." It "shows already," says Bushell, "the preoccupation of Chinese art with the motion and breathing life of animals and plants, which has given their painters so signal a superiority over Europeans in such subjects." When one remembers that in China the wild swan was traditionally the messenger of the heart, the phrase might be used also to typify Chinese poetry: "the motion and breathing life" of a world in which man is the animal and nature the plant. But the wild swan was not merely a messenger between young and passionate hearts. Chinese poetry begins, in a way, where ours ends. When I felt a certain monotony of subject matter in a section of the volume I was translating, the parting and separation of friends and the solace of the everlasting hills, I turned to the *Oxford Book of English Verse* and found there an equal if not greater monotony in the succession of poems dealing with the extravagant passions of youth. Wordsworth, in his lyrics, is the most nearly Chinese of our poets. The poetry of the Chinese is, like his, the poetry of the mature, or, better, of grown children. It sings not the rebelliousness of youth, but the wisdom of age; not the excitement of artificial life, except for the elevation brought by wine, but the quiet of nature; not the unsteady joys of passion, but the steadfast joy of friendship. It is attached to actual daily life and not reserved as an ethereal pastime. A Chinese poem sounds often like the heart of a letter—and so it was: a condensed and thoughtful message.

Tu Fu of the T'ang Dynasty is generally accounted by the Chinese as the greatest of their lyric poets, though it was said of him and Li Po, "How shall we tell, when two eagles have flown beyond sight, which one has come nearer the sun?" From Tu Fu's grandfather, Tu Shên-yen, the editors of the anthology I am translating selected a single poem, in which his quiet voice echoes all the way from the sixth century to undo a persistent delusion, prevalent among certain poets of the Western moment, that beauty is to be found only in the unfamiliar. Incidentally, the poem illustrates the difficult game of "harmonizing a poem," which poets sometimes played with their verse: one poet would respond to a poem from another by adopting the other's rhyme-words in the same or altered arrangement. Tu Shên-yen's poem is called

> *On a Walk in the Early Spring*
> *(Harmonizing a Poem by My Friend Lu*
> *Stationed at Ch'ang-chou)*
> Only to wanderers can come
> Ever new the shock of beauty,
> Of white cloud and red cloud dawning from the sea,
> Of spring in the wild-plum and river-willow. . . .
> I watch a yellow oriole dart in the warm air,
> And a green water-plant reflected by the sun.
> Suddenly an old song fills
> My heart with home, my eyes with tears.

"To understand the circumstances of mortality," says a writer in *The Nation*, "to know what such a being as man can expect, and then to contemplate such knowledge—that is as near as art can get to any steadiness of joy." And that is where T'ang poetry had arrived a thousand years ago. The T'ang poets do not fool themselves with illusion but, seeing things as they are, find beauty in them—and thereby bring the high, the deep, the everlasting, into simple, easy touch with the immediate. They are masters of momentous minutiae, the small things that make the big. They know and record the immense patience of beauty. There is sadness in that patience, but it is an honest, a hearty, an even relishable sadness. One feels that they had sent their souls out through all the intricacies that are now confusing this Western generation, through all the ways of experience and imagination, and had then recalled them to the pure elemental truths, had received them again, peacefully cleansed of illusion and restlessness, and content in the final simple beauty of their own dooryards. To be sure, they knew where to place their dooryards. But so might we all, if we would.

I was fortunate enough to spend three months on a Chinese mountaintop, with a poet and his family, in the kind of retirement the old fellows loved and wrote about, overlooking a landscape the like of which I had never seen from any dwelling on earth. There were Sung mountain paintings glimmering from our peak all the way to the Himalayas; there were tremendous rainbows, sometimes leaving a bright section in the heart of a towering white cloud after the rest of the bow had faded; there were countless bamboos glistening after brief showers; there were the cicadas, ten thousand Chinese actors on one note at top pitch; there were the waterfalls along our paths; there were slow changes of incredible mist, spellbinding the dawns and the twilights; there was always, below us, the vast plain—rippled with hills, varied with purple shadows of cloud, veined with jade-green rice fields; and there were remote silver gleams of river and lake and even of sea—the whole level eastward horizon seeming often the actual ocean and our mountain the brow of the earth. It is no wonder that I became imbued with the spirit of the poets who had lived in just such places—with the "huge and thoughtful" patience of China: the kind of patience that is wisdom; the kind of wisdom that is submersion of one's self and its little ways in the large and peaceful distances of nature. And just as that landscape moved and breathed, so do the Chinese poems from line to line. And just as man becomes natural and simple in a presence like that, so did the Chinese poets. And in all the chaos of contemporary China that spirit is alive. In Peking last winter, fine old Admiral Tsai Ting-kan said to a friend of mine, "The older I grow, the more contempt I have for the processes of human reason and the more respect for the processes of the human heart."

Dr. Kiang has said much the same thing to me. And against various odds, he has practiced what he preaches. Appalled at times by the stupendous task confronting those who would ameliorate conditions in China, he has begun, as the sincere and simple altruist always begins, with his own conduct and his own circumstances. Some years ago he founded a girls' school and gave his own dwelling in Peking to house it: the first girls' school in the country founded by a Chinese. He inherited a fine library and a distinguished collection of paintings. Some of the latter are in museums in Japan, the Nipponese having been the most intelligent of all the looters after the Boxer uprising. What was left of the library he has given to the University of California. His share of other property inherited from his father he has renounced in favor of his brothers. When Yüan Shih-k'ai usurped the throne, Kiang risked his life by challenging the act and finally fled to America. Now that he can be of service again in China, he has relinquished academic opportunities in the New World, to return to his own people. In other words, he is a man of the same nature as the noblest of the T'ang poets and, as such, better fitted to interpret them than if his only qualification were the title he won under the Empire, when literary knowledge and even poetic ability were requisite for passing the old Government Examinations.

When Dr. Kiang and I were colleagues on the faculty of the University of California, he led me to an anthology, compiled several hundred years ago, of poems written during China's golden age of poetry, between A.D. 600 and 900: *Three Hundred Pearls of the T'ang Dynasty,* an anthology better known among Chinese than *The Golden Treasury,* or any other collection of English poetry, is known among us. It is in the hands and heart of every Celestial schoolboy. One afternoon in Peking, I was to address a large audience and read some of my translations at the Higher Normal School, a Chinese institution for the training of teachers. Dr. Kiang was my interpreter for those of the students not proficient in English; and he was to read the originals of the poems. At the last moment we found we had not brought the Chinese book; and it had to be hastily bought at a shop close by. Laughing at my surprise that so important a volume was not in the school library, President T. Y. Teng explained, "We do not need it there: everyone has it."

The Chinese call this poetry, written thirteen hundred years ago, "modern poetry." In this "modern poetry," in spite of the constraint of rules and regulations unparalleled in the prosody of the West, I found the same human pith, the same living simplicity and directness, the same fundamental beauty, as in the ancient "unregulated" verse of the Confucian *Book,* and the added power of an austere and consummate art.

T'ang poetry, like all Chinese poetry—even of the contemporary poetic rebels, who correspond in spirit to our writers of free verse—used rhyme, or what we should call assonance. Rhyme in itself, however, is not enough. There are "drum tales," containing thousands of lines all on a single rhyme, which calls each time for an accompanying drumbeat; and these achievements are not considered poetry. Besides rhyme, there are rules of tone and balance which I have space here only to intimate. A Chinese character may be inflected, in the dialect preferred by *literati,* according to five tones—one level, two rising, one sinking and one arrested. The first three are called "even tones" and the latter two "uneven tones"; and there is an intricate pattern by which corresponding characters in adjacent lines have to be of opposite tone-groups, while yet of parallel syntax. A translator might conceivably divide the English vowels into two groups—a, e, i, and y on the one side and o and u on the other—and, opposing the vowels of the two groups in conformity with the pattern of opposed tones, arrive at an effect faintly akin to the music of the Chinese convention; but to translate three hundred poems in this manner would be a lifework. As to the parallel use of words of a similar nature, I am convinced that the result would monotonously offend the English ear, though I am not sure that a final translation may not be made a thousand years hence, faithfully following the Chinese order. In some of the four-line poems it is possible in 1921 to use the parallelism throughout and in some of the longer poems to use it now and then. For example here is a poem by Po Chü-yi, a slightly different version of which I have already published in *Asia:*

A Suggestion to My Friend Liu

There's a gleam of green in an old bottle,
There's a stir of red in the quiet stove,
There's a feeling of snow in the dusk outside—
What about a cup of wine instead?

I have in China, like two of the poets I quote, a friend named Liu—to whom I successfully sent this reminder.
    A poem by Liu Tsung-yüan shows the same method:

Snow on the River

A thousand mountains and no bird,
Ten thousand paths, without a footprint,
A little boat, a bamboo cloak,
An old man fishing in the cold river-snow . . .

Here you have the verbal parallelism, but nothing, of course, of the pattern of tone and rhyme.
    I agree with Arthur Waley that a rhymed English version is treacherous

ground. Let me give the carefully simple reading which Dr. Kiang has helped me make for the *Outlook* of Liu Fang-p'ing's

A Spring Heart-Break

With twilight passing her silken window,
She weeps alone in a chamber of gold;
For spring is departing from a desolate garden,
And a drift of pear-petals is closing a door.

And then the long-established version by Prof. Herbert A. Giles:

The Spinster

Dim twilight throws a deeper shade across the windowscreen;
Alone within a gilded hall her tear-drops flow unseen.
No sound the lonely court-yard stirs; the spring is all but through;
Around the pear-blooms fade and fall—and no one comes to woo.

When a Chinese poet wishes to present you with flat terms, whatever he may imply by them in the judgment of commentators, he speaks as Wang Chien does in

A Bride

On the third day, taking my place to cook,
Washing my hands to make the bridal soup,
I decide that not my mother-in-law
But my husband's young sister shall have the first taste.

But the heart of the poem, "A Sigh of Spring," beating forever in its last line, seems to have made on the eminent sinologue who was translating it as "The Spinster" either no impression at all or else too much of an impression.

The use of metaphor by the T'ang poets? In comparison with our use of it, they hardly use it at all. Their language is compact of it. But so, to a lesser degree, is ours. And it is surely as much an error in translating from the Chinese to drag out from an ideograph its radical metaphor as it would be in translating from the English to uproot the origins of our own idioms. It lands you in a limbo-language. If an English poet incidentally used the phrase, "at daybreak," and a translator made it appear to a

Chinese reader that the phrase read, "when night was broken by the day," the relation of the phrase to whatever else the English poet might be saying would be distorted and the balance of his poem would be broken by what in itself is a valid and arresting image. But the image is now a commonplace. Hence it should be translated into an equivalent phrase in the Chinese and not dislocated by an unintended emphasis. Dr. Kiang once said to me of an English translation, "Three heavy words in a four-line poem? One would tip it over."

Unfortunately the English poet or reader who approaches a literature like the Chinese or the Greek is so accustomed to our lavish use of surface-images that he feels ashamed of the nudity he sees and hastens to clothe it. Gilbert Murray, even, says in one of his introductions that, if he should translate a play from the Greek in terms as simple as the original, the effect in English, a language naturally ornate, would be so plain as to be bald. That approach seems to me mistaken and a little insular, as though English literature had nothing to learn; and it has caused, on the part of many translators and through their work, a misunderstanding of the spirit and beauty of Chinese poetry. We Westerners are forever expressing things in terms of other things, exalting metaphor too often above truth. The triumph of the great Chinese poets is the art by which they express a thing in its own innermost terms. And it is that very art, concealing itself, which may make them seem to the casual observer persons of slight attainment, not "literary" enough. A friend remarked to me, on hearing some of Wêi Ying-wu's verse, "There's nothing in that. That's what everyone feels and anyone could say." I doubt not that Wêi Ying-wu, had he overheard, would have been comforted.

Restricting myself, in order to keep within bounds, to the four-line poems in which the words stop but the sense goes on, I choose from Wêi Ying-wu

An Autumn Night Message to Ch'iu

As I walk in the cool of the autumn night,
Thinking of you, singing my poem,
I hear a mountain pine-cone fall. . . .
You also seem to be awake.

The poet here selects an exact touch in natural happenings that starts alive a sense of the nearness of a friend—a moment mystic, but not too mystic to be real. He makes no surface metaphor of it by saying that the pine-cone fell like a footstep. His metaphor becomes one only through your own application of it. It is at the very heart of his mood and of his meaning, not on the surface. And it is only as you also are touched by the pulse of it, that you feel what the poet feels when an unexpected sound brings him acutely the sense of life, of motion, of change, and so of human relationship. It is only by your becoming the poet, by his humanly taking you into himself, that you feel the communion of the earth and the presence of his friend. So it is with the concluding suggestion of the petals in the poem of spring. The poet tells what is happening, which is enough in itself to make a charming and wistful picture of a lady and her garden. It is left for you to form, if you like, the metaphor of a drift of loves, of memories, of regrets, closing like petals the door of her youth.

Giles constantly elucidates and sacrifices the poetic suggestiveness of the original. L. Cranmer-Byng, in his *Lute of Jade* and *Feast of Lanterns,* overdecorates and thereby forfeits clean selectiveness. To be sure, he makes beautiful Tennysonian lines, such as

> Till she of the dark moth-eyebrows, lily-pale,
> Shines through tall avenues of spears to die.

But Dr. Kiang assures me that those lines are by Cranmer-Byng, and not by Po Chü-yi, who says, more simply,

> Till under their horses' hoofs they might trample those
> moth-eyebrows . . .

I cannot judge yet of the interesting translations by Florence Ayscough and Amy Lowell; but, from the few I have seen, I should say that these authors, also, tend to inflate the poems with too much pomp and color. The contemporary writer who is contributing most of all to spread an erroneous idea of the great Chinese lyrics is E. Powys Mathers in his popular books of translations from the Oriental verse of many countries. I suspect that he may be translating them through the French and that the French versions, like the charming paraphrases of Judith Gautier, may be partly to blame. At any rate, he uses, in his book, *Colored Stars,* the French name Thou-Sin-Yu for Chu Ch'ing-yü, giving from that poet a whimsical, rather droll little poem, which possibly but not necessarily refers to a telltale among the ladies. Here is the poem, with nothing added, a version accurately checked by Dr. Kiang:

A Song of the Palace

> Now that the palace-gate has softly closed on its flowers,
> Ladies file out to their pavilion of jade,

Abrim to the lips with imperial gossip
But not daring to breath it with a parrot among them.

Mathers translates this very simple poem as follows:

In the Palace

What rigorous calm! What almost holy silence!
    All the doors are shut, and the beds of flowers are giving out scent;
    discreetly, of course . . .
Two women that lean against each other, stand to the balustrade of red
    marble on the edge of the terrace.
One of them wishes to speak, to confide to her friend the secret sorrow
    that is agonizing her heart.
She throws an anxious glance at the motionless leaves, and because of a
    paroquet with iridescent wings that perches on a branch, she sighs
    and is silent.

I make no comment—except that, fortunately, there is another English-man, Arthur Waley, whose honest translations are even more popular.

I am often asked whether, in making these translations, I have learned any Chinese myself. No. Wandering through out-of-the-way places in China, following at Si Wu and up through the Yangtze Gorges the very footsteps of the poets in whose work I was engrossed, I learned to ask in several dialects for a few necessaries; but that is a very far cry from being able to read. I learned that *shan* means mountain and that *shuêi* means water and that *shan-shuêi* means landscape. I learned that "mountain-water" paintings lack sometimes the mountain and sometimes the water, and I learned to translate the word as landscape. I am not even sure how to spell the word for water. I am spelling it as it sounded when I added to it the word for hot, which I herewith avoid spelling, and summoned, according to a middle or an upper gesture, a hand-basin or a pot of tea. But had I learned Chinese, I should not have fared much better as a trans-lator. I am assured that not even foreigners born in China and knowing the language from childhood are safe guides when it comes to Chinese poetry.

The Chinese themselves vary in their interpretations—not in a way that conflicts with basic and essential clarity, but in one that is only natu-ral, considering the absence from the poems of such grammatical details as person, tense and number. Sometimes I would lay before Dr. Kiang divergent readings from several Chinese whom I had the pleasure of consulting. Dr. Hu Suh, an influential young modernist of Peking Government University and author of widely read poems in the so-called "vulgar tongue," was a patient listener. And World-of-Jade—otherwise Nieh Shih-chang—the young student and friend who piloted me on many trips, was constantly reading the poems and making helpful suggestions. I remember, too, the charm and delight with which Princess Der Ling, former lady-in-waiting to the Empress Dowager, would recite aloud with me instantaneous translations of the poems, which she knew by heart, as I read my versions. For the most part we would coincide. Now and then she would take issue. And when I would carry her challenges and those of the others to Dr. Kiang, he would make sure that I knew the literal meaning of the successive characters, explain his own preference, give me sometimes my choice of the various interpretations, or even let me make one of my own. It is due him, for better or worse, to say that I generally chose his.

Among the scholars I met in Peking was the queued and aged Dr. Ku Hung-ming, a conservative in both politics and literature, a monarchist and a classicist. Attendant long ago at the University of Edinburgh and familiar with five languages, he is a witty opponent of foreign influence and a doughty upholder of traditional Chinese culture. I cannot do better than to call him as witness in favor of some of my contentions as to T'ang poetry, by quoting a passage or two from *The Spirit of the Chinese People,* his naïvely brilliant and stalwart book, written in English but published as yet only in Peking.

"The *classica majora* Chinese is not difficult," says he, "because, like the spoken or colloquial Chinese, it is extremely simple . . . plain in words and style . . . simple in ideas . . . and yet how deep in thought, how deep in feeling it is!" Consequently, "Chinese is difficult because it is deep. It is difficult because it is a language for expressing deep feeling in simple words." Dr. Ku then gives a translation of his own of a rather long poem by Tu Fu, and comments, "The above version, I admit, is almost doggerel. . . . The Chinese text is not doggerel, but poetry—poetry simple to the verge of colloquialism, yet with a grace, dignity, pathos and nobleness which I cannot reproduce and which perhaps it is impossible to reproduce, in English, in such simple language." A passage from another essay of his may explain to us in wider terms the warm, live presence of the Chinese poets: "The wonderful peculiarity of the Chinese people is that, while living a life of the heart, the life of a child, they yet have a power of mind and rationality which you do not find in the Christian people of medieval Europe or in any other primitive people. . . . For a people who have lived so long as a grown-up nation, as a nation of adult reason, they are yet able to this day to live the life of a child—a life of the heart. Instead, therefore, of saying that the Chinese are a people of arrested development, one ought rather to say that the Chinese are a people who never grow old. The real Chinaman is a man who lives the life of a man of adult reason with the heart of a child: the head of a grown-up man and the heart of a child. The Chinese spirit, therefore, is a spirit of perpetual youth, the spirit of national immortality."

This quality which Dr. Ku describes in the Chinese spirit, this directness, this pulse of the heart, is the quality by which the T'ang poetry endures. Sinister and devious the Chinese are not, except to shield themselves from even more sinister and devious foreigners, or to outwit brutal exploitation. They are not to be judged from the depraved conduct of scheming eunuchs, of profligate monarchs and courtiers, nor from the debased callousness of generals and soldiers; they are not to be judged by a foreigner who arrogates to himself racial superiority. They are to be judged from the spirit of the people at large; they are to be judged evenly and honestly. And then will be found in them the deep simplicity of the T'ang poets.

The clothes of poetry change from age to age: fashion, manner, decoration. The body of poetry is the same a thousand years ago, a thousand years hence. Poetry that depends on its trappings dies; but poetry that is bare and vital and true is imperishable. There are many Chinese court pieces and poems of official adulation that are overloaded with artifice and ornament. As curiosities, they may survive to astonish the eye of the literary tourist: jade for the jaded. But the power that makes the best of the T'ang poetry permanent is the honest bareness of its beauty, relating it to the poetic hearts of any race or time.

As artist and as human being, I cherish my three years' labor and the hope that it will help to interpret for the West not only the perfected artistry of the Chinese but the spirit expressed through that artistry—a spirit as nobly simple and as nobly sad, after all, as the spirit we Westerners must find fundamental in ourselves whenever we have time to be alone with it. Before there can be political equity in the world, there must be human equity, an end of racial ignorance and snobbery on all sides, an end of the superstition that superficial differences of skin and mold mean fundamental differences of mind and spirit. East and West, there is only one human spirit in the world, though knaves and fools would keep it divided. And it is the nearest thing we know to what we confidently call the divine spirit. At its best it is the spirit of beauty, whether in nature, in art or in the conduct of man. And still, through the centuries, the poets are its heralds.

New poets from the West are now assembling, as well they may, in the spirit-house of Wêi Ying-wu at Su-chou, where he greets them as, long ago, he greeted other poets:

Entertaining Literary Men in My Official Residence on a Rainy Day

Outside are insignia, shown in state;
But here are sweet incense-clouds, quietly ours.
Wind and rain, coming in from sea,
Have cooled this pavilion over the lake
And driven the feverish heat away
From where my eminent guests are gathered.
. . . Ashamed though I am of my high position
While people lead unhappy lives,
Let us reasonably banish care
And just be friends, enjoying nature.
Though we have to go without fish and meat,
There are fruits and vegetables aplenty.
. . . We bow, we take our cups of wine,
We give our attention to beautiful poems.
When the mind is exalted, the body is lightened
And feels as if it could float in the wind.
. . . Su-chou is famed as a center of letters;
And all you writers, coming here,
Prove that the name of a great land
Is made by better things than wealth.

—*Asia*, December 1921

The Persistence of Poetry

Definitions, rather than realities, have for centuries cost blood and brains. Therefore the tender heart sinks a little when it essays definition. Especially is it uncomfortable, trying to define poetry. For poetry is not so much a matter of hemming about, as of releasing. Can you bridle Pegasus with definition? Can Wordsworth by defining poetry as "passion remembered in tranquillity" prevent its being, on occasion, tranquillity remembered in passion? Do the "infinite capacity for taking pains" and "the first fine careless rapture" deny each other? Where angels might fear to tread, I have rushed in and have tried to devise a phrase which, though not necessarily implying the "sensuous" and the "noble" as exacted by Milton, would epitomize for my own satisfaction the nature and practice of poetry. I have made the phrase as brief as I could. Perhaps its very brevity will leave it vague enough to cover or suggest the reaches of poetry, better than if I had expanded the idea into words more specific and debatable. Here it is then. Two words. *Passionate patience*.

Of all the arts, music and poetry are those nearest to the heart, and most immediately echo the heart. Any definition of the elements of poetry must define also the elements of life nearest to the heart. No one would question passion as the prime element in live things; nor would anyone, I think, considering the cosmic silence which meets man's passionate and thwarted demands, question the element of patience as necessarily inhering in the life we have to live and try to understand.

Primarily, poetry like music—as a matter of fact with music—came out of the heart and lips of simple mankind. One who lives in New Mexico and wanders sometimes among Indians has an opportunity, rare in this modern world, of feeling and hearing poetry at its primitive source. Although the Indians have not themselves recorded their songs, they have followed the custom of all primitive folk and handed down words and music from father to son for many generations; so that we are undoubtedly hearing, in the choruses that accompany tribal ceremonies, a poetry which antedates our own coming to this continent. Besides those traditional racial songs, there are countless personal poems springing up yesterday and today from this or that individual in the Pueblo villages or the Navajo hogans. These poems come with their own music and are extremely simple. They are haunting, as such primitive rhythms always are, whether one hear them from a Navajo shepherd setting his heartbeat to coyote music on some invisible hill at night, or from a Hopi herdsboy singing his cattle back to the mesa, or from a Swiss mountaineer yodeling, or from a boat-boy on the Yangtsze River translating into ancient loves and hopes his own young emotions.

The modern European or American inherits a very different kind of poetry. Through a vast cumulation of books, there have come to him not only these original wellings from man's rhythmic heart, but also the subsequent literary adaptings of primal impulses to the complicated needs and tastes of a gradually cultured civilization. In medieval literature we have on the one hand folk-poetry and on the other hand poetry of the court. Now that republics succeed kingdoms we have forgotten the enforced flatteries due from minstrels to their patrons; and the folk-songs are no longer our own. The middle class is now the patron. The patron has become diffused and impersonal, but it still holds the purse and pays the poet. Its vanity is as great as that of the feudal lords, and its taste not necessarily better. The upper class, on our modern financial basis, has pretty well outgrown the uses of poetry; it has been twisted, for the most part, too far away from natural life, and the middle class now expects primal elements of poetry to be infused and tempered with those qualities of intelligence which are the due of sophisticated and cultured beings.

Culture brings with it a satiety and a fatigue. We know too much, or think we do. At least we have studied too much. We have killed the songsters and dissected their throats. There is nothing new under the sun. We compete with one another in meticulous shades of artificial taste. We are intellectually estranged from the simple sources of poetry. It would seem that in the noisy midst of a mechanistic civilization, poetry must perforce atrophy. Clearly, however, this is not what happens behind our busy and, on the whole, unpoetic lives. Any newspaperman, in touch with the more sensational events happening amongst our millions, knows how the passionate lover, the murderer, the suicide, or even the bandit, inclines to set down his crude emotions in crude verse. Any magazine editor knows from what thousands and thousands of the inarticulate in every American town and village come manuscripts of verse. Even a quarter of a century ago, when the public attitude toward poetry was far less serious, far less friendly, than it is today, the multitude dared secretly to express in verse its emotions and aspirations. Often in the emotional output there would be, and there continues to be, a thought, an impulse, a line, a phrase, of genuine worth or beauty. Unfortunately, busy editors cannot also be tutors. And though it would seem that these utterances from primitive individuals might contain the qualities which inform and beautify utterances from people racially primitive, the fact is otherwise. The environment of a comparative culture and of mechanistic progress intrudes on the simple person. In these days, a certain amount of instruction is necessary, except in the rarest of instances, for a poet to be a poet.

And here, between the impulse and the craft, we realize the extraordinarily delicate edge on which a modern poet must tread. Shakespeare, writing for both the aristocracy and the pit, trod this edge with a genius almost inexplicable. Although his language derived from sources that might have seemed above the ears of the herd, they could listen and understand, even while the Euphuists applauded. To this day, despite the most earnest efforts of pedagogues to annihilate in the mind of a college student an intuitive acceptance of the right and rhythmic beauty of Shakespeare, the profoundly human and poetic quality of the dramatist reaches modern listeners or readers as vividly as it did theater audiences in his own time. And this reach depends not at all upon Shakespeare's knowledge of Latin or Greek, nor upon his acquaintance with the earlier plays which he metamorphosed, nor upon the Elizabethan meaning of his terminology, nor upon anything except his passionate understanding of the emotional values of living and of the vibrations universal in man, and upon his ability so to phrase those emotions and vibrations as to make them, even in a language partly archaic to us, the living speech of human hearts. This passionate gift is genius. And in whatever time it happen, whether it be the time of Li Po or of Homer, of Chaucer or of Shakespeare, it is the rhythm by which men feel their own impulses, their own emotions, their own thoughts. A poet's office is to catch this rhythm and give it to the multitude which has tried to express itself in heart-felt words but has missed the soul-felt rhythm. When a master lives who can so use language that a whole vast sky of words seems as simple as a petal, then the genius arrives who in poetry expresses men to themselves. In our own day two lyric poets, one in England and one in America, have caught this semi-mystical accent. A. E. Housman, in forms and in an austerity of phrase which he might not have used but for his intimate acquaintance with Greek literature, has set down in imperishably distinguished verse, world-old and many times retold emotions. Edna St. Vincent Millay in a different language, more Shakespearean perhaps and yet with an occasional aside that might have been spoken in a village on the coast of Maine, has performed the same magic.

There are countless artificers, over-cultured and jaded, who with extensive knowledge of the world's poets and with the most highly self-conscious uses of prosody, fabricate words into strained and intellectualized meanings which pass for a season among the literary fashionables as poetry, but which are about as important to the singing heart of man as the latest sartorial trick from Paris. Amy Lowell was the high priestess of this cult. Indefatigable as she was in her hours of writing, self-convinced as she was in her theories of art, defiant as she was in her version of herself as a poet, diverting and intriguing as she was in witty polemics, she has already ceased to hold the imagination, except as an arresting and picturesque personality. There is a whole tribe of her nature who might, if they would, do better than she did, and yet who may be equipped, after all, to serve only as haberdashers for contemporary culture.

The Navajo Indians are supposed to be able, with concerted incantation, to make corn or cactus grow a month a minute. Around the seedling they hold a screen of blankets, while they sing their spell. When they move away, the seedling is a few inches high. And so it goes, spell by spell, until the plant or flower is complete. This kind of magic is for children, young or old, so credulous of miracle in the outside world that they will always lend themselves to the sorcerer. Poetry is another kind of magic. A true poet makes a flower of life grow in the heart. It may be a flower of good, it may be a flower of evil. It may be the morning-glory, it may be the deadly nightshade. The true poets are the priests of the inner miracle. There is all the difference in the world between these flowers in the heart and the outer flowers which are fabricated by craftsmen.

Like most of us who are schooled in this Western world, I was afforded in my youth a study of culture flowing mainly from two sources, the Greek and the Hebrew. I had come to feel that poetic literature must contain streams from one or the other of those two sources: on the one hand the clean, objective, symmetrical, athletic beauty of the Greek, on the other hand the turgid, subjective, distorted, elaborated beauty of the Hebrew. Like my fellow students, I had been offered nothing of the literature of the Far East. I am still doubtful that I could ever feel any real adherence to the ornate and entranced literature of India; but I have come by accident into as close touch with Chinese poetry as a Westerner is able to come without a knowledge of the Chinese tongue. And I feel with conviction, that in the matter of poetry, I have begun to receive a new, finer and deeper education than had come to me from the Hebrew or the Greek.

Centuries ago, cultured Chinese had reached the point of intellectual saturation which has tired the mind of the modern European. The Chinese gentleman knew the ancient folk-songs, compiled by Confucius. He knew also, all around him, a profoundly rich civilization, a more poised and particularized sophistication than we Westerners have yet attained.

Through the Asian centuries, everyone has written verse. In fact, from early imperial days down to these even worse disordered days of the republic, the sense of poetry as a natural and solacing part of life has lasted among the Chinese people. Whether or not the individual may form or enjoy his poetry in metrical shape, he is constantly aware of the kinship between the beauty of the world and the beauty of imaginative phrase. On any Chinese mountain-climb toward a temple, rock after rock with its terse and suggestive inscription will bear witness to this temper. So will the street-cries of the peddlers, or the names of the teahouses and on many hilltops and lakesides the casual but reverent jottings of this or that anonymous appreciator of natural beauty. When Whitman said, "To have great poets there must be great audiences too," he must have had in the back of his mind enriched generations like the Elizabethan in England or like almost any generation in China. In those great audiences each man, to the limit of his capacity and with natural ease, was a poet.

There is a simple secret in the Oriental ease. It is told in a pamphlet by an old Chinese scholar who till a few years ago was still living in Peking, and still with infinite passion adhering to the precepts of his ancestors and with infinite patience, acceptably expressed by the way among foreigners, adhering to his conviction that foreigners impair the health of China. His name is Ku Hung-ming. His pamphlet, written in English, one of the five languages of which he was master, is called *The Spirit of the Chinese People*. In it he advances, as reason for the eternal youth of the Chinese people, the fact that the average Chinese has managed to maintain within himself the head of a man and the heart of a child. On this brief he is absorbingly interesting, explaining the continuance of Chinese culture, the only ancient culture still racially existent. My immediate concern with his brief is more special. I detect in it something that he does not specify; a reason for the continuance of poetry as a live factor among his people and, more than that, the best reason I know of for the persistence of poetry anywhere among cultured races.

Music may be the most intimate of the arts; I am not sure. Except for simple melodies, music is beyond the reach of any individual who is not a technician. Painting and sculpture are obviously arts expressing themselves in single given objects, which although they may be duplicated and so circulated are for the most part accessible only to the privileged or to those who make pilgrimages. Poetry more than any other of the arts may be carried about by a man either in his own remembering heart or else in compact and easily available printed form. It belongs to anyone. It is of all the arts the closest to a man; and it will so continue to be, in spite of the apparent shocks given it by the noises of modern commerce and science and jazz.

It has been an age-old custom in China that poets, even the best of them, have devoted their earlier years to some form of public service. Century after century, Chinese poems reflect this deep devotion of their authors to the good of the state,—their unwavering allegiance to righteousness, even when it meant demotion or exile or death. In modern Western times there have been periods when poetry has seemed to be a candle-lit and thin-blooded occupation. I venture to surmise that poetry written in that sort of atmosphere grows with time less and less valid, less and less noticed. As a matter of fact, the outstanding English poets have been acutely concerned with the happiness of their fellow men and have given themselves warmly to public causes in which they believed. Similarly, present-day poets in America, with amazingly few exceptions, have clustered to the defense of noble souls at bay like Eugene Debs, or have been quick to protest against doubtful justice as in the case of Sacco and Vanzetti. This sort of zeal may not result in poetry of a high order immediately connected with the specific cause; but there is no question that but for this bravery, this heat on behalf of man's better nature, there would not be in the hearts of the poets so fine a crucible for their more personal alchemies.

These various remarks bind together, I think. I have been trying to focus my thoughts on the place of the poet and poetry, in a time of cumulated and over-materialistic culture. I have remarked that the art of a poet is by no means only craft, but inheres in his life; that there is a special gift by which a particular poet now and then expresses the poetic impulse in the hearts of other men; but that the element is common to us all, and is an element inextricably mingled with the element of life itself.

I have said very little about the craft, the skill, the technique of verse. At the risk of setting my general observations out of gear, I must before I finish say a word as to the method of Chinese poetry. I am not referring to the superficial tricks by which a Chinese poet makes his words balanced and melodious. The discovery which has largely undone my early convictions as to the way of writing poetry has really to do with use of substance rather than with turns of expression. Mencius said long ago, in reference to the Odes collected by Confucius: "Those who explain the Odes must not insist on one term so as to do violence to a sentence, nor on a sentence so as to do violence to the general scope. They must try with their thoughts to meet that scope, and then they will apprehend it." In the poetry of the West we are accustomed to let our appreciative minds accept with joy this or that passage in a poem,—to prefer the occasional glitter of a jewel to the straight light of the sun. The Chinese poet seldom lets any portion of what he is saying unbalance the entirety. Moreover, with the exception of a particular class of writing—adulatory verse written for the court—Chinese poetry rarely trespasses beyond the bounds of actuality. Whereas Western poets will take actualities as points of departure for exaggeration or fantasy or else as shadows of contrast against dreams of unreality, the great Chinese poets accept the world exactly as they find it in all its terms, and with profound simplicity find therein sufficient solace. Even in phraseology they seldom talk about one thing in terms of another, but are able enough and sure enough as artists to make the ultimately exact terms become the beautiful terms. If a metaphor is used, it is a metaphor directly relating to the theme, not something borrowed from the ends of the earth. The metaphor must be concurrent with the action or flow of the poem; not merely superinduced, but an integral part of both the scene and the emotion.

Wordsworth, of our poets, comes closest to the Chinese; but their poetry cleaves even nearer than his to nature. They perform the miracle of identifying the wonder of beauty with common sense. Rather, they prove that the simplest common sense, the most salutary, and the most nearly universal, is the sense of the beauty of nature, quickened and yet sobered by the wistful warmth of human friendship.

For our taste, used as we are to the operatic in poetry, the substance of Chinese poems seems often mild or even trivial; but if we will be honest with ourselves and with our appreciation of what is lastingly important, we shall find these very same poems to be momentous details in the immense patience of beauty. They are the heart of an intimate letter. They bring the true, the beautiful, the everlasting, into simple easy touch with the human, the homely and the immediate. And I predict that future Western poets will go to school with the masters of the T'ang Dynasty, as well as with the masters of the golden age of Greece, or with the Hebrew prophets, or with the English dramatists or romanticists—to learn how best may be expressed, for themselves and others, that passionate patience which is the core of life.

It is not necessary that culture bring about the death of poetry, as it did in the Rome of Virgil. The cynics are wrong who see in our future no place for an art which belongs, they say, to the childhood of the race. The head of a man and the heart of a child working together as in the Chinese have made possible with one race and may make possible with any race, even in the thick of the most intricate culture, the persistence of the purest poetry.

—Part of this essay appeared as Witter Bynner's introduction to *The Jade Mountain,* an anthology of 300 poems of the T'ang Dynasty, translated from the Chinese by Witter Bynner and Kiang Kang-hu. A portion of the essay was printed in *The Dial* under the title "Poetry and Culture," October 1928; the full essay was published as a chapbook by The Book Club of California, San Francisco, 1929

"The Tale of Genji"

A JAPANESE GALLANT

From the union of a Japanese Emperor with a favored gentlewoman of the wardrobe came a beautiful son—an epic for epicures.

The Tale of Genji begins, as far as I know, with a device new in literature. A group of young courtiers sit about, in the second chapter, comparing notes as to their amorous adventures, each instancing the experience which seems to him most extraordinary. Genji, the Shining One, who has been born, bred and betrothed in the first chapter, and is described as "so lovely that one might have wished he were a girl," listens with apparent deference and with no report of his own and then proceeds, through this first volume of the six-volume story of his life, to outdistance, on almost any night he chooses, the exploits of his fellows. Whether the "anecdotes and reflections" of the others were romantic, audacious, ignoble, pathetic, poetic or grotesque, the story he tells, by living it, tops them all in every illumined particular.

This structural device is new to us of the West only because for a thousand years there has been no Arthur Waley sufficiently discerning, sufficiently accomplished and sufficiently industrious, to translate for us, from the Japanese of Lady Murasaki Shikibu, a tale which, "already a classic in the year 1022," remains, according to Mr. Waley, "by far the greatest novel of the East" and, "even if compared with the fiction of Europe, takes its place as one of the dozen greatest masterpieces of the world."

On the night of the story telling, Genji, already married, heard himself warned against women:

Beware of caressing manners and soft, entangling ways. For if you are so rash as to let them lead you astray you will soon find yourself cutting a very silly figure.

Nevertheless, Genji "had in his heart of hearts been thinking of one person only." Nor was this person his noble wife. Nor was it another person whom he encountered the very next night at the house of one of his gentlemen-in-waiting and whom he carried off to his room with a delightful minimum of ceremony. The subject of his thoughts was his host's young stepmother, who, be it recorded in wonder, resisted Genji's further attentions, with all the fluttered and scrupulous pertinacity of a Victorian heroine, the difference being that she was governed less by moral scruples than by scruples of caste. Not to those days can we trace the origin of the cryptic answer: "the higher the fewer." "Noblesse oblige" had gayer interpretations than in later times: sexual favors were then a part of the graceful duties of high rank. The young wife's resistance, however, served only to lend an occasional sweet sting of sadness to Genji's other amours. He allowed himself little time and, after all, had little need for vain regrets, except as they soothed with shadow the bright light of his conquests.

Not only Genji's own impulses, his heart-breaking comeliness and his moving mastery as poet and ceremonial dancer, but the devoted vigilance of his attendants and the curious favor of the moon, were of the utmost use to him in varying his diversions. A certain servant, for example, was "touched at his own magnanimity in surrendering to his master a prize which he might well have kept for himself." Even Genji's father-in-law melted toward the boy's waywardness. One night Genji and his brother-in-law, Chujo, returned together from secret expeditions.

> They did not send for torchbearers to see them in at the gates, but creeping in very quietly, stole to a portico where they could not be seen and had their ordinary clothes brought to them there. Having changed, they entered the house merrily blowing their flutes as though they had just come back from the Palace. Chujo's father, who usually pretended not to hear them when they returned late at night, on this occasion brought out his flageolet, which was his favorite instrument, and began to play very agreeably.

With but two exceptions the ladies also were more than warm to the innuendo of his poetic messages, not only patrician ladies whose complaisance was expected, but ladies of the stricter caste.

> Even those who seemed bent on showing by the prim stiffness of their answers that they placed virtue high above sensibility, and who at first appeared hardly conversant with the usages of polite so-

ciety, would suddenly collapse into the wildest intimacy which would continue until their marriage with some commonplace husband cut short the correspondence.

Turning from these anonymous ladies to those others whom the chronicler distinguishes with names and importance, we find attached to Genji a prodigious network of intrigue. First came Fujitsubo who, succeeding to the affections of the Emperor after the death of Genji's mother, might in spite of her youth be called Genji's stepmother; then the stepmother and next the sister of the aforementioned gentleman-in-waiting; then his brother-in-law Chujo's lost mistress, Yugao, and finally Fujitsubo's niece, the ten-year-old Murasaki (not to be confused with Murasaki, the chronicler). At intervals moreover, during this four-year-period beginning when he was seventeen, he consorted with Lady Rokujo, widow of the Emperor's brother. In other words, he was lover, in part successively, in part simultaneously, to his stepmother, to his brother-in-law's former mistress, to his own uncle's widow and to his stepmother's niece. He also paid occasional attention to his own wife who, at the end of the first volume, dies bearing him a son while his stepmother lives in fearful anguish lest the Emperor recognize in a son born to her the features of Genji.

But I put a charming tale badly.

In a way it is worthwhile to strip from the beautiful bold bad figure of Genji his poetic ways and means, the glamour of his courtly associations and all the suavities of Japanese courtship, in order to realize that "the quest of the golden girl" was a more rapid and radical business in the days recorded by Lady Murasaki than in the days recorded by Cellini, Casanova, Fielding or LeGallienne. When Genji and his friends were only doing what everyone did and was expected to do, it may seem strange that they made so careful a pretense of secrecy. There can have been no real need of hypocritic deception or timid concealment. And yet it is not so strange. Might Romeo and Juliet have loved so well without their stealth? When in the world's history has open love been so tingling a joy as secret love? Perhaps delight rather than fear has been the mainspring of hypocrisy in England, as of poetry in Japan.

Returning from the moral isle to the poetic it is important to note that all of Genji's love-taking was done in more or less delicate verse. So also was his leave-taking. He seldom lacked the wisdom of the Emperor's dictum:

Affairs of this kind must be managed so that the woman, no matter who she is, need not feel that she has been brought into a humiliating position or treated in a cynical or offhand way. Forget this rule, and she will soon make you feel the unpleasant consequences of her resentment.

In one of his escapades, when Genji had spent much time courting a certain Princess because of imagined charms, he finally gained her presence.

What an absurd mistake he had made! She was certainly very tall, as was shown by the length of her back when she took her seat; he could hardly believe that such a back could belong to a woman. A moment afterward he suddenly became aware of her main defect. It was her nose. He could not help looking at it. . . . Not only was it amazingly prominent, but (strangest of all) the tip which drooped downward a little was tinged with pink, contrasting in the oddest manner with the rest of her complexion which was of a whiteness that would have put snow to shame.

Yet even to this stupid and ridiculous woman, who reminded him of Samantabhadra's white elephant, with its red trunk, he sent a poem:

Scarcely had the evening mist lifted and revealed the prospect to my sight, when the night rain closed gloomily about me.

And he added in a letter:

I shall watch with impatience for a sign that the clouds are breaking.

Here is one of his poems to the very different Lady Fujitsubo:

Now that at last we have met, would that we might vanish forever into the dream we dreamed tonight.

And here is one which, after the funeral of his much-neglected wife, he whispered into the ear of his father-in-law:

Because of all the mists that wreathe the autumn sky, I know not which ascended from my lady's bier, henceforth upon the country of the clouds from pole to pole I gaze with love.

Not only his verses but his writing of both Japanese and Chinese characters and various other little touches of breeding cogently affected the feminine heart. For instance, he knew how to impress the nun in whose care he found ten-year-old Murasaki; he knew how to pave the way toward adopting the child for his own purposes. Writing a poem to Murasaki he enclosed it in a letter to the nun.

Though she had long passed the zenith of her years, the nun could not but be pleased and flattered by the elegance of the note; for it was not only written in an exquisite hand, but was folded with a careless dexterity which she greatly admired.

Nonetheless she parried, writing for the child the following shrewd poem:

For as long as the cherry blossoms remain unscattered upon the shores of Onoe where wild storms blow—so long have you till now been constant.

Genji was the perfect philanderer. There were always more fish in the sea. In spite of the wide difference between his story and that of *Tom Jones;* in spite of all the perfume on Genji's sleeve and all the murmurings of his writing-brush, I find Murasaki's narrative persistently reminding me of Fielding's *Tom Jones,* with music by Debussy. The constant use of poetry, for epistolary and even conversational exchange among characters, is the main element that makes the Japanese narrative for us quaint and faraway; for in spite of occasional mists in the telling the story is vigorously alive. Its petals drift on eternal flesh and blood.

In what is to me the most memorable chapter of the book, the account of Genji's taking the mysterious Yugao away from her exposed and humble quarters to a sort of House of Usher, of her death there by his side and his remorseful visit to the mountain priest, Lady Murasaki exhibits something of the power of that later woman writer Emily Brontë in *Wuthering Heights.* The fox-spirits and the involuntary spell wrought by Lady Rokujo are no stranger than such Christian superstitions as ghosts and devils or such fell powers as Mrs. Eddy's malicious animal magnetism. Certainly nothing written in England before the twelfth century, and very little written in the eighteenth, begins to come as near America in the twentieth as does the essence of *The Tale of Genji.* Something of this modernity may be due to Mr. Waley's limpidly human translation, but most of it must inhere in the original.

Arthur Waley, with an already proven taste for Oriental masterpieces and a proven skill in bringing them vividly to English readers, has so translated *The Tale of Genji* that it reads like the wind. Only once was I halted, against my will, by this sentence:

Was it being four years older than him that made her so unapproachable, so exasperatingly well regulated?

I quote the whole sentence, in order that I may praise even while I question. I should like to quote many other passages, such as

The crowds flashed by him like the hurrying images that a stream catches and breaks. . . .

The Emperor's envoys thronged thick as the feet of the raindrops.

or

Among the leaves were white flowers with petals half unfolded like the lips of people smiling at their own thoughts.

Thanks to Lady Murasaki and to Mr. Waley, many a lady in the Western world will be taking Genji into her heart and many a gentleman will understand why. As the Shining One passes by in the rich procession of these volumes it will be pertinent to remember a sentence from the last chapter of the first volume:

If even these strangers were in such a taking, it may be imagined with what excitement, scattered here and there among the crowd, those with whom Genji was in secret communication watched the procession go by and with how many hidden sighs their bosoms heaved.

—Review of *The Tale of Genji*, by Lady Murasaki, translated from the Japanese by Arthur Waley, Boston: Houghton Mifflin Company. Published in *The New York Herald Tribune Books*, September 27, 1925

Laotzu

LEGENDS as to Laotzu are more or less familiar.

Immaculately conceived by a shooting-star, carried in his mother's womb for sixty-two years and born, it is said, white-haired, in 604 B.C., he became in due time keeper of imperial archives at Loyang, an ancient capital in what is now the Chinese province of Honan.

Speaking wisdom which attracted followers, he had refused to the end of his life to set it down: considering the way of life and the ways of the world, he had decided that a great deal was done and said in the world which might better be spared. His choice, however, was not, as has been widely assumed, vacant inaction or passive contemplation. It was creative quietism. Though he realized the fact that action can be emptier than inaction, he was no more than Walt Whitman a believer in abstention from deed. He knew that a man can be a doer without being an actor and by no means banned being of use when he said that "the way to do is to be." Twenty-five centuries before Whitman, he knew the value of loafing and inviting one's soul; and the American poet, whether or not consciously, has been in many ways one of the Chinese poet's more eminent Western disciples, as Thoreau has been also, with his tenet, "Be it life or death, we seek only reality." But Whitman and Thoreau loved written words, whereas Laotzu felt that written words by defining, by limiting, could have dubious effects. Aware of the dangers inherent in dogma, he was reluctant to leave a set record of his own spoken belief, lest it become to followers an outer and formal rather than an inner and natural faith, an outside authority rather than intuition. He laid down no rigid laws for behavior: men's conduct should depend on their instinct and conscience. His last wish would have been to create other men in his own image; but he gently continued in life, by example presumably and by spoken word, suggesting to his neighbors and his emperor how natural, easy and happy a condition it is for men to be members of one another.

> How do I know this integrity?
> Because it could all begin in me.

> One who recognizes all men as members of his own body
> Is a sound man to guard them.

Legendary or true, it is told that Confucius, impressed by Laotzu's influence on people, visited him once to ask advice, ironically enough, on points of ceremonial etiquette. Baffled by the answers of the older man, to whom etiquette meant hypocrisy and nonsense, Confucius returned to his disciples and told them: "Of birds I know that they have wings to fly with, of fish that they have fins to swim with, of wild beasts that they have feet to run with. For feet there are traps, for fins nets, for wings arrows. But who knows how dragons surmount wind and cloud into heaven? This day I have seen Laotzu and he is a dragon."

The end of the life legend is that, saddened by men's tragic perversity, their indisposition to accept "the way of life," to use life with natural goodness, with serene and integral respect, Laotzu rode away alone on a waterbuffalo into the desert beyond the boundary of civilization, the great wall of his period. It is narrated that when he arrived at one of its gates, a warden there, Yin Hsi, who had had a dream of the sage's coming, recognized him from the dream and persuaded him to forego his reluctance and to record the principles of his philosophy. The result is said to have been the *Tao Teh Ching,* tao meaning the way of all life, teh the fit use of life by men and ching a text or classic. And from the gate-house or from somewhere, this testament of man's fitness in the universe, this text of five thousand words, comprising eighty-one sayings, many of them in verse, has come down through the centuries.

In written history there is little basis for these legends. Record of the philosopher appears first—a brief account ending, "No one knows where he died"—in the annals of Ssu Ma Ch'ien, born five hundred years after Laotzu; and some Western scholars, like some of their Eastern predecessors, have believed that long-lived Laotzu was a myth and that the sayings attributed to him were a compilation of the sayings of a number of men who lived during the next two or three hundred years. Gowen and Hall in their *Outline History of China* say that the *Tao Teh Ching* "is very probably the work of a later age, perhaps of the second century B.C., but is generally regarded as containing many of the sayings of the sage." In an essay accompanying the Buddhist-minded translation by Wai-tao and Dwight

Goddard, Dr. Kiang Kang-hu is more specific. "Three Taoist sages," he writes, "who lived two or three hundred or more years apart, according to history, are commonly believed to be the same man, who by his wisdom had attained longevity . . . The simpler and more probable solution of the confusion is to accept the historicity of all three but to give credit for the original writing to Laotzu and consider the others as able disciples and possibly editors. The book in its present form might not have been written until the third century B.C. . . . for it was engraved on stone tablets soon after that time." It might, he thinks, have contained verses by later Taoists "without detracting from the larger credit that belongs to Laotzu." The earliest known manuscript dates from the T'ang Dynasty, a thousand years later. In *A Criticism of Some Recent Methods of Dating Laotzu,* Dr. Hu Shih has shown that the methods of internal evidence used to impugn the authenticity of Laotzu's writings might have cast similar doubt on the writings of Confucius or of almost anyone. Mark Twain's comment that *Hamlet* was written by Shakespeare or by some one else of the same name is pertinent. The *Tao Teh Ching* is a book, an important and coherent book; and its value comes not from the outward identity or identities but from the inward and homogeneous identity of whoever wrote it.

More relevant is a divergence of judgment as to the book's value. Herbert Giles, the able, pioneering British sinophile, tender toward Confucian orthodoxy and finding in Laotzu "direct antagonism to it," wrote in his *Chinese Literature* published at the turn of the century that "scant allusion would have been made" to the *Tao Teh Ching,* "were it not for the attention paid to it by several more or less eminent foreign students of the language."

Perhaps pedantic Giles was annoyed by the fact that Laotzu could speak of scholars as a corrupting nuisance. Other scholars more imaginative than Giles have differed with him; and current tendency gives the mystical ethics of Laotzu a surer place in import for the world than the practical proprieties of Confucius. Certainly *Tao* has had profound influence on a great part of the world's population. Apart from the superstitious and the misled who have taken over the name for religious sects and have perverted its meaning into alchemy, geomancy, occultism, church tricks generally, a majority in the Oriental world has been fundamentally informed by Taoist quietism, whether or not they realize the source of the patience, forbearance and fortitude which characterize them. Not only has Laotzu's creative quietism been the foundation of China's age-long survival; what was originally good in Japanese Shin*tao*ism has also derived from him. And the Western world might well temper its characteristic faults by taking Laotzu to heart.

Herrymon Maurer in a postscript to *The Old Fellow*, his fictional portrait of Laotzu, notes how closely the use of life according to Laotzu relates to the principles of democracy. Maurer is right that democracy cannot be a successful general practice unless it is first a true individual conviction. Many of us in the West think ourselves believers in democracy if we can point to one of its fading flowers even while the root of it in our own lives is gone with worms. No one in history has shown better than Laotzu how to keep the root of democracy clean. Not only democracy but all of life, he points out, grows at one's own doorstep. Maurer says,

"Laotzu is one of our chief weapons against tanks, artillery and bombs." I agree that no one has bettered the ancient advice:
"Conduct your triumph as a funeral."

"In this life," reflected Sarah, Duchess of Marlborough in an eighteenth-century letter to her granddaughter, "I am satisfied there is nothing to be done but to make the best of what cannot be helped, to act with reason oneself and with a good conscience. And though that will not give all the joys some people wish for, yet it will make one very quiet." Laotzu's quietism is nothing but the fundamental sense commonly inherent in mankind, a common-sense so profound in its simplicity that it has come to be called mysticism. Mysticism or not, it seems to me the straightest, most logical explanation as yet advanced for the continuance of life, the most logical use yet advised for enjoying it. While most of us, as we use life, try to open the universe to ourselves, Laotzu opens himself to the universe. If the views of disciples or commentators have sifted into his text, the original intent and integrity shine through nonetheless. All the deadening paraphernalia wished on him by priests and scholars cannot hide him. He remains as freshly and as universally alive as childhood. Followers of most religions or philosophies, feeling called upon to follow beyond reason, follow only a little way. Laotzu's logical, practical suggestions are both reasonable and simple.

However, if metaphysical or scholarly terms seem necessary for understanding, Dr. I. W. Heysinger relates Laotzu's basic concept to that of Roames, Darwin's pupil and co-worker: "the integrating principle of the whole—the Spirit, as it were, of the universe—instinct with contrivance, which flows with purpose" and to the philosophy of Lamarck. I myself have found Socrates and Plato in it, Marcus Aurelius and Tolstoi. More modernly it is at the heart of Mrs. Eddy's doctrines or of Bergson's creative evolution. Many a contemporary cult would do well to stop fumbling at the edges of Tao, to forget its priests who invented the ouija board and to go to its center.

Concerned with this center, Dr. Lin Yutang says in *The Wisdom of India and China:* "If there is one book in the whole of Oriental literature which should be read above all the others, it is, in my opinion, Laotzu's *Book of Tao* . . . It is one of the profoundest books in the world's philosophy . . . profound and clear, mystic and practical."

He says this in the preface to his own English version of *The Book of Tao.* I had hoped that this version would be enough clearer than others in English to explain for me the influence of Laotzu on many of the T'ang poets, with whom I had become acquainted through Dr. Kiang Kang-hu's literal texts. With all admiration for Dr. Lin's Chinese spirit and English prose, I found myself little better satisfied with his presentation of Laotzu in Western free verse than I have been with other English versions, most of which have seemed to me dry and stiff, pompous and obscure. And that is why I have been led to make my own version.

Though I cannot read Chinese, two years spent in China and eleven years of work with Dr. Kiang in translating *The Jade Mountain* have given me a fair sense of the "spirit of the Chinese people" and an assiduity in finding English equivalents for idiom which literal translation fails to convey. And now, through various and varying English versions of the *Tao Teh Ching,* I have probed for the meaning as I recognize it and have persistently sought for it the clearest and simplest English expression I could discover. Above all I have been prompted by hope to acquaint Western readers with the heart of a Chinese poet whose head has been too much studied.

I have used, incidentally, even when I quote in this preface from those who use other orthography, the spellings Laotzu and *Tao Teh Ching* as preferable for the English or American ear and eye. And perhaps I shall be taken to task for using two or three times an unorthodox interpretation of text. But might not Laotzu's expression, for example, to "stand below other people," usually translated to "humble oneself below them," have been an ancient origin of our own word, "to understand"?

"There can be little doubt," says Walter Gorn Old, "that any translation from the Chinese is capable of extreme flexibility and license, of which, indeed the translator must avail himself if he would rightly render the spirit rather than the letter of the text; and the spirit, after all, is the essential thing, if we follow the teaching of Laotzu. It is safe to say that the more literal the translation may be the more obscure its meaning." Some of the *Tao Teh Ching* sayings, I am told, jingle repetitively with a surface lightness like that of nursery rhymes; and I have now and then ventured such effects, besides using rhyme whenever it felt natural to the sense and stayed by the text. Dr. Heysinger, deft and honest though his version is, sometimes lets the exactions of prosody dilate and dilute his writing.

Dr. Lin Yutang's faithfulness, on the other hand, like Arthur Waley's, stays by expressions significant to Eastern but not to Western readers; and Laotzu should, I am convinced, be brought close to people in their own idiom, as a being beyond race or age.

As to other translations, Walter Gorn Old's has been popular in England and its comparatively direct wording is accompanied by brief friendly essays of both Buddhist and Christian tinge, Arthur Waley's is painstakingly accurate and scholarly but difficult for any but scholars to follow, and there are several which are overcolored with Buddhism. Despite some fourteen offerings, and despite the fact that "the wording of the original," according to Dr. Lionel Giles, keeper of Oriental manuscripts in the British Museum, "is extraordinarily vigorous and terse," Westerners have not yet, in my judgment, been given a sufficiently intelligible version of Laotzu. Now that East and West have met, I suspect that every coming generation of Westerners will, in its own turn, in its own preferred words, try to express Laotzu's conception of the way and use of life. Though he himself said that words cannot express existence, he himself trespassed into them for his own generation.

Together with this absence of a forthright and congenial English translation, there are two other principal reasons why Laotzu has not as yet endeared himself to many Westerners. As religion on the one hand, as philosophy on the other, Taoism has been adulterated and complicated by its Oriental adherents. "The Taoist religion," writes Dr. Kiang, "is an abuse of Taoist philosophy. We find nothing essentially in common between them and, in many respects, they are conflicting." He elaborates upon this abuse, as he might have done upon ecclesiastical abuse of the philosophy of Jesus; but he does not, in my Occidental judgment, sufficiently emphasize the disservice done Laotzu by academicians. As the master himself said of the sensible man he commended,

> The cultured might call him heathenish,
> This man of few words, because his one care
> Is not to interfere but to let nature restore
> The sense of direction most men ignore,

and as he said also,

> False teachers of the way of life use flowery words
> And start nonsense.

Even Laotzu's most famous disciple, Chuangtzu, playfully complicated his master's firm, calm teaching; and the do-nothing idea has been so stressed a misreading as to alienate or puzzle many a Westerner who, seeing Laotzu steadily and whole, would have understood him and responded. Quakers, for instance, would be better Quakers for knowing Tao. Not all Westerners are natural addicts of the strenuous life.

But finally Dr. Kiang is right. Worse than the disservice done the sensible master by some of his scholarly followers has been the wrong done him by the religionists who have preempted him.

Laotzu knew that organization and institution interfere with a man's responsibility to himself and therefore with his proper use of life, that the more any outside authority interferes with a man's use of life and the less the man uses it according to his own instinct and conscience, the worse for the man and the worse for society. The only authority is "the way of life" itself; a man's sense of it is the only priest or prophet. And yet, as travelers have seen Taoism in China, it is a cult compounded of devils and derelicts, a priest-ridden clutter of superstitions founded on ignorance and fear. As an organized religion, its initial and main sect having been established in the first century A.D. by a Pope named Chang Tao-lin, Taoism has even less to do with its founder than most cults have to do with the founders from whom they profess derivation. Even in modern China a Taoist papacy is paid to exorcize demons out of rich homes. To symbolize the patches of a beggar's cloak in Buddhistic ritual, fine brocades are cut into squares and then pieced together again in aesthetically broken design; Christ's cross has been made the pattern for palatial temples; and Laotzu's faith in the naturally and openly beneficent flow of life has been distorted into a commanding but hidden breath of dragons, his simple delighted awareness of the way of life has been twisted into a quest for the philosopher's stone. Thus men love to turn the simplest and most human of their species into complex and superhuman beings; thus everywhere men yearn to be misled by magicians; thus priests and cults in all lands and under virtuous guise make of ethics a craft and a business.

Confucius had the wisdom to forbid that a religion be based on his personality or codes; and his injunction against graven images has fared better than a similar injunction in the Ten Commandments. Hence Confucius continues unchanged as a realistic philosopher, an early pragmatist, while Laotzu and Jesus, his ethical fellows, have been tampered with by prelates, have been more and more removed from human living and relegated as mystics to a supernatural world.

Confucius prescribed formalized rather than spontaneous conduct for the development of superior men in their relation not only to the structure of society but to themselves. Laotzu, with little liking for organized thought or recruited action, no final faith in any authority but the authority of the heart, suggests that if those in charge of human affairs would act on instinct and conscience there would be less and less need of organized authority for governing people or, at any rate—and here he is seen as the realist he remains, as a man aware of necessarily gradual steps—less need for "superior men" to show. In our own time we have had evidence of the tragic effects of showy authority. In this dislike of show, rather than in any fundament of ethics, lay most of what Giles considered Laotzu's "direct antagonism" to Confucian orthodoxy. The trouble was that Confucius so ritualized his ethical culture that conduct of life took on forms similar to those of religion, whereas Laotzu spurned both religious and civil ceremony as misleading and harmful spectacle, his faith and conduct depending upon no outward prop but upon inner accord with the conscience of the universe.

Faith of this sort is true mysticism. Yet nothing could be further from the realistic core of Laotzu's way of life than Wilder Hobson's description of it as "that great mystical doctrine which holds that by profound, solitary meditation men may obtain knowledge of the Absolute."

Laotzu was concerned, as man must ever be, with the origin and meaning of life but knew and declared that no man's explanation of it is absolute. His book opens,

> Existence is beyond the power of words
> To define,
> Terms may be used
> But are none of them absolute.

In at all considering the origin of life he was a mystic, as anyone must be, theist or atheist, who ventures either positive or negative guess concerning what is beyond the mind of man to know; and insofar as Laotzu's sayings probe this region he differed again from Confucius who, contentedly agnostic, restricted his philosophy to known nature and empirical bound. Laotzu, on the other hand, fused mysticism and pragmatism into a philosophy as realistic as that of Confucius but sweetened by the natural and sufficient intuition of rightness with which he believed all men to be endowed and by which he believed all men could discover their lives to be peaceful, useful and happy. He was by no means the solitary, unneighborly hermit, occult with meditation. He was as natural, as genial, as homely as Lincoln. Having a sense of proportion, he had a sense of humor and, as much as any man who has lived, was the everlasting neighbor. At least this is my reading of him from the one record by which he may be appraised.

It is worthy of note, moreover, that his philosophy anticipated and contained the humanitarian philosophies which have succeeded it, conflicting with none of them, deepening them all. It is a fair guess that neither the great Indian nor the great Jew would have found anything unacceptable in Laotzu's mystical uses, which have been made no more mystical by the one, no more useful by the other. Connecting not only mystically but practically with the springs and ends of our action, our thought, our being, it is a fundamental expression of everything in the heart and mind of men which respects, enjoys and serves the individual good by respecting, enjoying and serving the common good.

Though without the help this time of Dr. Kiang, who is beyond reach in China, and though mindful of Arthur Waley's distinction between scriptural and historical translation, I wait no longer to offer my reading of a poet whom I trust other readers will find with me to be neither occult nor complex but open and simple, neither pontifical nor archaic but lay and current, in his calm human stature.

—Introduction to *The Way of Life According to Laotzu: An American Version,* New York: John Day Co., 1944.

The New Atom

Dear Sir:

Although the Chamber of Commerce has sent its members the following communication from a group which is initiating the Santa Fe Citizens' Committee on Atomic Information, I wonder if you will not circulate it in your columns to help notify Santa Feans of an important occasion and opportunity: the open meeting at Seth Hall, Saturday evening, December 8th, at 8:30, when several of the distinguished scientists from Los Alamos will speak and answer questions. Those of us who attended the preliminary meeting at the Laboratory, where facts were presented in terms laymen could understand and where counsel was given with impressive earnestness, came away clarified and moved.

The members of the Chamber of Commerce, the churches and the various organized civic, professional and social groups in Santa Fe are invited to join a townwide Citizens' Committee on Atomic Information to cooperate with scientists at Los Alamos in spreading here and elsewhere knowledge of the potentialities of nuclear energy and quick search for the best and most constructive method of controlling it. It is said that most of the scientists at Los Alamos, as well as throughout the country, are convinced that the solution and safeguard for ourselves and all civilization is international control, while many laymen and scientists feel that the present form of control is for the best. These men, with their common sense, are aware that lack of international cooperation may mean international suicide, but their hopeful human spirit, racially composite and decent, and their belief that this world deserves to continue living and to become harmonious inspires them in their belief.

It might be if our government had not heeded Albert Einstein's letter in 1939, warning us that Germany was already blocking exports of uranium from Czechoslovakia and was intending control of uranium deposits in the Belgian Congo, and if scientists had not persuaded the government to set up in June 1940 its Office of Scientific Research Development, that very few American citizens would be existent today and be privileged, as we are, to receive similar warnings even more urgent and portentous. We Santa Feans who have long been mystified neighbors of these men should now be their usefully respectful associates, should be promptly and proudly active in impelling for them as immediate and wide a hearing as their knowledge, their eminence, their record and their grave warning demand.

Witter Bynner

—*The Santa Fe New Mexican,* December 5, 1945

String Too Short to Be Saved

Sɪʀ: Noting among "Letters to the Editor" objections to Lin Yutang's statement that "the material must be the basis for the spiritual well-being" [*SRL* Aug. 26], I am reminded of a remark I heard more than once years ago from Dr. Anna Howard Shaw, who was not only a suffrage leader but a Methodist minister and a Christian wit, to the effect that in the Lord's prayer ". . . give us this day our daily bread" precedes ". . . forgive us our trespasses. . . ."

It seems to me that Mr. Lin is making a point which not only Americans but perhaps others in the world might need to hear. A great part of the basis of modern life is material waste.

I remember well the satisfaction we children used to feel in New England when we carefully untied all string which came on packages and wound it carefully on little wooden shafts for future use. We even spread out the flaps of envelopes and twisted the resultant paper into neat squills, which stood in a little vase on the mantel over the fireplace, later to be lit from the embers and used instead of the old fumacious sulphur matches. The whole accent of life and activity was on preservation and use, and the good business of our fingers helped considerably not only in keeping children happy but in ridding our elders of wasteful or harmful thoughts. When people waste substance, as they so largely do in the world now, the step is short toward a psychology where the waste of life seems a natural part of the world's order.

Westerners would do well to give a more attentive ear to the soundness of Eastern thought as it comes to us through Mr. Lin's balanced mind. I grant that wasting of life has occurred on a stupendous scale in the Orient, the reasons being obvious; but I maintain that happiness or serenity of spirit has widely survived in the Orient because of its being partly based on such material measures as Lin Yutang recommends.

Witter Bynner

—*The Saturday Review of Literature,* April 30, 1950

Remembering a Gentle Scholar

In suggesting that, after an interval of many years, I again contribute to *The Occident,* its editor wrote me that the autumn issue "is to focus upon Asiatic literature" and added that "this theme was given impetus by a sense of its necessity in our present Western thought."

With more time and space, I should have liked to dwell on the theme as it relates to that necessity, our present political involvement with Asia making acutely necessary our understanding of the Oriental spirit; but I hope that a brief factual account of my connection with Chinese poetry and philosophy will not only record experience pertinent to the theme and to the impetus prompting it—as well as incidentally pertinent to the University of California—but will help to indicate the fact that human emotion and thought are of sympathetic kinship the world over and that such thought in Chinese philosophy as has lasted from the 6th century B.C. and in Chinese poetry from the 6th, 7th and 8th centuries A.D. is basically close to what is likely to last of "present Western thought."

In 1918, when I was a member of the faculty at Berkeley, I met a fellow member, Dr. Kiang Kang-hu, to whom I was at once drawn. What he had recently done as a man of principle and brave action was enough to evoke my interest even before I learned to know him as a gentle scholar and stimulating companion. He had been secretary to Yüan Shih-k'ai, China's first president after Sun Yat-sen's provisional presidency and patriotic withdrawal. When in 1916, Yüan schemed to make himself emperor, Dr. Kiang, denouncing the plot and instrumental in blocking it, had to flee for his life and, landing in the United States, speedily learned enough English to become an able and popular teacher at the University of California. Like most Americans, I had been trained exclusively in the

European culture which stems from Athens, Rome and Jerusalem. Until 1917, the best part of which year I spent in Japan and China, I had known next to nothing of the world's Asiatic background; and now at Berkeley I was finding myself moved by it as it reflected in Dr. Kiang, especially by fragments of Chinese poetry with which he would now and then illuminate his conversation. I had been superficially familiar with the ethical teachings of Confucius, had respected his sense of order, his successful rejection of divine attributes, and his intelligent concern with one world at a time, but had been a bit chilled by his preoccupation with domestic and social etiquette, his elaborate anticipation of Emerson's findings that in some respects manners are morals. Through glimpses of the calm, kind, almost democratic thinking, the intuitional sense of oneness in man, nature and eternity, which permeates many of the T'ang poems, I began seeing for the first time into an ancient society of individual spirits not shackled by dogma, by fixed commandment or code, not shadowed by jealous deity. Against the burdens and buffets of life, these poets had found an inner peace and a good will toward men at least as sure and sweet, it seemed to me, as any peace or good will found in a later world.

Jesus says, Leave all else and follow Me, which no all-powerful God would need to say and no man, impotent against change, should assume to say. His followers say, God died for us. It's the Me and the me. T'ang poets, living their Taoism, had eased meship into the whole current of life itself, no god or man intervening. They acknowledged the melancholy natural to man over his predicaments, but had not let it become anything like the morbidly mystical egotism in which Christianity has mythologized it. Wang Wêi says, I shall

> some day meet an old wood-cutter
> And talk and laugh and never return.

Han Hung asks,

> Who need be craving a world beyond this one?
> Here, among men, are the Purple Hills!

Mêng Chiao asks,

> What troubling wave can arrive to vex
> A spirit like water in a timeless well?

Liu Chang-ch'ing confesses,

Mingling with Truth among the flowers,
I have forgotten what to say.

A wisdom was here, I thought, relaxed and open, of which Christian
civilization—perhaps Buddhist civilization also—stood in need for a sim-
plifying and cleansing and strengthening of life; a wisdom which, I felt,
some unnecessary screen had been hiding from us of the West. Perhaps the
screen was the fact that, through priesthood and pathetic credulity, Tao-
ism had degenerated from a pure philosophic faith into superstition and
claptrap, much as the teachings of Jesus have done; some of the Christian
mythology seeming to me as savage as that of Greece but less engaging.
Perhaps Jesus needs Laotzu over here, I wondered, and Laotzu needs
Jesus over there. I tried to find Laotzu in translations of his sayings; but
the translations only clouded him for me, whereas Kiang's oral Angliciz-
ing of T'ang poets, and of their Taoism, illumined him. So I asked Kiang
if he and I might not try collaborating in translating poems by Wang Wêi.
I wish we had then thought of trying to translate the source, the *Tao Teh
Ching* itself. But Kiang proposed an 18th century anthology, *Three Hun-
dred Pearls of the T'ang Dynasty* (618 to 906 A.D.) the compiler of which
had remarked in his preface, "This is but a family reader for children, but
it will hold good until our hair is white": a collection of far wider popu-
larity in China than, say, *The Golden Treasury* here. *170 Chinese Poems,* the
first book of translations by Arthur Waley, Britain's distinguished Sinolo-
gist, had not then appeared and resounded, or I might have quit my
project; and earlier translations, except a few by Helen Waddell, had not
held what I wanted. Ezra Pound's small sheaf, *Cathay,* printed in London
three years before, contained passages arrestingly fine, as well as prophetic
of Waley's direct manner; but Kiang, wondering why the American poet
should call Li Po only by his Japanese name, Rihaku, recited off-hand
versions of the same poems Pound had chosen, which I found, even in
Kiang's halting English, still finer.

So we went to work, believing that in a year's time we could string
the three hundred Chinese pearls on English thread. Two years later we
sailed for China together, planning continuance through the summer of
our far from finished task. By a freak of fortune we lost each other. He
was to spend a fortnight with relatives and on business in Shanghai. He
had given me as his address a Chinese hotel there; but he had advised my
going ahead with the Arthur Davison Fickes, our travelling companions,
to Si Wu, the lake resort near Hangchow where he would join us later,
for escape from Shanghai's terrific heat. When we still had to flee heat,
we wrote giving him our address on Mokanshan, a comparatively cool
mountain, still farther from Shanghai. His hotel, being full as we learned

afterwards, not only had no room for him but apparently took no interest in his mail, though he called there again and again and I wrote there again and again all summer, he thinking as ill of an American as I of a Chinese. In the autumn, we met by accident on a Shanghai street. Since he had left with me his rough literal texts of the poems and I had been hard at work on them, we were able to go over them for accuracy, as we had done before and were to do again many times.

The publishers' announcement of *The Jade Mountain* for 1921, when we had expected it to be ready, led to an amusing literary panic of which I knew nothing until 1946 when, asked to review a volume of correspondence between Amy Lowell and Florence Ayscough, I discovered how hard Miss Lowell had driven her collaborator in order to issue their translations from the Chinese ahead of ours. As it happened, *Fir-Flower Tablets* appeared in 1921 and *The Jade Mountain*—after eight more years of work on it—in 1929.

Meanwhile the popular welcome given Arthur Waley's and Shigeyoshi Obata's translations, as well as magazine publication of nearly all our three hundred "pearls," had shown a marked Western interest in Chinese poetry, not as something exotic or picturesque but as a record of human feeling and thought so simply and rightly expressed as almost to conceal its artistry. I often wish that among our own contemporary poets there were more of the T'ang awareness that "a poem can be tipped over by one heavy word." In poetry, apart from political comments, officially commanded tributes or playful literary games, those old boys used no ponderous or intricate symbolism, no foppish babble, but the grace of an art in which a man's mind never grows childish and a child's heart never dies.

It is of course gratifying to me that Dr. Kiang's work and mine, as translators, stays alive; and I attribute its vitality to the fact that in spirit and expression the poems remain as close as we could keep them to what the originals mean in China. Mr. Waley, who knows Chinese, greeted the book warmly and took generous pains to point out a number of initial errors which have been corrected in later editions. I trust that the vogue of flashy, deliberately false translations, like those of Powys Mathers in *Colored Stars,* is past. I used to argue with Miss Lowell and Mrs. Ayscough against their exaggerated use of root-meanings in Chinese characters, so that under their hands what was natural, direct, every-day expression in the Orient would become in English odd or complex or literary. The temptation to dart toward such glitter is easy to understand; but I early agreed with Kiang that for translators the bright fly concealed a hook. I quote from one of Mrs. Ayscough's letters: "Take, for instance, *yu,* formed of the two radicals 'the wind' and 'to speak'; instead of just saying 'a gale,' Miss Lowell has rendered this 'shouts on the clearness of a gale.' One must be careful not to exaggerate," continues her collaborator, "but it makes lovely poems." Though it may gratify Mrs. Ayscough's weakness for "lovely poems" and though Chinese scholars may have sensitive feelers for the roots of their written characters, such translation does not give the reader or auditor in English the equivalent of what a Chinese reads or hears in the original. Poets write for people, not for etymologists. Whether or not Po Chü-yi, as is said, tested his poems by reading them to his cook, they are as human and simple as if he had done so and can be finally as appealing in Canton, Ohio, as in Canton, Kwangtung. On Second Avenue in New York I noticed years ago a Chinese restaurant called *The Jade Mountain* and, told by a waiter that the owner had taken the title from a book of translated poems, I hoped it was because they were well translated. But it was more probably because of magic in the name, Kiang Kang-hu. I had already been shown respect by the proprietor of a Chinese restaurant in Santa Fe due to my connection with "a great scholar." These days when Kiang is mentioned in The New Canton Cafe, my friend there shakes his head sadly and observes, "Maybe he was too ambitious, but he is still a great scholar."

It happened that, during the Sino-Japanese war, Dr. Kiang joined the puppet government at Nanking as Minister of Education. He wrote me that he considered his act not political but a means of serving his people in captivity, as a scholar should. Unfortunately, when he became later a captive of the Nationalists, they did not relish his explanation and sentenced him to death. Because of appeals from many sources, including two American generals who had met and admired him, the sentence was commuted to life imprisonment. There had to be more appeals before he was permitted brush and paper for writing.

It was after his imprisonment that, still unsatisfied with English versions of the *Tao Teh Ching,* even with Arthur Waley's and Lin Yutang's which were published after my earlier research, I decided that I must attempt one by myself, must try to uncover in Laotzu's book the secret of his profound influence on China's loftiest thinkers and doers. Without Kiang's help, except for the general perception due to our eleven years of collaborating, I pondered and worked for many months, digging out from a dozen or so translations in English what I felt Laotzu must have meant; and for better or worse the resultant "American version" has maintained remarkable popularity in the United States through the past decade. Innumerable letters have certified a readiness among all sorts and conditions of Americans to add Laotzu's wisdom to the wisdom of the West.

Partly because Arthur Waley had thought my turns of expression too smooth and had questioned some of my interpretations, partly because I feared that I had been presumptuous, but finally because I would rather have my readings in *The Way of Life* approved by Kiang than by anyone else, I needed most the letter which came from his Nanking prison, dated August 13, 1948, four years after I had sent him the book. I have heard nothing from him since; and for several years his wife and children have received no answer concerning him from Chinese authorities. But through the silence I hear again, in his letter, the gentle scholar I first heard in Berkeley thirty-five years ago.

"As to your interpretation of Lao-tse" (he uses the older English spelling, instead of my Anglicized form, comparable to our spelling Kung Fu-tze, Confucius) "I can only say that it was entirely your insight of a 'fore-Nature' understanding that rendered it so simple and yet so profound. Lao-tse's text is direct, and we have to go around about it. It is impossible to translate it without an interpretation. Most of the former translations were based on the interpretations of certain commentators, but you chiefly took its interpretation from your own insight, which I term the 'fore-Nature' understanding or, in Chinese, Hsien-T'ien. This Hsien-T'ien understanding is above and beyond words. As the Chinese say, 'All human beings are of the same heart, and all human hearts are for the same reason.' If this reason was not sidetracked by anything of an 'after-Nature,' then everyone would come to an identical or similar understanding. So the translation could be very close to the original text, even without knowledge of the words. I am grateful to you indeed for your kind dedication, but rather shameful for not being able to assist you in any way."

Though he does not commit himself to my interpretation, this gentle comment from Kiang Kang-hu has assisted me in more ways than one. I have tried to thank him in China, and I thank him here.

It is a warming phenomenon that our having been to all purposes at war with the present government of China's mainland—this fact has not turned our people against the Chinese as people. Russia, behind China, has been our real dread. And I doubt that the Chinese people will long be docile to foreign-inspired masters. Docility to any master is not in their nature nor in their history. Although the Soviet system, insofar as it means local government by guilds, originated in China, the Soviet system as developed by Russia into a police state is alien to Chinese character and tradition. From earliest times scholars and poets have held high place in Chinese government and, though often punished for individualism and candor, have seldom feared to criticize and to oppose and undo tyranny, as Dr. Kiang opposed and helped to thwart the attempted tyranny of Yüan Shih-k'ai. It is notable today that not only a statesman like Syngman Rhee but many thousands of Korean and Chinese soldiers are gallantly, stoutly opposing both Communist tyranny and our own powerful, disgraceful and unprecedented tyranny in imprisoning and tormenting our declared friends. I have a feeling that our own people at large are ashamed of our captains and bargainers. At least there is no surging popular sentiment among us favoring assault on the people of China. And I am convinced that under similar circumstances our feeling would have been less civilized fifty years ago, that among people in the Occident an understanding of people in the Orient has subtly and surely arisen and that this understanding is due more than we realize to the fact that Asian thought and art has reached and touched the West, that we now know Chinese civilization, for instance, to be not only the oldest civilization still vigorous but to be a civilization profoundly informed as to lasting values.

At the moment the element which controls China would seem to have set its face against the wisdom of philosophers and poets who have made China great in the past and who have lately come alive anew in conveying a sense of its greatness to a wider world. But are we less fluctuant, we in the West?

Three years ago I was calling on the Minister of War in London. He had recently returned from an official trip in the Orient and said that during his stay there he had written a poem which was to have been published in *The London Observer*. The Prime Minister, happening to notice a proof of it on the War Minister's desk, had to ask and be told what it was. He advised that it be withdrawn, since poetry writing was beneath the dignity of a Cabinet Member. He probably did not even know that for centuries Chinese Emperors, Premiers and Generals had been proud to write poetry, nor had he any suspicion that his own successor as Prime Minister in Britain would receive a Nobel award for literature.

Cabinet Members come and go. But Li Shang-yin, a gentle scholar, continues saying, as he said in the 9th century:

> Literature endures, like the universal spirit,
> And its breath becomes a part of the vitals of all men.

And Kiang Kang-hu continues quoting, even in prison: "All human beings are of the same heart, and all human hearts are for the same reason."

—*The Occident,* undergraduate publication, University of California, Berkeley, Winter 1953.

On Translating a Classic

It might be wondered, when what little Greek I had learned at college was forgotten, why and how I came to venture a version in English of a Euripidean play.

In 1914, Isadora Duncan with her six dancers had for some time been bringing Greek figures and friezes to life on the stages of several nations. Almost everyone connected in those days with any of the arts knew Isadora; and when she had been given use of the New Theater near Columbus Circle in New York, later called the Century Theater, we often heard her wish for a "right translation" of a Greek play to produce there. She had removed orchestra seats to make a deep-aproned stage on which she offered almost daily, at public performances, her rehearsals and experiments in dance and drama. Charging dearly for what lower seats were left but only ten cents for a gallery seat, she attracted substantial and ardent audiences to an exciting laboratory unique in American history. After her production of *Oedipus Rex*—the lead well played by her brother, Augustin—she kept begging me to try my hand at a version of *Iphigenia in Tauris,* which, she said from some knowledge or other, "though superbly simple in the original, had never been humanly translated into English, but always with stilted inversions and scholarly heaviness, and the sense subjected to the sound."

She made me try it, the choruses first. Scenes of the play were to follow and be combined into growing length for performance, as fast as I could write them. We had put on the stage all of the choruses, for Margherita Duncan and Helen Freeman, besides the six girls and herself, before someone discovered and reported that by living in the theater's large, luxurious dressing rooms Isadora and her group were breaking New York's fire regulations. So the whole experiment ended. But I finished the play, which was published as a single volume in 1915 and again, as part of my *Book of Plays,* in 1922. Both times, forgetting that we had omitted certain sections of the choruses which Isadora had thought too remotely allusive to be understood or effective, I neglected to restore them for print. They are included, however, in the present volume. I must add that in making the text for Isadora I relied only on close study of all English versions available. In revising it through the past two years, I have kept the choruses more or less as they were, a sort of musical accompaniment to the drama, but have otherwise written and discarded some seven manuscripts, with the devoted intent that what I could do for it might become ever simpler, clearer, and worthier of the humanist who wrote it.

For general accuracy, this new version has had the supervision of Richmond Lattimore, who instigated my endeavor to make it a still more human play in 1955 than the earlier version seemed to be in 1915. I repeat at this time the original dedication to my friend Barry Faulkner, the then young painter who helpfully watched the growth of the first version forty years ago.

—Prefatory note to Witter Bynner's translation of *Iphigenia in Tauris* included in the introduction by Richmond Lattimore, *The Complete Greek Tragedies, Euripides II,* edited by David Grene and Richmond Lattimore, Chicago: University of Chicago Press, 1956.

PART THREE

Letters

After WB graduated from Harvard in 1902, he went for the summer to Europe and then began as an editor at McClure's *magazine, one of the most prominent publications of its period. While there he edited the poetry section, worked on the fiction, and acted as an assistant to S.S. McClure (1857–1949), the editor in chief. The following letter exists only in a copy made by WB with a note at the top of it in his hand: "WB's letter with S.S. McClure's signature— written in Henry James' manner." WB's friendship with Henry James (1843– 1916) began during James's 1904–5 visit to the United States and centered on their meetings, luncheons, and talks at The Players, WB's New York club. WB recounts these events and records conversations of James's in articles included in the prose section. The Colonel Harvey mentioned in the first line is George Harvey (1864–1928), the owner of the* North American Review *and* Harper's, *which published James's articles about his visit to America. These articles appeared in 1907 as* The American Scene.

TO HENRY JAMES

McClure, Phillips and Co.
New York City
June 30, 1904

Dear Mr. James:

About your defection to Colonel Harvey, it was good of you to write me so careful and gentle a letter. In spite of a certain amount of what I should call perplexity rather than grief,—since the thing is all *done* and less use in crying than in pondering a lesson for the future, to be sure—I cannot help liking the spirit of your letter, and, after all, no other attitude profiting me, appreciating your position in the matter and my own right to be only patient. You will, at least, may I not presume thus far, not assure away all your time and friendliness. Though our audience, owing in great degree to the fact that it is a very large one, is also a very difficult one, and makes selection of material for *McClure's* magazine a matter intricate with motives and considerations, I had hoped there might be a chance for us to feed the general some palatable caviar. Perhaps the doubts in the case are another argument in favor of what you have done to fix your feet on financial terra firma.

Surely, though, come and see us. Indeed I shall rely upon your good faith to let me know of your coming, in time for me to see you promptly, easily, and on the elected day, among the fewest possible fatiguing stresses!

Very sincerely yours,

S. S. McClure

WB had gone late in 1906 to visit the sculptor Augustus Saint-Gaudens (1848–1907). WB knew him through his extensive sculptoral works and then through his son Homer (1880–1958), a student at Harvard with WB and a close friend. Over the next few months, WB established a place for himself— a bedroom and study—in Homer and Carlota Saint-Gaudens's house, which eventually became his permanent residence until he moved to California in 1918. (Although the house was in Cornish, New Hampshire, the mailing address was across the river in Windsor, Vermont.) With Cornish as his base, WB began a series of lecture tours on poetry that took him all over the country for the next ten to fifteen years.

The following letter is to one of WB's closest female friends, Hersilia A. Mitchell-Keays (1861–1910)—Celia Keays, or St. Celia, as she was called by WB. She was the source of inspiration for "Celia," who is the all-pervasive poetic ideal in WB's The New World *(1915) and* Grenstone Poems *(1917). Older than WB, the mother of three young men—two at Harvard about WB's age— she was a counselor or surrogate mother at most, but she was never WB's lover. The widow of a minister from Grand Haven, Michigan, after his death she brought her three boys to Boston, where she wrote novels on such subjects as divorce and the responsibility of wealth. She was ill for several years and eventually died of tuberculosis on April 12, 1910. WB spent many years trying to dramatize her novel* The Road to Damascus *(1907), which finally appeared as* His Father's House *in Los Angeles in June 1912, to some considerable local success.*

TO HERSILIA A. MITCHELL-KEAYS

c/o Augustus Saint-Gaudens
Windsor, Vermont
January 18, 1907

***

Shall I tell you about Saint-Gaudens? I think I will, instead of putting it in the diary. So will you keep it? I couldn't see him the first day. But the next afternoon he sent for me. I'm afraid he saw my stricken heart, in my face, when I shook that long thin hand.—The little bones were as limp as spaghetti! The body was tensely resting, wherever it touched the sofa, lest it rub through. There were hot-water bottles—and between the knees and between the shins, cushions! The very touching of toe to toe was a torture to his nerves! On the road home from a dreadful trouble, he encountered neuritis and has fallen under it completely shattered. They have stopped giving him the morphine he has long been relying on. They are fooling him with empty capsules, for bromide. To his mournful agitation, they are, however, giving him coffee. He has already asked me three times, whether I don't find coffee bad for me. The first time, I didn't realize and told him "yes";—but he forgot and asked again. He is only feebly aware of things. I could see, as I greeted him, the light in his pinched gray face, of a successful recovery of the phrase he had planned to say to me. He has been seeing almost nobody. Out it came:—"You and I, Bynner, have changed places, since I last saw you!" (I had been rheumaticky)—Then the light went out—and he added "What helped you?—did you give up coffee?" etc. It was only a few minutes before I was afraid he was going to cry; so I left. His wife, in her way, is kind;—but her attention consists of snappings and snarlings and intermittent whinings, not so much against him as against man, woman, child, and God! There was something fearfully pathetic in Carlota's saying to me: "Why is it that every time he sees me, he cries?"

The next time I saw him, I played to him, and, save the mark, *sang* to him! Somehow it struck right. He wanted more. And yesterday, though I didn't realize it, he expected me at four, had his sofa moved accordingly, a cushion put on the piano stool, anticipated the event several times— and—the fool woman with him (a cousin) hadn't the sense to telephone me! The day before, he had been brought out of himself to the extent that when I'd played the sextette from *Lucia* and didn't know the tenor's solo in the last act, he whistled the long aria all through,—unintelligibly to me, and at times almost inaudibly, but *all through,* while Homer and I sat silent. I believe his ambitions and intentions are strong enough to raise the dead. All I could think of was Lazarus. But in the eyes comes now and again, above the starved-looking nose, an inward vision of *life,*—of self-creation!

Before coming here, I had, of course, three happy days in Keene,— Barry Faulkner[1] and I quite at one, and making of farewell a memorable ten-mile walk over glaring roads in a wind that on the hilltops was a very knife.

My mode of life has become regulated in a way that would amaze you. It's breakfast at seven-thirty, and a high degree of unhappiness; then work from nine till twelve in a screened-in nook of my own in the Saint's studio, with an inspiring gaze now and then at his incomplete, but none the less thrilling, Phillips Brooks;[2]—the Bishop preaching from a lectern, right arm extended; behind him, with a hand on his left shoulder, a calm, faraway Christ, and beyond & over Him a tall, severe Cross, standing against the mid-most of a dome-capped semicircle of Corinthian pillars, which holds and frames the whole. It's one of his very finest. After lunch comes either more work, or snowy frolic. It was eight below zero yesterday; but we climbed again & again to the top of a long winding series of hills, over which to slide on skis. You should see the appalling headers I take; clean into the air and bang on my face;—and then I don't know till next morning how maimed I am! I've had for three days now a spot mottled black & blue on my thigh, the size and height of a soup plate. Oh but it's fun! Evenings are short and sweet; bed by eleven. Last night we sleighed, for half an hour, our breath making little icicles on the furs, to dine at Maxfield Parrish's.[3] He was cooking a goose in front of a burning pile of logs in a twelve-foot fireplace. He was cordial to the extent of cocktails, champagne, wine sauce, and white menthe,—and full of quips as quaintly colored and outlined as his more fantastic paintings, a sort of personal slang, breezy, constant and most expressive. To be sure, when he referred to the hindquarters of the goose as the "steerage," and a little later, patting the place where the dressing ought to be, called it a "bustle," I couldn't help asking if there were "only one bustle in the entire steerage."! You can judge what fun I might have with him listening, instigating, and roaring!

***

1. Barry Faulkner (1881–1966) was a student at Harvard with WB and became a lifelong friend. Their correspondence, although not regular, never ceased, but as the years went on it became apparent that their natures were not congenial. WB wrote one of his *Guest Book* (1935) sonnets about Faulkner and called it "Pettyfogger." One line sums up the characterization: "He'll borrow just as little as he'll lend." As early as 1903, WB wrote in his journal: "Good, clever letter from Barry Faulkner, though in the mood of a sparrowish old maid."

Faulkner lived in New York and New Hampshire, never marrying, a cautious man. He was a painter whose murals are in the National Archives in Washington, D.C., the RCA Building in Rockefeller Center in New York City, and the John Hancock Building in Boston.

2. Phillips Brooks (1835–93) was the minister of Trinity Church, Boston, and one of the most influential clergymen of the period. The statue of him by Saint-Gaudens is in Trinity Churchyard.

3. Maxfield Parrish (1870–1966), painter and illustrator, lived in Cornish.

Windsor, Vermont
January 30, 1907

✳✳✳

The Saint—about whom you ask—was out here for ten minutes. . . . He was carried out to criticize and direct the work of his assistants on the Phillips Brooks, and on a strikingly beautiful relief—adaptation of the profile of the Sherman Victory, for the next penny. The latter is as chaste and noble a thing as the best Greek coins, *far* superior I should say to anything we have yet had. The other work going on under these pathetic little visits, during which eight or ten sentences exhaust him,— are a new Lincoln, seated (for Chicago), a John Hay,[1] a Mark Hanna[2] (nice and ugly) and a group of glorious Caryatides (for the Albright Gallery). The quality which singles itself out for me more and more as the gift above and beyond what other men can do, it not the composition, the modelling, or the technique in any palpable respect,—but an indefinable, expressiveness on his more imaginative faces—a forward look of peaceful waiting. The figure for the Adams tomb in Washington, the Shaw face, peaceful in its very advance to war, the Caryatides, and now this strangely fine Christ, in the Phillips Brooks monument, all have it.[3] And as I looked diagonally across the room from my work and saw his own face rising out of its weakness and wretched apprehensiveness to the contemplation of his work, I saw that same look, that strong, vivid, peaceful, forward look. It's as though he hadn't been able to understand life under its outward form, beyond the creative convictions of his work, and as though something in that work, something deeper than understanding, had set his gaze forward and his unrest at peace. The labor of his life and the deep silence of his faith have together become genius.

He has been having setbacks. He thinks they are drugging him. When I tell him that they've told me how few drugs are now being used as compared to a while ago, he suspects it was told me to reach him. He thinks, too, that he is mortally sick and not being told. He is so actively anxious to live and work that you feel as though he were newly stricken with his whole sickness many times a day. His family proceeds on the assumption that he will recover. I have a throb now and then that he won't. His pain is so evident and so constant!

***

1. John Hay (1838–1905) was a secretary to Abraham Lincoln and Secretary of State under William McKinley and Theodore Roosevelt.

2. Mark Hanna (1837–1904) was an Ohio industrialist and a major Republican political figure, considered instrumental in securing McKinley's election in 1896.

3. These refer to some of August St. Gaudens' most famous sculptures: the figure for the grave of Mrs. Henry Adams in Washington, the relief in the Boston Common of the Civil War officer Colonel Robert Shaw and his Black regiment, some Greek female figures for columns at the Albright-Knox Gallery in Buffalo, New York, and the Phillip Brooks statue referred to above.

Throughout the early part of his life, WB tried to write plays as well as poetry. He attempted several full-length works, many one-acters, and the story and lyrics for a musical version of Everyman *as a woman, called* Anygirl *(1917). The final outcome was not a career in the theater, but still he had some success. He did a version of Euripides'* Iphigenia in Tauris *(1915) for Isadora Duncan, parts of which she performed and which since has been performed by many college groups. Reference has been made to his dramatization of Mrs. H. A. Mitchell-Keays's novel* His Father's House. *His own one-acters were all performed: "Tiger" (1913), with the most success and scandal—it was a verse play on prostitution; "The Little King" (1914), a verse play about the young Dauphin during the French Revolution; and "A Night Wind," about love in a coffee shop in Greenwich Village, and "Cycle," an anti-war play, both published in 1922 in his volume* A Book of Plays. *His great success came later, in 1926, when he wrote a comic verse play about Mabel Dodge Luhan (1879–1962), called* Cake.*

The following letter refers to Cecil B. De Mille (1881–1959), who later became one of Hollywood's most famous directors. WB knew him and his family in New York City and wrote with him the well-received one-act play discussed in this letter, "Kit" (1907), and later The Mechanic *(1907), a full-length play that was never performed and has not survived.*

TO HERSILIA A. MITCHELL-KEAYS

The Players
16 Gramercy Park
New York City
July 5, 1907

Young De Mille is worth *everything* to me just now; for his constructive instinct and methods (I'll learn 'em!); for his knowledge of what will and won't do on the stage; and for a trick of inspiring me to work like a madman. Just contrast this with my natural methods!—On Tuesday morning, he said, "So-and-so has a vaudeville sketch for next year which isn't very good. If we could get a good one ready for her manager to show to her in Washington on Friday night—we'd stand a large chance of its being taken." "All right," said I. We then went without luncheon (except olives and crackers) while we thrashed out our plot from the popular elements of love, duty, and the West! He 'phoned the manager to come and listen to the plot. I had an excited headache and two Bromo Seltzers. The manager came, listened, and liked it. De Mille was then to make a scenario and mail it to me; I was to return with the thing *written* at three the next day. But I went ahead that night without the scenario and had two thirds of it written by 3.30 a.m. I was up at 7 a.m. and, adapting some of his scenario to fit my version, read it to him at 3 p.m. It wasn't *broad* enough either in humor or emotion. He gave me pointers till 4 p.m. I worked again that night (Wednesday) till 2 a.m., copied the whole on my typewriter, and left it at his address, done, at 4 p.m. yesterday, fourth of July! This afternoon at 4 p.m. came Mrs. De Mille's opinion that it was a "winner without any question"; and it had been given to the manager to take to the "star"; copies meantime having been made,—of which you shall see one. As I said, contrast this with my usual methods!

TO HERSILIA A. MITCHELL-KEAYS [1]

Chairback Mountain Camp
Maine
June 15, 1908

***

I'm very tired, and anxious besides to be in bed for the reason that I am alone in the cabin this gusty night, De Mille having taken his pack for a three-day tramp in the woods. There's a dead loon in camp, shot by a clever fool, and down the lake a live loon, calling. Big drops of rain sound like footsteps and the creak of the wind now and then like the lifting of the latch. Shadows glue their faces to the windows;—and yet a revolver is to me a fearsome bedfellow. Something's whimpering on the lakes— and there again, and nearer, comes that hollow scream of the loon. I wish I were in bed, in spite of the bedfellow; and I wish I were awake and it were morning.

1. This letter describes an incident from which WB took his poem "The Dead Loon," the one clear result of the trip. This poem appears in the poetry section.

TO EDNA KENTON[1]

Windsor, Vermont
January 12, 1910

***

Yes the V.V.'s[2] intrigue me immensely—overcultured as only Middle Westerners could be (if you'll please intelligently understand me) from a sudden immersion in Parisian Paradise. In restless halflights they nibble at forbidden fruits—which in whole light are just apples!

***

1. Edna Kenton (1876–1954) was a writer of fiction, history, and criticism. This paragraph is in a letter to her soliciting a manuscript for Small, Maynard.
2. Carl Van Vechten (1880–1964) was one of the prominent cultural figures in New York City in the early years of this century, first as music critic, then as novelist, and finally as photographer. He was to become a major influence on WB and a lifelong friend, with his second wife, the Russian actress Fania Marinoff (1890–1971)—though at first WB did not accept Van Vechten, as this passage about him and his first wife, Anna, indicates. In a letter written later this same year, WB describes Van Vechten as not worth knowing.

The next letter is one of many to Haniel Long (1888–1956), the poet and critic, whom WB often called Niel or Shorty. After WB's friendship with Arthur Ficke, his relationship with Long was one of his oldest, most important, and most difficult associations. The story of their friendship is confusing, and at times painful. At first WB was a liberating father-figure for this young man born in Burma and raised by missionary parents, but very soon Long began to develop his own style—somewhat withdrawn, quiet, gentle, mystical—not at all like WB's. In

1913 Long married Alice Knoblauch (1890–1956), a well-educated woman who had traveled extensively in the Orient and Europe, whom WB found difficult to accept. In spite of their various and growing differences, Long and WB continued to share their great interest in poetry and found in their friendship a stimulating if difficult exchange. While teaching English at the Carnegie Institute of Technology in Pittsburgh in the late twenties, Long had a physical and nervous breakdown, and he and his wife decided to move to Santa Fe, where he could devote himself entirely to writing. In the early thirties, after WB's close friend Robert Hunt came to live with WB, WB and Long became more and more privately critical of each other's life, but they never openly quarreled until 1948, when an unpleasant social incident that Long found unacceptable produced a complete withdrawal on Long's part. After this he did not visit WB for almost eight years. Friends finally brought them together on WB's seventy-fifth birthday on August 10, 1956. By then Long and WB were both ill and had lost most of their sight. The meeting was a superficial reconciliation. Then Alice and Haniel Long died, she on October 14 at St. Vincent's Hospital in Sante Fe and he on October 17 at the Mayo Clinic in Rochester, Minnesota. WB was asked to read Long's poetry at the joint funeral service and he did so as if their relationship had been restored to what it had been.

It is very likely that WB and Long were lovers early in their relationship and that WB could not accept the loss of this or Long's rejection of him for Alice and their domestic life. The depth of WB's feeling about Long can be measured by the poem "Episode of Decay," first published in Against the Cold *and included here in the poetry section. The two characters in this macabre and bitter incident are meant to be Haniel and Alice Long.*

Long himself wrote a number of books, including Pittsburgh Memoranda *(1935), an account of a group of Pittsburghers—Carnegie, Frick, Stephen Foster, and several other famous and little-known people;* Interlinear to Cabeza de Vaca *(1936), a prose poem; and* Malinche (Doña Marina) *(1939), the story of the Mexican girl who aids Cortez, from love, and thus contributes to the destruction of her people. It is some measure of Long's quality as a writer that Henry Miller so admired the* Interlinear *that he wrote an introduction to it for a British edition. May Sarton included a description of Haniel and Alice Long in* A World of Light *(1976).*

Long is an interesting writer. It is possible to consider Interlinear to Cabeza de Vaca *as one of the exceptional historical fictions by an American in this century, and to find* Pittsburgh Memoranda *a document so far-reaching in its suggestions about the role of art and environment in American culture that it is only now able to be understood. Like WB himself, with whom he shares such a long and complex relationship, Long has received far less critical attention than he deserves.*

TO HANIEL LONG

Ithaca, New York
March 28, 1911

***

. . . I was petted a little by Isadora Duncan[1] in Buffalo. We had not met; and [she] . . . received me with exclamations of self-pity, lamenting over the lodging of a cinder in her eye. "To think that I should have been seeking my poet all over America and should at last be able to set on him only one good eye!" She draped a shapely arm over the other—which was in fact swollen and unsightly—and murmured against time and fate. "I was beautiful in Atlantic City," she pouted, a baby in face and affectations, "and, since I had written you that I was there and wished for you, you should have come. Each morning and evening I looked through my window to see if there were not a troubadour on a white horse speeding up the boardwalk. And there was nothing but vulgarity."

Then she bade us sup with Damrosch[2] and herself at the hotel and sent a manager with us to lead us safely to their private dining room, where, on my protest to Damrosch that we hadn't time for supper, he insisted on serving us champagne in which to drink the lady's health, who, arriving shortly after in deep brown furs and a rosy scarf caught diagonally across the unfit eye, first greeting us, then looking in gentle dissatisfaction upon her chair at the table, said to the waiter: "Take this away and bring a sofa": a request that induced from him only amazement of visage and imperfection of service in that he brought instead, to her disgust and to the table, a capacious armchair. Of which she inquired in a still small penetrating voice: "Is that what you call a sofa?" And of which, when he explained that the hotel was being all torn up and that there wasn't a sofa on that floor, she made the best, protesting wearily "What?—not a sofa on this floor?" and dismissing the misfortune by accepting the armchair for a less picturesque pose than she had intended on the sofa and by writing for me with a gold pencil, proffered by a tall dumb handsome man with a naughty eye but a prophylactic profile, on the cloth of the table where the champagne stood palely bubbling, her prospective itinerary, places and dates, among which with delightful misspelled allurement was "Cinsinatto," whence she is to return for a final N.Y. performance on the 31st and a farewell supper to be attended by

Yours faithfully
(having served this long sentence!)

***

1. The relationship between WB and Isadora Duncan (1878–1927) was not a close one, but WB admired her and supported her as an artist. In 1914, he began writing for her a translation of *Iphigenia in Tauris,* which she performed parts of before her theater in New York City was closed because of some confusion with the management, or the orchestra, or the police department. As is often the case with Isadora Duncan, the facts are a mixture of impressions, but the result was that WB could not complete the translation before she ended her run. The purpose was to create a version of a Greek play that had in English the naturalness and force of the original. Bynner published the play in 1915 and revised it in 1956 for the University of Chicago edition of collected Greek plays. It was included as one of the first versions of a Greek play translated expressly for performance on the modern stage.

2. Walter Damrosch (1862–1950) was a composer of several operas, conductor at the Metropolitan Opera, and the music director of the New York Philharmonic.

TO ALBERT BIGELOW PAINE[1]

Windsor, Vermont
December 3, 1911

I have just come across an old letter of Mark's written to me in his hand, October 5, 1906. Whether it is of any use to you I don't know, but loving its importance to me, I send it to you.

Perplexed between two courses—editorship and a livelihood on the one hand and poetry and poverty on the other, I consulted with Mark. I finally acted on his advice and severed every part of my connection with *McClure's.* As yet I have no regrets. Here is what he wrote me when I reported my step:

Dear Poet:
    You have certainly done right for several good reasons; at least, of them, I can name two:
    1. With your reputation you can have your freedom and yet earn your living. 2. If you fall short of succeeding to your wish, your reputation will provide you another job. And so, in high approval I suppress the scolding and give you the saintly and fatherly pat instead. . . .

The scolding I had anticipated was for disregarding his suggestions that I remain enough longer at *McClure's* to lay aside a little money, a thing I had improvidently postponed doing.

1. Albert Bigelow Paine (1861–1927), editor, dramatist, and novelist, was the authorized biographer of the three-volume *Mark Twain, A Biography* which appeared in 1912. He was also the editor of Twain's letters, which appeared in 1917.

On another occasion when I had written a poem to Clara,[1] he pretended great indignation that the first poem I had written to anyone in his household should not be to him and threatened that he would "fix me." At dinner shortly after he "fixed me" by producing from his pocket a slip of paper on which he had set down what he said was his only poem. He read the lines and then gave me the paper, which I have fondly treasured. As I copied his letter with his own inconsequent punctuation, so I copy his poem with the extra syllable in one line (I wonder if it wasn't an intentional, appropriate ejaculation?)—

> Of all sad words of tongue or pen,
> The saddest are these: "It might have been."
> Ah, say not so!—as life grows longer, leaner, thinner,
> We recognize, O God, it might have Bynner!

Apropos of an altercation we had with Harper's (he took me with him to Lauterbach, his lawyer) I was sufficiently struck with his sublime profanity to respond with a poem to himself:

> *To Saint Mark*
>
> Archangel of Profanity
> Of Blasphemous Urbanity
>   Shall be your name and post!—
>
> You shall be king of carpers
> At all the heavenly Harpers—
>   You'll make a bully Host!
>
> At every feather-tip, an oath
> Ascended from the behemoth
>   Shall hang and sparkle plain,
>
> And the Creator, staying near,
> Shall beg you—with attentive—
>   To take His name in vain.

I wonder if you could help me in my desire to have myself the original of that poem?

***

I wonder if this contribution is of any service? At any rate, I have done my duty and pleasure.

1. Clara Clemens Samossoud (1874–1962), the daughter of Mark Twain and a concert singer, was a good friend of WB's in the early years of this century, but they were never romantically connected, as has been intimated by some writers.

TO WOODROW WILSON

Windsor, Vermont
August 1, 1916

Can you not personally prevent the party called democratic from being the only party opposing the true democracy of national Equal Suffrage, an issue vital to thousands of your friends.

Arthur Davison Ficke (1883–1945) whose name appears in the next letter and throughout these letters, became a friend of WB's at Harvard and the friendship was the most important and lasting in WB's life. Both poets and men of the world, equally urbane and witty, stylistically they were not alike: WB was more expressive and democratic, and Ficke quieter and more aristocratic. They always claimed to dislike each other's poetry—except when they wrote the Spectra poems as Emanuel Morgan and Anne Knish. They disagreed in many areas and took pleasure in doing so because they knew that difference was an expression of both their natures and not of animosity. Ficke wrote WB in 1931: ". . . certain things grow clear in the course of time. I, for example, am really at home with only two people in the world. One of them is you." It was Ficke who first took WB to Japan and China. Together they wrote to Edna St. Vincent Millay (1892– 1950) and then each, in his own way, fell in love with her. Ficke wrote verse; a novel about Mexico, where he had first gone with WB; and a book on Japanese prints, which he collected. He married twice. From Iowa, a lawyer by profession, he gave up the law for poetry and lived most of his life at Hardhack, a house in Hillsdale, New York, near Edna St. Vincent Millay and her husband, Eugen Boissevain (1880–1949). For many years Ficke suffered severely from tuberculosis, which, along with cancer, caused his death. He wrote of himself, during a particularly bad siege of his illness, these two remarks, separated by almost a year:

Pain is the only thing that can make us conscious of the present moment. The rest of the time, we are thinking of the past or the future, and the present has no existence for us.

Granted that man is a very imperfect being, living in a universe that does not conform to his desires—still I feel that the show is a good one, and that I have been fortunate in seeing it.

TO EDNA ST. VINCENT MILLAY

New York City
January 1, 1922

The Millay Fingers

Promethean bringers
Of desire
Are these ten singers
In the lyre.

These wind-blown fingers
With the earth conspire
as in raindrops lingers
Fire.

Beloved Edna:

Your call, with its breath of you, stirs through my days.—Instead of going to China in the spring, I shall come to Europe, and we'll talk deep. Perhaps for either of us marriage would be jolly. Perhaps not.—Uncannily I feel the beckon to be rather for Arthur than for
Hal [1]

1. WB had asked Edna Millay to marry him in December 1921, and she had accepted, but the situation was probably not as it appeared: WB may have sent off a letter to Millay in Vienna as a lark, or perhaps when he was tight. More sober, as WB is in this communication, he fears the situation and realizes she loves Arthur Ficke. In the end, Ficke's good sense prevailed. He insisted, in duplicate letters to each written in January 1922, that the marriage of any one of them to another would destroy the relationship of the three. The result was that Millay and Ficke remained close to each other and WB was their constant correspondent and companion. The odd trio, and the respective spouses, remained good friends for life. WB also refers to the proposal in the letter of March 14, 1922.

TO ALICE CORBIN HENDERSON [1]

Hotel Seymour
New York City
January 21, 1922

When I had almost decided that I was not going to the coast, and therefore should be forced to miss Santa Fe, along came your enticing note. Whether I go to California or not, I shall come to Santa Fe, after all. Your suggestion of practical assistance for the trip is very welcome, and I shall, of course, be glad to come for "gate receipts."

I have been giving a comprehensive talk on "A Year in China" or "The Heart of China," whichever you prefer as a title. It contains both amusement and meat. I illuminate it here and there with Chinese poems. On several occasions I have given a talk exclusively on "Chinese Poetry," which is somewhat more special and technical, but has easily reached non-professional audiences. I do not know your group there, but I suggest that the first of the two lectures would be safe anywhere.[2] I am sending you a copy of the December *Asia*, also a page of poems from the *New York Evening Post*. There is still another group in the February *Poetry*. Since I shall be speaking in Dallas, Texas, on February 11th, you had better set your date somewhere between the 14th and 18th—any one of those days. I shall certainly stay in Santa Fe for a week or more. Do not let Willard Nash[3] escape before I arrive. I am agog for the happy meetings and discussions we shall have together, and thank you again for sending the word which seems to have enchanted a wish into a reality. You may always reach me at this address, though I am leaving New York the day after the Poetry Society dinner. I am glad you approve of our speakers. I made a decided effort. With heartiest regards, I am

Yours faithfully

1. Alice Corbin Henderson (1881–1949), poet and editor, had been involved with Harriet Monroe in the founding and editing of *Poetry,* but in 1916 was forced to come to Santa Fe to cure her tuberculosis. For a number of years she continued to assist Miss Monroe from Santa Fe, but she also became occupied in writing her own poetry. She was the center of the circle in Santa Fe which included WB, Haniel Long, Arthur Ficke, and many others over the years. Her husband was the painter-architect-designer, William Penhallow Henderson (1877–1943). Their daughter, Alice, married the son of Mabel Dodge Luhan, John Evans (1902–78), on December 20, 1922, with WB as best man. She divorced Evans in 1933, and in 1938 married Edgar Rossin (1901–48).

2. WB refers to the talks he gave based upon his experiences in China. He had been giving these as he traveled around the country on one of his many lecture tours. The tours were his principal means of support, along with the smaller amounts received from publications, such as those mentioned here.

3. Willard Nash (1898–1943) was a painter and friend of WB. It was to see him that WB

first considered visiting Santa Fe. Nash was one of the group of painters who settled on the Camino del Monte Sol and called themselves Los Cinco Pintores. Nash, his painter friends, and the Hendersons formed an artist colony congenial to WB. Nash's work was shown in 1932 and again in 1935 at the Whitney Museum of American Art in New York City. In 1936 he moved to California. At his death WB took up a subscription to buy a nude by Nash for the Museum of New Mexico, thus aiding the artist's reputation and his widow. The painting was accepted, but the director refused to hang a nude.

TO HANIEL LONG

Sunmount
Santa Fe
March 14, 1922

***

Have I whispered that I may come back here from California, whither I go on April 15th, and take an adobe house for the summer? It's primitive and peaceful—not so beautiful to me as middle California, but a stimulating change. How I do happen along, and what fun it is! Why should I marry? Ask Alice?

A laughing note comes from E.[1]—and I feel at least as gay as she. One had preceded it, in which she had saddened me. For the very last time, I fancy, I have made my bow to matrimony.

Big love to my Longs!

1. Edna St. Vincent Millay.

TO ARTHUR DAVISON FICKE

Sunmount
Santa Fe
April 5, 1922

I suppose you were right. I was judging from outside—and from a love which has grown up round you and Evelyn together and hates to be disturbed. I have just written Eve as best I could. It was the more difficult letter, so I wrote it first.[1]

Far be it from me to impugn love. I bow to it always. But the very fact that I haven't married shows my doubts as to its undeviating permanence. You, too, have been in love and thought it permanent. That's why I cautioned you. And Gladys is younger. What if she were to change first? But you know all that—and you choose. And I guess you're wise to choose as you're choosing and to be frank about it with Evelyn. The uncanny part of the whole thing is that Gladys always reminds me of Evelyn. What a world!

I had answered your wire before I knew of any of this. Tempted as I was to join you and grieved not to be well enough, I am now a little glad. I'm an old softy, you see; and after our two Oriental trips I shouldn't have been at ease under the new conditions—at any rate, not quite so soon. It's not that I'm a moralist. It's not that I don't like Gladys. I'm an old softy, that's all.

As to Edna, she is now laughing at me, as if she had been laughing all the while. Perhaps she was. I hope so.

This semi-breakdown of mine has given me time to think hard, and I am determined not to marry anyone if I can help it. Perhaps when I see Edna, I'll not be able to help it. But perhaps she will be. And there you are.

A mad world, my masters!

I am just back from a visit to Mabel Sterne (Dodge, that was).[2] She is said to be living with an Indian now. He was there at any rate: chauffeur outside, guest inside. I like him well enough and have no scruples. In fact, there was an Indian girl in the house who danced with me and was very beautiful. . . .

***

I was going to ask you to let me dedicate "Tiger" to you in the new volume of collected plays. What do you think? Do you dislike the play? I like it myself. It was never dedicated. Is there any angle from which the dedication might be unwise? Would Eve feel left out? Would a dedication to the two of you be preferable or crazy? Would she want her name connected with a play like that anyway? I'm all mixed up. Please wire me your judgment, so that I may wire Knopf. If everything were normal, I should like to dedicate it "To Arthur Davison Ficke." How would it be, "To Anne Knish"? Am I just tired or is it a curious problem?[3]

Good night, old dear.

***

1. Ficke had decided to divorce his first wife, Evelyn Blunt (1880–1954), and marry Gladys Brown (1890–1973), which he did in 1923.

2. Mable Dodge Sterne (1879–1962) married the American Pueblo Indian Antonio "Tony" Luhan (1880?–1963) in 1923 and lived the rest of her life in Taos. She was a great influence in the community, brought many important artists and writers to New Mexico,

and wrote very well of the area. Her career in Florence, New York, and Taos became the subject, in part, of WB's play *Cake*.

3. WB simply dedicated his play "To Arthur Davison Ficke."

D. H. Lawrence (1885–1930) and Frieda von Richthofen, his wife (1879– 1956), were important characters in WB's life: Lawrence for a brief but significant period in 1922–23 and Frieda for the rest of her life, which was largely spent in Taos. Lawrence and WB were deeply attracted antagonists; Frieda and WB shared a natural affinity which always remained strong.

The Lawrences first arrived in Santa Fe by train on September 10, 1922, and were met by Mabel Dodge Sterne and Tony Luhan. The trip to Taos was too long to make that day and Mrs. Sterne asked WB if he would let the Lawrences stay in his house. It is with a description of their arrival at his house that WB later began his book on the Lawrences, Journey with Genius *(1951), which recounts his association with them and their trip together to Mexico in 1923. This description is included in the prose section. WB wrote three poems about D.H. Lawrence, all reprinted here: "Lorenzo" and "D.H. Lawrence" in* Caravan *and "A Foreigner" in* Indian Earth.

TO ARTHUR DAVISON FICKE

530½ College Street[1]
Santa Fe
September 18, 1922

On their way to Mabel Sterne's the other night, the D. H. Lawrences rested in my "dark bed"—but I in the studio! If you come, we'll run up to Mabel's. You'll like the Lawrences and be much intrigued by Mabel.

1. WB had stationery printed with his name and his new address. The address eventually became 342 Buena Vista Street, for the same house.

TO MABEL DODGE LUHAN

Santa Fe
September 29, 1922

Let us remark in passing that poor Alice Corbin has a case of Lawrengitis.

TO BARRY FAULKNER

Santa Fe
[September, 1922]

***

D. H. Lawrence and his wife proved to be, at least on so brief a meeting, simple, human, jolly creatures. Like many of the writing Englishmen, Lawrence has that curious blond voice, that almost petulant treble. It is a petulance that whines into a grin. They all have it. Apart from that, and in spite of his gnomish beard, he was as likable and easy as a kid. His wife, a capacious and vibrant German, was even more magnetic, with the large and ready charm which almost all German women have for me. It was as if she were the earth, and he the house. The house of course gets the notice. Before long, mainly out of loyalty to you, I shall tackle another one of his books. Since *Sons and Lovers* I have read nothing but his absurd rubbish on *Psychoanalysis and the Unconscious*. I suspect that he is more of an artist than he lets himself be, that he is, as it were, afraid of himself.

***

TO PORTER GARNETT[1]

[Mexico]
April 13, 1923

***

I suppose Haniel has told you that we are in Mexico with the D. H. Lawrences. I had long been intending a trip here. They came down through Santa Fe from Taos and urged us to accompany them. I had a few misgivings, which have since been borne out. The man himself, and his wife, from a brief earlier meeting, I had liked well enough, but I had never liked the spirit of the man in his books. He had seemed to me a sort of Freudian prig—anything but immoral—and I still find him so. Give me a promiscuous lover anytime instead of a promiscuous hater. Promiscuous hating is really a more degraded form of immorality than the other. Fortunately there are two phases of Lawrence which one may easily and simply enjoy. By nature, except as he has tampered with himself, he is an impulsive boyish gentle soul; and as a writer he is by nature eminently gifted. The trouble with him is that he has let his intellect and his more intemperate inclinations elaborate a code of thought and conduct which permit him all sorts of rather pretentious self-indulgence. I think I should like the man very much indeed if he were a real self instead of a fabricated self. What is left of the reality under the fabrication, together with a rather neat wit, make him supportable. When his hearty German wife is with him and they take semi-seriously their constant petty bickerings, I am amused and at ease. When I am alone with him, I have a hard time not to be bored. A contrast between the stature of this man and that of Meredith[2] shows to what a degree the English novel and the spirit behind it has deteriorated. It has come down from generous genius to a bitter knack.

We are due for a few more weeks together. This morning I thought I should have to contrive a pretext for escape; but this afternoon I feel better. The Lawrences' attitude toward Johnson and myself is genial and charming—with always a shadow lurking as to what he will say about us later. So far I have hardly heard him say a decent word about anyone—even those supposed to be his close friends. It is curious to think of literature falling into such clutches.

***

1. Porter Garnett (1871–1951) was a friend of WB's from his Berkeley days. He was a prominent Bohemian Club member, and he later ran the Laboratory Press at the Carnegie Institute of Technology.

2. George Meredith (1828–1909), one of the best known 19th-century English novelists and poets, was considered by WB to be one of the three major influences upon his literary career (along with Walt Whitman and A. E. Housman). WB met Meredith in 1902 on a trip to England and wrote an essay on that visit that is reprinted in *The Works of Witter Bynner: Prose Pieces*.

TO WILLARD JOHNSON[1]

Hotel del Jardin
Puebla, Mexico
Thursday, April 19th, I think,
1923

***

D. H. revived somewhat but cursed the land and despaired of its people. One instant he does that and the next instant wishes a hacienda hereabouts for six months—then curses again. If ever there were a sick soul, it is his. He froths at all objective sentiment but sentimentalizes himself into a sort of God who creates the earth and not only on the seventh day but every day finds it bad. Poor Frieda! If she calls an idea "hellish," he swarms on her with venom for being vulgar and in the same breath is calling the same idea "shit and nonsense." "Always do what I say, never do what Frieda says. I have premonitions about things. She's a fool." This man whom a generation is thinking intellectual is as set about with super- stitions as a parlor of palmistry. In fact his whole scheme of things is only a new superstition, a new humbuggery as impressive as phrenology. I am ashamed of an age that for a moment takes him seriously. Personally my distaste for his half-baked violence is changing into pity for his sick ego- tism. This morning I had decided to quit the party and return to my other invalid. This afternoon I decided that I had better complete the round. Perhaps I am a better dose for him than he is for me. I never combat him with words but only by continuing to be what I am and to believe more than ever in almost everything that he condemns. His code, without his knowing it, is exactly that of the American businessman. He wants what he wants when he wants it. He does not know where he's going, but he's on his way. He hits at any competitor. He is gathering up the earth but has no use for it. He's a pathetic figure. It takes all my religion to keep me from turning on him with contempt. No, no, no—he's not vicious. He's the pathetic man who has loved his own soul so well that he has slain it.

If anyone reads him fifteen years from now, you may publish this. It may be needed.

What an answer to your note!—which I found here an hour ago.

Your slowness of recovery worries me. But it reassures me that we followed the only wise course. The Southern trip would have been im- possible for you within any reasonable time.

Frieda, for the past three days, has been in bed with a cold. I hope my turn is not waiting till we reach Orizaba tomorrow night. Apart from that contingency we shall spend Saturday and Sunday in Orizaba and Cor- doba, returning to Mexico on Monday. I hope you'll not be too lonely and restless. . . .

***

1. Willard Johnson (1897–1968) was as a student at Berkeley one of the founders of *Laughing Horse,* a satiric magazine which he took with him from Berkeley and published at infrequent intervals for many years. A small, quiet man, non-demonstrative, "Spud," as he was called, served WB as secretary and companion. In 1923 WB and he went to Mexico with D. H. and Frieda Lawrence. Johnson had a year in New York on the staff of *The New Yorker,* but finally went to Taos and worked for Mabel Luhan, edited the local paper, wrote a column for the newspaper, and became a wry, monk-like creature, greatly loved, although always from a distance. He and WB remained friends but were not, after this early period, close.

TO ALICE CORBIN HENDERSON

Hotel Arzapalo
Chapala
[July 3, 1923]

All right—a quick, personally written word, from my bed! I've turned in early, because we're setting out tomorrow on a two-day boat trip on this much-affording lake. It's faintly possible that I shall back out in the morning from such close contact again with the Death Worm. As we live here in Chapala, I manage very well. We see each other only an hour or so a day. Spud is very happy with him—but not I. He's too dank. He almost smells of death, being completely dead at the core. His fevered surfaces may fool one generation but not two.

I had looked forward to a month here without him. He had definitely planned departure. Now, alas, he lingers. In a curious way he likes Spud. In a deeper way he detests me. He is afraid ever to be irritated with me, to show his irritation, lest there be such a slop of lava that the party will break up. And, somehow, he likes the party. Our wills have tussled and mine has more than held its own, which both angers and draws him. He is having his revenge on me in a novel—which Spud is copying and I am not allowed to read.[1] I see now how he has been defeated by people all through his life and has consequently lashed their paper images with his poor fury. What a sick man he is and what a weak man! Bits of him are likable and might have been developed into a whole firm man, if he had not so perversely enjoyed his weaknesses. He is good at phrases; and he is always at ease with animals, because they can never intimately oppose him. . . .

1. *The Plumed Serpent* (1926); WB writes to Lawrence about this novel on January 19, 1928.

Bynner's co-translator of The Jade Mountain *was Kiang Kang-hu (1883–1954). He was an essential part of the success of the translation: he made the literal translations from which Bynner worked; checked each for accuracy of translation into English poetry; checked any facts as to history or the locations mentioned in the poems; supplied all the scholarly information; and, most critically, brought his great knowledge of Chinese culture to bear on all aspects of the project. He was himself a fascinating and intriguing man.*
Born in Kiangsi Province of an old and prominent Mandarin family, Kiang

received an excellent education, including language study in Japan and Belgium, and served his government in several posts until he began devoting himself to idealistic and liberal causes. He was the organizer and chosen head of the Chinese Socialist Party and the editor of a socialist journal. One of the young people who worked for him as an office assistant (to learn about socialism) was Mao Tse-tung. When Yuan Shih-k'ai became President of China after Sun Yat-sen, Kiang was proscribed and around 1913 was forced to leave China. He began teaching at Berkeley and left to the university 13,000 volumes which remained in his family's private library. He worked on the Oriental Collections at the Library of Congress and then in 1920 returned to China with WB. He went to observe socialism in Moscow and Berlin, traveled throughout Southeast Asia studying the educational and political systems, and in 1922 founded Southern University in Shanghai; in 1924 he reorganized the Socialist Party. By 1929 he was in the United States again, and then at McGill University in Montreal to head a new department of Chinese Studies.

In 1932 he wrote to WB: "I may resign and return to China just to suffer with my people. I want to dispossess everything in the World so I can be what I am again. This is too strange to tell anybody; I hope it will not alarm you." He did return to China and eventually took the post of Minister of Education in Wang Ching-wei's puppet government run by the Japanese. When the Nationalists returned to power in 1945, he was arrested and put in prison. He barely escaped being killed. The Communists would not release him when they came into power. He asked to be able to serve his government from jail, but was refused. He was permitted to write, and he prepared an autobiography that has not been published. He is believed to have died in jail on December 6, 1954. WB made many attempts to have him released from prison but he could do little. It is likely, however, that WB's letters helped prevent Kiang's execution.

TO KIANG KANG-HU

Hotel Arzapalo
Chapala
July 20, 1923

✳✳✳

I wish you would give me further news of your affairs: about the government nearly sending you as ambassador to Russia, and about your university. Thanks for the news about your family. My congratulations to your wife on her achievement.

✳✳✳

Thanks for your comment on the Li Po translations. I enclose you a letter from a Chinese student, S. Y. Chu, with a reference to Li Po's "A Song of Chang-Kan."[1] In it you will find some penciled queries which I wish you would answer. Long ago, by the way, I sent you a complete list of the poets in our anthology asking you to fill in such dates as I lacked. I wonder if that list failed to reach you. I enclose another.

The book progresses a little more rapidly; and as I have said before, the delay is advantageous for us in the fact that many of the poems are appearing in magazines and giving the volume, before its issue, a growing prestige.

The question of notes troubles me. It seems to me that figures set here and there against words in the text are disfiguring and distracting. Hence I am rearranging our note system and am thinking seriously of a geographical index at the back of the book in which those interested might find the modern equivalents of T'ang places.[2] The difficulty would be that some of these T'ang names, like Wu, mean in different poems, different places. In the case of such names I should have to differentiate and make specific references to the poems in which they appear. I mention this because I wish you would take pains on the group of manuscripts I am sending you today under separate cover, to set down the modern names of places for such use as I propose. You may either return me the manuscripts with your comments or send me the comments in a letter carefully listing them under the titles. From time to time as I can supply you with copies, I shall send you other groups of the poems, hoping thereby to save extensive revision on the proofs, and consequent expense. Please notice that I wish your supervision on the printed poems as well as those typed.

Having just spent a week in a hospital after an operation,[3] I'm not feeling very energetic. Otherwise I might write you a better letter. Let me only say that as compared to the United States, Mexico reminds me of China. Not so systematized as the United States, but fresher and freer. I feel that Mexico may be a barrier against the blighting southward progress of Anglo-Saxondom.

Hoping to be in China within two years, and sending you all my affectionate greetings, I am

Faithfully yours

1. Li Po (circa 700–762) was one of the major T'ang poets and one whom WB especially admired. WB wrote a poem about him, "To Li Po," reprinted in the selections from *Take Away the Darkness* in the poetry section.
2. Such a section appeared in *The Jade Mountain* as "Topography."
3. WB was operated on in early July with an infected fistula.

WB's mother wrote him on December 8, 1924, about living in Santa Fe: "Also, I think the whole atmosphere too narrow a one for you and your gifts. . . . Frankly I do not think you have advanced intellectually since being there . . . the environs are not developing you. . . . You have too many gifts to bury them under a Santa Fe bushel." She ended her remarks with the definitive statement: "My perspective is better than yours." WB answered her in the following letter.

Santa Fe
December 12, 1924

***

Your coffee-spurred letter arrived yesterday and amused me. Not that I don't listen to what you say. I know that I have been through a stagnant sort of period; but I know also that it has had nothing to do with Santa Fe. The war would have reached and dispirited me anywhere—even in China. And Santa Fe has given me better restorative than I have found elsewhere in America. There is a fundamental soundness in the blending of these three cultures. As I try to do everywhere, I have followed the Confucian doctrine of giving a share of myself to my community. Then comes the Taoist doctrine of withdrawal after service, for the cultivation of one's own soul and sensibilities. After the age of forty, no man should live in a city. . . .

***

TO MARGARET SANGER [1]

Santa Fe
February 21, 1925

It is unthinkable that you and your associates should be harassed by the laws and officials of a civilized government, particularly a government which involved its people in the devastating conflict of the great war, or the Great Murder as an Englishman has aptly called it. A better understanding among all nations of the principles you advocate and of the motives you forward, would be a fundamental contribution toward the establishment of peace. Your method is much better than the war method for the regulation of mankind. It is indeed an important factor in the good will toward men which is inseparable from peace on earth.

1. Margaret (Higgins) Sanger (1883–1966), one of the early American leaders in the birth-control movement, was indicted in 1915 for sending information on contraceptives through the mails and the next year was arrested for running a birth-control clinic in Brooklyn. WB did not know her personally.

TO MARIANNE MOORE [1]

Hotel Mólgora [2]
Chapala
July 30, 1925

***

. . . Emanuel Morgan [3] has led me into devious ways, about which other people are sorrier than I. I wonder if you would read a verse play of mine—part verse—with a view to its possible use in *The Dial*. I promise you that it is I who am making the suggestion and no practical joker. I had not thought of it as *Dial* material; but after your letter, I think of it as exactly that. Perhaps you will too—and will advise me to omit most of the fifth act. It is a satirical fantasy called, for want of a better title, *Cake*. The chief characters are a Lady and a Eunuch; others are a Chinese Mandarin, Mary Magdalen, Judas, a Swami, and a Negro. On the whole, it's not so mad as it sounds; in part, it's madder. Oddly enough, the real quality of the play, unless I am very wrong, is in its chuckles. I am garrulous about it, because it was burned by a little boy and in less than thirty-six hours rewritten by a larger boy. This happened only a few weeks ago.

***

1. Marianne Moore (1887–1972), poet and essayist, and WB were acquaintances only through her editorial work on *The Dial* and WB's submission of poetry and, in this case, a play. Actually *The Dial* accepted very few of WB's poems.
2. The Hotel Arzapalo had been bought and for this one year was called Hotel Mólgora.
3. Emanuel Morgan is the name WB used in writing the Spectra poems. See the essay on the Spectra poems in the prose section.

TO PAUL HORGAN [1]

Santa Fe
October 26, 1926

Where this paper came from I don't know.[2] I found it among W. Johnson's effects. It serves.

First of all, going back to an old letter of yours, let me say that B. Hunt's arrival,[3] visit and departure have all been amazing to me, almost mythical. He had said that he would stop off a minute on his way west, after his several weeks with you. Then he wrote that he would be here a fortnight earlier than planned; then he came three days earlier still, without warning—so that I was away on a trip, and he spent the weekend alone at the house, keyed in (and perhaps up, a little) by Rita. Soon after this he took a great shine to my friend Davey James[4] and was absent and invisible for a week—drunk, I fear, a good part of the time. Finally he returned to College St., behaved admirably, and wanted a job. When I landed him a pleasant prospect in an architect's office, he decided to go home and suddenly went, leaving all his toilet articles. Since then I have had no word from him.

It is only fair that you know all this; but I wanted him to tell you himself. Perhaps by now he has done so. I pray you not to berate him in any way. That's not what he needs at the moment. I might have scolded him on various counts; in fact I did scold him,—sufficiently, I think. He went home, gentle and sober. Bibulous as you may think my house, it has its bounds. After exceeding them a while (not in my company), he lived strictly and sweetly within them; and my summary is that I am very fond of him and hope he will come again—if only to disprove that he is a legend.

I sound priggish in some of this but, as you know, am not.

***

Either in this envelope or in another following it, I'll enclose evidence of the sport it affords me to be a politician even these few minutes.[5] My own election is impossible, thank God, in this solidly Republican county; but the powers decided that my candidacy would help Hannett,[6] in whom I believe. So I am campaigning: third State House speech tomorrow night, others at country *bailes,* and letters in *The New Mexican.* I wish you were [here] to smile and help.

Edna Millay arrives tomorrow.

***

1. Paul Horgan (1903–95), friend of WB's from 1926 until WB died in 1968, was a literary executor of WB's estate until, by court order, it was assigned to establish The Witter Bynner Foundation for Poetry. A novelist, short-story writer, historian, and essayist, Horgan won two Pulitzer Prizes and a number of other awards for his two-score published volumes. He served as director of the Center for Advanced Studies at Wesleyan University from 1962 to 1967.

2. WB was writing on stationery that carried the heading "Harvard Club of New Mexico."

3. This is the earliest reference to Robert Hunt (1906–64), who was to come in November 1930 to visit WB and never to leave, except for war service. WB first met Robert Hunt in the summer of 1926, when he came to visit his friend Paul Horgan, who was serving briefly as WB's secretary. Horgan and Hunt had met at the New Mexico Military Institute in Roswell, where they were fellow cadets.

4. Not identified.

5. WB ran for the state legislature on the Democratic ticket. He lost to the Republican candidate, Roman L. Baca, 4,419 to 2,370.

6. Arthur T. Hannett (1884–1966) was governor of New Mexico from 1925 to 1927.

TO IDELLA PURNELL STONE[1]

Santa Fe
November 10, 1926

Tomorrow morning I'm off on a three-day Indian trip with Edna Millay; but I must perforce take a little of the night to calm you, if I can, concerning my character and calumniators.

First of all, bless you for being prompted to write what seems to me one of your best poems and, always, thanks—no, not thanks, just cheers, for the candor and realness of your friendship.

No one knows better than you that there is in me an element of tenderness toward my male friends which verges on the sort of physical attachment the detractors talk about.[2] I am well aware of the fact that, were I less fastidious, I might have gone the way of certain of our friends. And that awareness makes me tolerant of their presence and also of their right to their own ways of living. On the other hand, my spirit cannot help being troubled for them, and I visit on them what they consider Puritanic preaching. There is so much depravity round about us, in the conduct of some and the imagination of others, that I don't wonder at suspicions of me, when I consider my complete willingness to incur them. Dr. Gombert[3] saw me in New York with a young writer, Glenway Wescott,[4] who is an avowed homosexual and at the same time one of the most brilliant persons I know. Sometimes I think him a very fine person. Certainly I respect his courage and his dignity. There are many others whom I know and see and am not afraid to be seen with. And I don't care a whoop what anyone says about me. I've lived too long to be responsible to anyone but myself. And I can face myself with very little shame.

The Goddard girl's[5] story is different. It derives from a girl she lived with here—a poor, vicious, drunken creature who maligned me in the one way she thought might hurt and did it merely because I showed too openly that I couldn't bear her. I thought Alice a better sort.

∗∗∗

1. Idella Purnell Stone (1901–1982), poet and editor, was a student in WB's Berkeley verse class. Her father was a dentist in Guadalajara, Mexico. While working there in 1923, at the U.S. Embassy, she started a magazine, *Palms,* to which WB contributed extensive advice, his own poetry, and the poetry of many others.

2. WB discusses the subject of male friendship in Chapter 42, "Comrade," in *Journey with Genius.*

3. Not identified.

4. Glenway Wescott (1901–1989), the American novelist and critic, met WB first in New York City and again in Santa Fe. Wescott had lived briefly in Santa Fe before WB arrived.

5. Not identified.

It seems the advice in the following letter has to do with Hunt's having frankly said something about his life to his parents. It is probably that this was an admission of his homosexual nature. WB's reaction, telling him not to be open publicly but to be honest with himself, may throw some light on WB's letter to Idella Purnell and suggest that what he said to her followed a code of public conformity and private honesty which remained his pattern for life.

TO ROBERT HUNT

Contoocook Manor
Antrim, New Hampshire
August, 1927

You've made a mistake, I think, but a good mistake. For your own immediate relief from unbearable interference in your conduct of life, you probably had to speak; and you are clear now from that kind of bother. Alas, another kind will follow. Before, they were directing you socially. Now it will be morally. Before, though, it was at close quarters. Now it's at a distance. That's a gain.

On the whole, however, I disbelieve in admitting the unsympathetic to knowledge. Let them surmise what they will, and you can still shrug your shoulders. Once they know, they shrug theirs, and it's not a pleasant shrug. I say this, because I fear lest your windy impulses may blow you into regrettable candors, candors which can only cause you eventual discomfort. Hold back, old dear. This is not advice to be cowardly—it's advice toward wise, unharassed happiness. Don't indulge your sudden fevers for sensation. Be square with yourself. Accept the liking of those who like you. Like those you like. And to hell with the rest. Am I right?

Be sure of my liking, anyway—and of my liking your liking. That's fixed.

As to a bookshop in Santa Fe, somebody, alas, has stolen a march on you and done the very thing you propose. I might inquire, when I return, as to possibilities of combining or taking over.

***

The Plumed Serpent, *the novel D. H. Lawrence was writing in 1923 when he was in Mexico with WB, was published in 1926. WB's response to the novel involved his conflict of ego with a fellow artist and the fact that Lawrence portrayed him unflatteringly as Owen Rhys, a minor character.*

TO D. H. LAWRENCE[1]

January 19, 1928

Not wishing to dictate what I had to say about *The Plumed Serpent,* I waited. And now's a chance on this leisurely motor trip to California.

You must know, without my saying so, that I think the first half of it a consummate piece of noticing and writing. You are much better about Mexico there than you are in *Mornings.*[2] But, after that, I'm ready to quarrel with you.

It's a fundamental quarrel. You are forever hunting out in mankind some superior being (sometimes yourself) and attributing to him mystical or semi-mystical qualities of godly leadership. In this way you try to justify man's ways to God, or to yourself. There is always a physical tinge in it—an animal admiration—and often, arising out of that, a blur of spiritual admiration. You carry over, from Egypt or from England, a need of *religion:* or of authority. Touching on it, you become vague and feminine. Fair enough.

Distrusting your gesture toward religion, I see well how you must detest mine. For years, I have innerly believed that no man, not even the authoritative or prophetic leader, has any importance at all except as he foresees and furthers the ultimate amalgamation of all life into one total, completed consciousness which will somehow fulfill these imperfect and vain fragments of the totality, these individualities which we jealously restrict, when for right and happy growth we should be enlarging them toward that final merged realization of the only self.

Your way of thought for us seems to me to make man not more but less; and I don't doubt that my religious groping has the same effect on you.

Apart from this fundamental difference between us (a difference of similarity) I resented, with perhaps too personal or perhaps sufficiently reasonable irritation, the intrusion into your book of an outside influence—a presence of weakness, after your own presence had been strong. It almost seemed as though you had dropped the pen, and left behind that miraculous half-book of real observation and authoritative writing, and let Mabel take it up and proceed to impose upon your pages her idiotic bunk about Tony's spiritual qualities and to infuse into your magnificent vision her queasy female notions generally.

You emerged and shone your clear self in the narratives about destroying the Roman images and that unforgettable fight at the hacienda; but the rest of your finish sounded like Mabel. I could feel her suave presence impressing Orage,[3] or something of the sort, on the gullible. It wasn't you. She missed your person, old boy; but she caught your book—or part of it.

Now flay me.

1. This letter exists only in a copy that WB made about 1955 to send to Edward Nehls, the scholar who was preparing the three-volume *D. H. Lawrence: A Composite Biography* (1957, 1958, 1959).

2. *Mornings in Mexico* (1927).

3. Alfred Richard Orage (1873–1934) was an editor of the *New Age,* a periodical of the Fabian Society in England. He became a disciple of the Greek-Armenian mystic George Gurdjieff (1872–1949) and came to the United States in 1924 promoting Gurdjieff's teachings.

TO ROBERT HUNT

Santa Maria Inn
Santa Maria, California
January 26, 1928

Nobody better than you jewels a moment with your heart and eyes and sets it in a handclasp. Your triple gift: your prescience, your presents,[1] and your presence! What moments they made!

How do you continue, old darling?

Was there too harsh a reality in anticipation come true and in a class missed? I hope not.

Tell me, will you, c/o Albert M. Bender . . .

Love to you and thanks.

1. Robert Hunt had given WB a present of a lacquered box.

TO ALBERT M. BENDER [1]

Hardhack
Hillsdale, New York
February 24, 1929

By the time your word replies to this, I shall be in New York City again. Meantime I am resting in New York State—at Arthur Ficke's, hemmed in by a country deep with snow. We see Edna Millay, stay the night there because we are glad that the roads prevent our leaving—and we listen to new sonnets as lovely as the old. And how sweetly they swing in that bell-like voice. And how good the world is, after all, that can give me these true, song-hearted friends and yet leave me homesick for my own hills! It's a rich world—the crumbs from its great table are sufficient to swell Lazarus with indigestion. Especially in California!!

* * *

Love to your coast from this one and from the mountains between.

1. Albert M. Bender (1866–1941) was one of the most interesting and unusual patrons of the arts in the long and distinguished history of San Francisco patronage. Born in Dublin, the son of a rabbi, he was a considerable success in running his own insurance agency and began helping artists early in life. He gave directly, sometimes out of his own pocket, usually not obtrusively, and he helped anyone, without particular regard for any qualification but need. He set up an art library at the California School of Fine Arts, gave Asian objects to the Palace of the Legion of Honor, and over one thousand separate items to the San Francisco Museum of Art. Mills College and the University of California also received his assistance, as did galleries in Washington, D.C., Paris, and Dublin. He made WB a few loans, but in this relationship he showed another side of himself: he simply enjoyed giving presents, most often books, but also ties or scarves or handkerchiefs. WB and Kiang Kang-hu dedicated *The Jade Mountain* to Bender.

By August 1930, WB was suffering from severe depression. He had written Haniel Long about this state on August 21 and admitted how badly he felt and how he did not want anyone else to know. He gardened a great deal, went to the Indian country for the Snake Dance and the Gallup Ceremonial, and then to the Santa Fe Fiesta in September, but nothing changed.

This letter to Arthur Ficke speaks of Robert Hunt's arrival in Santa Fe and, simultaneously, the lifting of WB's depression and the beginning of a new poem. On this day, WB wrote another friend about the change: "It had been a corpse-like summer. I have felt like a dead but agitated carcass, pulled around among people by an invisible hand with invisible strings, and all to no purpose; but new

blood is returning into the veins of the corpse. I feel another world around me,
am writing again; I like, once more, to look at the landscape."

TO ARTHUR DAVISON FICKE[1]

Santa Fe
November 12, 1930

***

You will be interested to know that Bobby Hunt suddenly descended on me ten days ago. He encountered someone who had a return ticket from California, expiring on October 31st. He seized it on the eve of its expiration and landed here to my great delight. He had been working twelve to fourteen hours a day for six months as Assistant Manager and Treasurer of the Paramount Publix Theatres in Portland, Oregon, had broken down under the strain, and was convalescing at Palo Alto when this chance came to come to Santa Fe. It is extremely pleasant for me to have him here.

***

The vague depression that has held me, more or less, all summer, has now entirely lifted. With its lifting, I began a new long poem,[2] which I am eager to have you see. I think, though, that I will finish it and let you see it entire, rather than send you any portion of it. I have an idea you will like it better than anything I have done.

***

What a devil of a time you are having! My note, doubtless, sounded too blunt in the matter of your coming back here. If so, please realize that it was only because I was rushed and yet wanted to say something. You will remember my saying repeatedly to you and Gladys that I have seen person after person cured out here, who have then gone away, and sooner or later lost the cure and had to return. In spite of all the doctors and their theory that fresh air anywhere is as good as it is anywhere else, other places do not seem to do the job. You have had your own experience at Saranac. I have known similar cases in all sorts of regions other than this. When you know that this place really set you up once, put you back on your feet, and set you at work again on your writing, why the devil don't you throw aside all other considerations and accept once more the benefit about which you are sure, instead of dallying with doubtful possibilities. All other considerations, dear boy, are of no importance in comparison with your regaining your health. The depression you have been under is nothing except a result of your ailment. The other trouble of which you told me is equally a result.

Please think very seriously of what I say. It may be inadvisable for you to take the trip at present, I don't know about that; I have a strong feeling that you would risk less with the trip than you would by staying in a moist climate. Caring for you as I do—more, as you know, than for any of my friends—I am most anxiously earnest in my advice. You may not particularly care for Santa Fe; but isn't it a better prospect to make up your mind to live here to resume your inner vitality, to be alive and happy again with new, strong impulses in your life and work, than to fret along in places you like better, always near a menacing shadow.

Please don't trust the Eastern doctors. They sent you to Saranac once. Trust old Halbert a little.

1. A copy of this typed letter was sent to Albert Bender, with this note written by hand at the end. "Dear Albert/He needs all the love we can give him. It's rope to a drowning man./ Ever/Hal." Ficke had tuberculosis.

2. *Eden Tree* (1931).

***

TO ROBERT HUNT

Hotel Seymour
New York City
Almost the New Year not quite

I must tell you first—just for fun—that two guys have written a book called *Sex in the Arts*[1]—no, they have edited it—a symposium—and someone named Robinson has dealt with the poets and has found "contemporary poetry the languishing victim of an almost universal mother-complex." "The dominant note in modern poetry is the utterance of this futility—the futility of romantic, substitutive love to satisfy psychic needs of men. The most distinguished poets of our age are in the grip of this malady. Conversely, no poet of importance is free of it. And syllogistically, no person who is free of it is important." Aiken, Eliot, Millay, Bynner, and Robinson are his specific examples.

Hullo, mother, I send you a tiny New Year's greeting and only would it were not tiny. December cheated me completely. Can you manage awhile? Tell me all!—including details.

Here things look worse and worse. Mother buys me a coat and a pair of gloves. I'm buying the rest—Budd shirts at 87 cents a shirt, etc. *But* we'll have to stint ourselves much more than we've anticipated, if signs are true. How, then, can you fatten?

As for me I weigh 183 and *ought* to starve. If you were here I might like New York—

***

March 4, 1933

Well, the nightmare has come, as you know; and I, the perfect fool, while advising everyone else to act, failed to act in time myself. On Friday afternoon I said to myself: "This is the end. Tomorrow I withdraw everything from all banks (three)." On Saturday morning I arose at eight and at nine-fifteen found all banks closed. On Friday I could have salvaged three thousand dollars.

As it stands, our position is precarious. I have two thousand cash available, from all sources. Our life at Santa Fe takes ordinarily five hundred a month (but not that much since your management—about three hundred it was). Apparently we'll have to let all the servants go presently and do the work ourselves. Can we? I don't see why not. If you think we can, it's safe for us to return. Advise me what you think. If we can keep just Rita, will you help? There's the house & wood for you and the coal and garden for me. Otherwise it might be wisest for you to stay with your family and I with mine—until we know the extent of the disaster. I am heartsick. There's only one thing I want. Home. And you know what that means.

My income this month is $5.00! Jesus!

[P.S.] Will you stand by?

1. *Sex in the Arts: A Symposium* was edited by John Francis McDermott and Kendall B. Taft and published in 1932. The chapter called "Modern Poetry" was written by Henry Morton Robinson.

WB returned to Santa Fe for the summer and fall and was again in New York on December 23, 1933, where he soon resumed writing to Hunt, who had remained in Santa Fe. It appears that Hunt wrote WB at the Biltmore Hotel so that the letters would not arrive at WB's mother's apartment, where WB was staying. This arrangement permitted Hunt to be free to write as he chose.

Hotel Seymour
New York City
January 12, 1934

***

Tonight I went alone to *Thunder Over Mexico*[1]. Except for the cruel scene of running horses' hooves across the heads and shoulders of agonized buried men (one of them screaming), a scene almost too cruel to bear, the film was a disappointment. Apart from the cutting, Eisenstein's directing was a disappointment, *too* stylized and repetitious; too self-conscious and arty.

Speaking of the "arty,"—Cocteau[2] certainly wins with *Le Sang d'un Poète*. Note the nudes!—the nigger a man with a woman's behind and the boy a superbly built athlete with a deep hole of a wound under his left shoulder blade. The picture is mad but exciting. You'd like it, I think. Grand effects—not only by the nudes. The latter entered roughly into my almost monastic life. But perhaps "monastic" is just what I don't mean.

***

1. *Thunder Over Mexico* is one title for Eisenstein's film on which WB had seen him working in Mexico. See the second note to the letter of January 27, 1939.
2. Jean Cocteau (1889–1963) wrote and directed *Le Sang d'un Poète* in 1933.

January 25, 1934

1-2-3-4-5-6 and so go the numbers of life; but why, please, did you have to show Arthur's letter to Haniel?[1] It beats anything that I can think of. It's the last thing I would have wished—and I remember thinking, when I enclosed you the letter, sharing it with you,—"but I don't have to tell Bob that—he'll know. I can trust Bob to know that, without my telling him. He'll know. He'd even be annoyed if I told him, it's so obvious." And yet, apparently, it wasn't that obvious. I suffer. Two ways. Three ways. You shouldn't have done it. Why? why? God in heaven! It did no good. It was just for you. Oh, Bob!

I'll go on now, of course, and tell Arthur that you showed the letter and I'll show Arthur the letter which came from Haniel in response. Once opened, it's opened; but I thought it was just for you. It should have been. It did no good, the showing. Why did you? Not that I don't know.

1. Arthur Ficke had written the following to WB about Haniel Long's book of poems *Atlantides* (1933): "All I can say is that it seems to me one of the outstanding examples of the reason why poetry is so discredited an art in our day; and that it perfectly confirms a theory . . . that all art is merely the successful cure of a neurotic state. . . . The trouble with Haniel as a writer is that he states his conclusions in EXCLUSIVE terms. . . . I fear he will continue to masturbate in verse. . . . Let us try to pull poetry out of this mire of private self-pity, and make it symbolic for all men."

TO ARTHUR DAVISON FICKE

Hollywood, California
January 27, 1939

***

. . . For a fortnight we have been luxuriating in a different difference from New Mexico. Ensconced in a comfortable five-room apartment, near Frieda and the Huxleys,[1] we have—except for them, whom I like and see quietly—been hidden from people and been blessing the prize of privacy. Night before last, because an English friend—who preceded us here from Santa Fe and is bent on securing fine films for the English Academy—offered us a showing of vast unknown parts of Eisenstein's Mexican film, I weakened and summoned twenty or thirty Angelenos and Hollywoodsies to a projection room.[2] They disliked the film—unwarrantedly—almost as much as they did one another—I hope unwarrantedly—for it was a good film and they were good people. And now I half regret my charity; for our door is open, our presence known, our privacy undone. Once more the phone, once more the phonies. Let a few know, all know.

***

I revert to our toying with the Eisenstein film;—an impressive stretch of uncut material, magnificent in many spots and probably most intelligent in the man's plan, which was lamentably prevented. I liked seeing how a director takes the same scene over and over till it finally follows his intent, and I realized how much harder it is for men like Eisenstein and the Flahertys[3] to work with peasants, who become under such scrutiny far more stagy than professional actors. Huxley complained that Eisenstein *made* his people *act,* Huxley not realizing that whereas professionals could easily appear to be simple and not acting, it is almost impossible for a director to make simple folk refrain from self-conscious miming. Frieda complained that the scenes were morbid, overlooking Eisenstein's valid attempt to show inheritance in present Mexico not only of Aztec physiognomy but of Aztec blood lust, religious cruelty, and callous comradeship with death. Though I know well, since I was with Eisenstein when he was taking some of the later shots, how recklessly he threw away money advanced through Upton Sinclair, how I wish that the latter might have managed to let the Russian cut and combine his nearly two hundred thousand feet of film into the epic intended!—instead of which it is reliably rumored that Eisenstein was barred at our border by charges of immorality, "moral turpitude," brought from California and was barred, apparently forever, from his film.

At dinner, before we saw the picture, were Marie Seton,[4] the English-woman, Henry Eichheim,[5] Santa Barbara composer who wishes to set poems from *The Jade Mountain,* and Edgard and Louise Varèse.[6] We'd have had Stokowski[7] too but that there seems to be some sort of tension between him and Edgard. Louise maintains a dogged youth and jittered with joy over news of you. Edgard, after his grave illness of some months ago, looks like a Don Juan not wasted but worn. They were excited over the latest novel by my great friend Edwin Corle, *Burro Alley.*[8] I recommend your reading it, especially with your knowledge of Santa Fe; but I more especially recommend his earlier *Fig Tree John* and *People on the Earth,* the best fiction I know about Indians. And don't let the subject deter you. Corle is coming in from the mountains on Monday with his wife, Helen Freeman, whom I think you used to know when she was great pals with Mitchell Kennerley or playing with Norma Millay in *Patience.*

1. Aldous Huxley (1894–1963), the English novelist and critic, visited WB in Santa Fe and WB usually saw him when in Los Angeles.

2. The history of Eisenstein's Mexican film is long and complicated, and is still not complete. Steven P. Hill of the University of Illinois has given the editor the following information. Mr. and Mrs. Upton Sinclair were financing much of the film in Mexico and with 70 to 80 percent of the film shot, the Sinclairs said they could not raise more money. Eisenstein left Mexico in February 1932. The Sinclairs and Eisenstein argued and he did not come to Hollywood to edit the film. After some delay, Mrs. Sinclair managed to have the footage edited; a film of 65 to 70 minutes was released in 1933 as *Thunder Over Mexico.* In 1939 Marie Seton (see below) purchased 177 minutes of footage and edited the film as closely as possible to what Eisenstein had intended. This version was called *Time in the Sun.* In 1970 the Soviet government acquired the original footage and is said to be working on a version. Eisenstein and his followers tended to refer to the film as *Qué Viva Mexico.*

3. David Flaherty (1897–1966), a friend of WB's, worked on the films his brother Robert (1884–1951) directed, including *Moana of the South Seas* and *Nanook of the North.*

4. The showing WB refers to is one that Marie Seton (1910–), an English writer of

biographies, including one on Eisenstein, arranged at the start of her project on the Mexican film.

5. Henry Eichheim (1870–1942) set six of *The Jade Mountain* translations to music, according to WB's letter to Alfred Knopf of March 13, 1939. Eichheim had been to the Orient and had a special interest in its music.

6. Edgard Varèse (1885–1965) was a French-American composer who came to the United States in 1916 and started the International Composers' Guild for the advancement of experimental music. Louise Varèse (1890–1989), his wife, was an American and a major translator from the French of works by Rimbaud, Proust, Bernanos, Saint-John Perse, Michaux, and Simenon.

7. Leopold Stokowski (1882–1977), the conductor, was known especially as an interpreter of modern music. He was at this time in Hollywood working as the music supervisor for *Fantasia* (1940).

8. Edwin Corle (1906–56) wrote the novels that WB mentions in the following years: *Fig Tree John* (1935), about nineteenth-century Apaches; *People on the Earth* (1937), on the same theme; and *Burro Alley* (1938), about night life in Santa Fe. Helen Freeman (1885?–1960), Corle's first wife, was an actress and had read some of the choruses of WB's translation of *Iphigenia in Tauris* in New York, in 1915.

9. Mitchell Kennerley (1878–1950) was at one point WB's publisher and the publisher of other young poets. He also operated an important art gallery in New York City.

10. Norma Millay (1893–1986), Edna's sister, acted with Helen Freeman in Gilbert and Sullivan's *Patience,* a production that opened on December 29, 1924, at the Provincetown Playhouse.

WB recorded in his journal these two visits with Edna Millay in 1939:

June 29: Edna St. Vincent Millay—after three years, is it, or four?—a mime now with a lost face, gaunt, haggard, red-splotched—like a slattern in the back room of a London bar. Sweet, shrill bird-notes left in the jargon and a wish in the face—but nowhere to fly on to sing. She gropes. She thinks immediately of going home, of escape—the slump. Before even eating she plots solitude with her sad self—face sagging, eyes blearily absent, even the shoulders looking like yesterday's vegetables.

July 1: But today we visit Steepletop,[1] finding Edna nude in her pool and gay. Though her eyes are still lost and her expression that of a harassed Irish chambermaid, in manner and speech she is now her old-time chirping, flitting self,—very much of the bird ilk. Her pool in its evergreen maze is a lyrical creation. Her own setting is undoubtedly a restorative to her.—She tells me that her recent tour of the United States (with Gene, a maid, and constant hard work) netted her nothing. In fact she came out with a loss. But it's good advertising. *Huntsman, What Quarry?*[2] has sold 60,000 copies. She spoke of it to me slightingly—"only one or two good poems": a new attitude. Hitherto she has acted as infallible as a pope.

1. Steepletop is the name of Edna Millay's house in Austerlitz, New York, on the Massachusetts border near Stockbridge. The property is now the Millay Colony for the Arts.

2. *Huntsman, What Quarry?* is a collection of Millay poems published in 1939.

WB's long association with Ezra Pound (1885–1972) began when Pound's father sent the young Ezra to WB to determine whether Pound's poetry warranted the investment of a European trip. WB said it did and also arranged for Pound's first three published American volumes, at Small, Maynard & Company. The two poets were not close and Pound clearly did not admire WB's verse but, as WB said, at least Pound never fought with him as he did with all his other friends. They remained friends even after the war and WB vigorously supported Pound during his years of imprisonment and afterward.

Besides these personal associations, WB and Pound shared an involvement with Harriet Monroe and the early years of Poetry, *a part in the development of the American school of poetry in the early years of this century, and a different, but deep, commitment to China and to its poetry. Also, it is likely that WB and Pound appreciated each other's flamboyant and highly personal life style. There is a warmth and a sense of humor in their correspondence with one another.*

TO EZRA POUND

Hotel Nido
Chapala
April 2, 1940

That challenging face of yours reached Santa Fe two months ago, to judge by the postmark, but then decided to see Mexico for itself and followed me here with eyes peering out of the envelope.[1] The latter had been opened by the Customs Bureau in Chicago and not properly resealed. Literally one eye was out of the wrapper—figuratively like a chicken from its shell. But you're here and I'm glad you are. My records indicate that a photograph of a portrait of my more patient phiz went to you long ago accompanying a Chinese deer: one of my paintings brought back in 1917.

It was a disappointment to me that our paths didn't cross when you were in the States. It would have been a good pow-wow—with plenty of disagreement for sauce. But I think you'd have liked the clear starkness of New Mexican country and laughed at the madness of my Santa Fe house. So, if ever these unholy wars permit, come again and come farther.

[P.S.] During my stay here I've put together a new book of poems to appear in the autumn. Would you rather have a copy of that when it's out or a copy of *Selected Poems*, from ten earlier volumes? Or neither?[2]

1. Ezra Pound had made a visit to the United States in 1939 and sent a letter to WB with a photograph. The letter and photgraph were received much later in Mexico. It is likely that

WB asked for the photograph as he regularly did this of his friends. The photos all hung in one room in his house.

2. WB refers to his new book of poems *Against the Cold* (1940).

TO ARTHUR DAVISON FICKE

Chapala
September 1, 1940

* * *

At the end of April I sent my trunk by express to an agent at the border, thinking that we were leaving the next day. Then, as I think I wrote you, I saw that the house I wanted in Chapala was for sale and I found that the price was within my means. So we began the business of buying it. It has taken ever since to put the deal through and we have died a dozen times of impatient nerves. Tape in Mexico is not only red but green and white besides and could easily braid the equator. Now that governmental permits and personal bills of sale are at last in a safe-deposit box in Guadalajara, we have almost ceased to savor the house—but not quite. With incredible effrontery—because I am told that often the government, giving no reason, refuses permits to foreigners—we jumped into building a sort of Kubla Khan double terrace on the roof at the rear of the house. When it was almost done, a pillar of brick and mortar still wet was struck by a beam carelessly swung. Down came the mirador onto the roof of the terrace and the entire two-story structure stormed upon the original roof of the house while Bob and I were eating lunch underneath. Fortunately the old house was strong. Fortunately, though we had just returned from Guadalajara and would normally have been up in the air inspecting progress, we were late for our meal and were eating. Fortunately, though four workmen were on the roof of the mirador and five others on the roof of the terrace and all of them plunged down in a debris of thousands of bricks and fourteen steel beams, not a man was killed and only one of them badly injured. Fortunately the work was being done on contract—though I at once offered, as I should, to meet doctors' bills. Jesus, what a day! The entire town crowded into the house, with women wailing. Corteges, with women still wailing, followed the car each time Bob drove one of the wounded back to his home. And, believe me, they enjoyed it more than we did. Again with effrontery, because we were not owning the house, we recommenced construction. Twice thereafter I went to Mexico City to wangle a permit from the government. Through an able, slick friend there and by careful financial oiling, I managed after three months to obtain the permit. Meanwhile we had built a little miracle of beauty atop the house. From it we have a panorama of the lake seen over roofs, unequalled anywhere in town. The point is—you having asked where the house is—we are in the heart of the village. You remember the Hotel Niza, alongside the Nido where we used to eat on occasion? We are exactly across from its front entrance. The house looks like little or nothing from outside but is magical once you pass the portal. It was an old house, long established on the plaza. Grandmothers whom I know were born here. From dim time back it has been haunted. An uncomfortable old gentleman roams the premises. But an eminent Mexican architect dared to reconstruct it into a vacation house for his brothers and sister and did a distinguished job.[1] The ghost, so they say, still roamed. Still does. Villagers believe that he pushed over the pillar. Perhaps he did. But his were not the hands that robbed us three days after we moved in. Never having encountered dishonesty in Chapala, Bob and I left our bedroom doors open, unlocked. Someone climbed the workmen's ladder at the back and took watches and money from our bedsides, ten inches from our heads. Thank God we didn't wake. Next day one of the workmen, a fellow from Tizapan, failed to appear on the job. He left town. But the authorities arrested Ysidoro![2] And I had a devil of a time getting him out of jail. Such drama as went on at the Presidencia while they proved to me that he was the only one who could have been guilty! To this day the authorities dislike me because I not only refused to believe them but took the poor boy back with complete charge of the house. They sent emissaries to his little shack on the hill and searched all his belongings—finding proudly a Gillette razor, which Tim had given him—and they concluded by tearing from the bosom of his wife a package which she screamed against their taking. It happened to be a token we had brought to Ysidoro from Tlaquepaque: an enormous and lifelike male member in the shape of a pistol!

Then neighbors gave us many caged birds—Bob's pet abomination. And two of them died for no reason. Again the ghost. Then, worst of all, Bob contracted jaundice. In bed for six weeks, with a loss of thirty pounds. This time I was frightened. He was himself the ghost. All in all, it's been a siege. But last Saturday I placed all the papers in the safe-deposit box. Bob is alive again, though thin. There's a crucifix over my door. And we're leaving!

＊＊＊

1. Luis Barragán (1902–88) is said to have been the architect of this reconstruction of the house that WB bought.
2. Ysidoro Pulido (1907?–56) was the young boy whom WB met on his first visit to Chapala in 1923 and described in *Journey with Genius*. He was one of the many children who

shined shoes and did errands and who so angered D. H. Lawrence. Ysidoro never left WB: every time WB was in Chapala, Ysidoro was his servant. When WB bought his own house in 1940, he built one behind it for Ysidoro, whose family still remains there. WB called him "Dizzy," because he did so much chaotically: he included in his exploits two or more wives, several children, mistresses, a great capacity for drink, a candy business, and the making of fake Indian images, which he sold to tourists as ancient treasures, or—even better— buried them and then took tourists on special digs where they amazingly uncovered his new treasures.

TO [MR.] LORRAINE M. GEORGE[1]

Santa Fe
February 13, 1941

Your letter reaches me just as I am leaving for Mexico, and I have not time to answer you as fully as I should like to do. But let me try to give you a few points briefly.

Having a most faulty memory as to dates, I cannot give you the year in which I first met Gibran; but it was before he had been introduced to the American public, and I remember being most impressed by the power and beauty of his tentative writings in English.[2] He was already an established writer, in fact, a living classic in Arabic, and I persuaded him to put together a group of his own translations of one of his books. Again my memory is shaky, but I should say it was *The Prophet*. Thereupon I introduced him to my publisher, Mr. Knopf, who at once liked and accepted the manuscript. This was the beginning of his great popularity as a writer in English.

Perhaps the best illustration I can give you of the man's personal quality is an episode which took place at the house of Mrs. Simeon Ford (Julia Ellsworth Ford)[3] through whom I met him.

One night at dinner there the maids failed to bring on one of the courses, and after a considerable wait and several bell ringings, Mrs. Ford rose and went to the pantry. There, behind a screen, stood two maids. When reprimanded, one of them explained, "But, Mrs. Ford, how can we go about our business when Mr. Gibran is talking? He sounds like Jesus." And he did. Odd as it was in many respects, the core of it was Christ-like. And it is a sorrow to remember that at the end, caught by a fatal disease, he withdrew into isolation in his studio and assuagement through drink. As you probably know, he had been locked in his studio for a day or two before they found him dead.

✳✳✳

1. Lorraine M. George (1920–   ), a student at Baylor University in Waco, Texas, was writing a master's thesis on Kahlil Gibran.

2. Kahlil Gibran (1882–1931) was a Lebanese-American artist, poet, novelist, and essayist who wrote books of a mystic nature on life, love, and death. He is most widely known for *The Prophet* (1923), the best-selling book that Alfred A. Knopf (1892–1984) so successfully published year after year and that helped finance his publishing house. WB and two others introduced Gibran to Knopf.

3. Julia Ellsworth Ford (1859–1950) was another of WB's older women friends. A wealthy woman, she was able to devote her life to her special interests. She wrote children's books—one, *Snickerty Nick* (1919), with some verses by WB; she was a patron of artists, including W.B. Yeats; she painted; and she collected a considerable library of fine books, which she left to Yale University.

TO LOURINDA RHOADES [1]

Chapala
May 19, 1941

Though I have occasionally enjoyed the crooning, runing method of reading poetry—almost universally favored by British poets—I prefer, for hearing and for speaking, the simpler method followed by most Americans. Lindsay [2] was magnificent in his hog-calling manner but was *sui generis*. And most of his poetry was written for declamatory utterance. On the whole, I have tried to write poetry which, when read aloud, would sound like someone telling a friend something of grave or tender import, naturally, earnestly, sincerely—just as one would talk at a close and good time. I don't mean that the clipped, elliptical way of speech used by too many of us should be used for poetry. I only wish that the value and beauty of the sound of words might be felt more in daily converse, that we would leave off our sense of so much difference when we come to formalized rhythms and our expectation that the poet should be a sort of classic actor. Daily speech is far fuller of poetry than most of us stop to realize, especially nowadays when Wordsworthian use of it in verse is out of favor. How to read aloud the conceited verse which holds much present attention would be beyond me. But Shakespeare, for all his grandeur, can still sound as natural as a child.

1. Lourinda Rhoades (1918–   ), now the Reverend Lourinda Rhoades Sanford, was then a graduate student at the University of Wisconsin.

2. Vachel Lindsay (1879–1931) was an American poet noted for his great ability to recite his poetry publicly, especially "The Congo."

TO EDWIN TYLER BYNNER [1]

Santa Fe
December 31, 1941

Odd holidays these have been for us. Many days ago, Bob tried to enlist in the Navy at the office here in Santa Fe and was turned down after physical examination.[2] He persisted, went to the office in Albuquerque, passed there the preliminary examination, and yesterday entrained for Denver for the final look-over. Add to these facts the fact that for a week he has been in bed with one of his phenomenal Niagaran colds, a doctor called out of bed even on Christmas night, and the poor boy up for his first meal Sunday night, the very evening before his morning departure. And then the final twist, the fact that if he is accepted in Denver he will go immediately west into service for a committed two years, perhaps more, without even ten minutes of return to the bereaved household.

You should have seen Mrs. Ponce, the cook, and Rita at the top of the steps when we drove him downtown yesterday morning. They were like women at the foot of the cross, tears down the cheeks and hands wringing in air.

Bobbie had declared resolutely for a week that he would not allow any of us to drive him to Albuquerque where he was to entrain,—that he was to take the bus and go solo. But when we drew up at the bus station yesterday morning, his face was so woebegone that for once in his life I expected him to do as he did, viz.: cave in at the suggestion that we drive him down to Albuquerque. Which same we did, Dick Parish[3] and I. I don't think you know Dick. He was in the Navy in the other war, contracted TB, and has very few tendons left to hold him together but is a devoted friend of Bob's and mine, on tiptoe in the all-right directions.

We landed in Albuquerque with two hours to spare before Bob had to report, gave him three bourbons which led him to express his jitters at the general prospect,—not the possibility of entering the Navy but the uncertainty of the whole situation. It was dour business returning to the house and not knowing whether he would be back in many months.

Dick made the suggestion which I, in a stupid sort of daze, had not considered: going to Lamy at 7:20 when the train would be pulling through on its way to Denver. I grabbed a bottle of bourbon and a couple of wool socks and we arrived in time for the train. Out came Bob to the platform at the head of seven intelligent-looking huskies, saying to us as though he had been in the service all his life, "I've been put in charge of this group and would like to introduce them," and crisply and exactly came their names. I proffered the bourbon to his grave answer, "I think not.

Mr. So-and-so is afraid that alcohol might increase the blood pressure." I proffered the package. Said he, "Is it anything that I should not open in the presence of my men?" I shook my head and he took it. In a few seconds, from the vestibule, having herded his men inside, he gave me an enormous wink.

It is now twenty-seven hours later and I have heard nothing as to the Denver decision. Before the letter is sealed I shall be able to report.

The servants are still in the depths, in fact, Mrs. Ponce had left the house before I came back and refused to feel its gloom longer, putting upon Rita the whole burden.

Life otherwise goes on as usual.

Just as I inquired of the Governor as to my duties as State Chairman in the United China Relief[4] and the personnel of my Board, I noted in the paper that there appears to be another state chairman. It is a woman who has served perhaps in that capacity or perhaps as county or city chairman for some time. Unfortunately, the Governor is critically ill with peritonitis and I can get no clarification as to where we stand. I should be only too glad for anybody else to be state chairman and let me help. On the other hand, I do not wish to shirk.

∗∗∗

1. Edwin Tyler Bynner (1885–1959) was WB's brother. "Tim" was an employee for over fifty years of one company, Woodward Baldwin, a New York cotton firm.

2. Hunt had tubercular scars.

3. Not identified.

4. WB's immediate contributions to the war effort included his state chairmanship of the United China Relief and personal reports to the Office of War Information. For the China Relief he worked diligently to arrange for fund raisers in the major cities and towns and then publicized these activities in Albuquerque with an exhibition of his Chinese paintings and a lecture on Chinese people and poetry.

Hunt was eventually rejected for service because of tubercular-scarred lungs. Finally, he decided to go to San Francisco in July 1943 to work on the docks for the Navy as a checker of supplies. He returned to WB who was in Chapala in October 1944 and they remained there until August 1945.

TO ROBERT HUNT

Chapala
August 21, 1943

✳✳✳

And now what do you suppose is happening? In tackling the chapter connecting religion with poetry, I found myself irritated by the feeble quality of Lin Yutang's translations of Laotzu—just as poor as any of the previous poor ones on which he tried to improve. I needed the Taoistic sayings in what I had at hand; and suddenly I realized that I'd have to make my own versions of them. And I've begun. In fact a tenth of the *Tao-Teh-Ching* already faces me in my own versions—and I see that they will make a chapter in themselves. So that's that.[1]

✳✳✳

1. WB refers to Laotzu's *Tao-Teh-Ching,* one of the important works of Chinese philosophy that WB translated in 1944 as *The Way of Life According to Laotzu: An American Version.* There are many versions of it, including ones by the prolific Chinese-American writer Lin Yutang (1895–1976) and by the English scholar Arthur Waley (see below), but WB's has been among the most popular and remains his most widely read book. It appears in part in this volume and in whole in *The Works of Witter Bynner: The Chinese Translations.*

Chapala
August 28, 1943

Your letter of August 18—the final one, I guess, from Santa Fe—saddened me at first but not afterwards. I knew how you felt: about leaving, about people, about yourself, about me. I could almost project myself into it as you sat there and share the feelings. They were vivid.

But when this reaches you, all that will be long past. Whatever may have followed, that particular depression is over and I hope it has had no successor. It communicated itself to me, so that I had a troubled night, the first of the sort since immediately after you left. But I plunged into an absorption of work and shook off for a while the sadness, which was with me again, though less heavy, in the morning. I have been working for nearly a week till four or five a.m. and rising at nine or ten, so that physically perhaps I wasn't steadied against the impact of your mood. When you write me that all is well with your work and prospects I shall be back again to the good swing I was in with the Laotzu and myself. In first draft

I have done nearly half his book. And it's being damn well worthwhile in more ways than one. In translations familiar to me his meanings have been like fish scales glistening on a gunwale. I dare to hope that I can put some of them back on live fish. As I wrote you, I need the Waley,[1] which is probably the best.

∗∗∗

Coming back to your personal reflections, I am glad that you read and took to heart the paragraph about Ezra Pound. You do occasionally incline to dodge irritations with friends by grabbing at ease with strangers. But whatever harm there may be in the procedure is undone or offset by realizations. I have spoken to you several times about your need of finding new friendships to take the place of those which the accidents and mere course of life and death dissolve. But I know well that friendship cannot be created by prescription. . . .

∗∗∗

One more point as to ourselves and our friends. I am more patient than you, you more generous than I. This is an interesting point—and it goes not only toward other friends but toward each other. However our own friendship is firmly rooted, a hardy perennial that should last us our lives.

∗∗∗

1. Arthur David Waley (1889–1966) was an authority on the Orient and a greatly respected translator of Chinese and Japanese. Waley had praised WB's *The Jade Mountain* when it appeared. The two finally met in 1950, when WB traveled to Europe.

Chapala
April 24, 1944

Day after day I've looked at the envelope bulging with good letters from you and realized that . . . I've given you no response for a hell of a time. . . . Besides the fact that I've not been feeling too well (not arthritis or colitis but a sullen stomach) and have been furthermore dejected by Knopf's declination of my Laotzu. All in all it's been hard to lift a hand. Probably the Laotzu situation had more to do with the stomach than I realized. Fear that my year's work down here was poor or wasted work has undoubtedly gnawed at my innards. But this morning comes an enthusiastic acceptance from John Day and my spirits lift. The book is dated for early fall and I'm going at the final revision with joyous vim.

Richard Walsh, president of the company, writes, "I am very keen about your Laotzu and surely want to publish it. Pearl Buck likes it too and asks me to tell you so. I am putting it on our list for early fall." Pearl Buck is his wife.[1] And this is what pleases me most: "We both take the exactly contrary opinion to that expressed by Mrs. Knopf[2]—we think that what Laotzu has to say is of particular importance to the Western world right now." This is much better than to have let the Knopfs publish it without heart, as they would have done if I had insisted.

1. Alfred Knopf who had published all of WB's books to date refused *The Way of Life*. He did not think it would have an audience. Also he was uncertain of WB's attempt to create a simple, direct, and readable "American version," a phrase WB wanted as part of the title. Richard Walsh (1886–1960) at The John Day Company took the book. He was a friend from Harvard and married to the novelist Pearl Buck (1892–1973) whom WB had first met in China.

2. Blanche Knopf (1894–1966), Alfred's wife, was extensively involved in the publishing firm.

It was on October 21 that Arthur Ficke wrote WB a "final" letter telling him he had cancer, and WB answered him at once. Ficke was not to die until November 30, 1945.

TO ARTHUR DAVISON FICKE

Chapala
October 28, 1944

No, I had not suspected this. But I had thought the other ailment worse and hope I may be right. I had been very sad and very anxious and very fond. In other words, the grave news is no graver than the apprehension I had been coping with. And Gladys says that this is not a "vicious" but a "borderline" case; so perhaps—and oh, may it be true!—we are better off than we should have been with a tubercular throat. It is good, though, to be solemn for a moment, however many other moments be ahead for us, and to face together, with a deep exclamation of thanks, the long, rich, happy friendship we have had. If one of us has to move along first—and two seldom go at the same time—I could wish it were I. Even though we have been apart these latter years, I cannot think of the visible world without you in it. Of all my friends you are the most firmly, solidly and comfortably rooted in me. How enjoyably we have respected each other! Bless you for saying much the same thing to me. I need such assurances more than you do. I have let the outer world bother me more than you have. Except for Tim and Bob, I stand in my own household, so to speak, pretty much alone. And you have Gladys, two birds with the wings of one.

This is no lamentation, not at all—not for either of us. We are singularly fortunate men. You, more than I, in maturity, have been afflicted physically; but we have both maintained that inner health which is Tao.

And so it gladdens me to be reminded that you led me to Asia. Do you remember that blinding moment in Davenport when I realized—entirely through you—that, come what might, I was going to the Orient? You were the light that made Paul—but no St.—of the Saul. And the heights we saw from Mokanshan! The butterflies never molded. We only thought they did. And Sarasota—the meatless shells that still sustain! The days of our years together, from college to now and forever, are writ on leaves of gold. Grant yet the appendix—the goldenest part of all—Hillsdale, Santa Fe, Chapala, somewhere! The Tlalocan days, as I live here again, come very close. . . .

And another aspect! I believe that all my life, through our semi-humorous tepidity toward each other's ways of writing, I have been doggedly struggling for your esteem. After those vain years with my novel, I yielded envious awe to *Mrs. Morton*.[1] To this day I cannot write prose and know it well. You can. Your letters have the pace of rivers. And so, to receive from you unmeasured encomium at last, for the *Laotzu,* makes me a bit giddy with relief. Not only as a man but as a writer, I have pleased my friend. Whoever else may like the *Laotzu* will be anticlimax. This time I was fairly sure—but oh, how welcome the word from you!

***

[P.S.] Keep me posted as to progress.
Thanks, thanks for that letter.

1. Ficke's novel is called *Mrs. Morton of Mexico* (1939). WB's efforts to write a novel were never successful.

TO ALICE CORBIN HENDERSON

Hotel de Cortes
Mexico City, Mexico
January 26, 1948

It grieved me not to see you in Santa Fe; but my stay there between trips was very short, and I understood why you didn't appear at our one— necessarily large—party.

I especially wanted to tell you about my call on Ezra Pound.[1] I will when I return. The doctor assured me that he is committed for good— his own good,—that he's a paranoid and thereby safe from further prosecution. Ezra rose like a great bear full of joy,—crying, "Witter!—after forty years!" And it *was* that.

You and I know that he's no crazier, really, than he always has been. But he's as sane too as he ever was. And when I told him that you spoke of him warmly, he challenged, "Why doesn't she write me?"

So do,—at St. Elizabeths Hospital, Washington, D.C. You may say anything. He does not think that he was traitorous but only continuing his honest and proper criticism of the U.S.A. in a country where, as he says, he was allowed free speech. He does not seem to think the war fact had any importance. Truths should go on. And they put him, our Army did, in a cage and exhibited him in Italian squares. The doctor verified this. (But perhaps you'd better not mention it in your letter.) "The sun was strong through the bars of my gorilla cage," he told me, "and it's left me blurred. Sometimes I'm blurred." Then, waving his arms like a very gorilla, he leapt in the air and embraced me again. At least his eyes were not sad. That I definitely saw. Write him.

1. Having been accused of treason and judged "insane and mentally unfit for trial" by a panel of doctors, Pound was placed in 1946 in St. Elizabeths Hospital in Washington, D.C., an institution for the criminally insane. He remained there until 1958. See the January 13, 1958 letter to Herbert Brownell, Jr., which illustrates WB's effort to have Pound released from St. Elizabeths.

TO KIANG KANG-HU

Santa Fe
September 24, 1948

You have no idea how much good your paragraph did me about my rash version of *The Way of Life*. Only yesterday came a new statement of sales of the book, showing that in six months people have bought as many copies as they would of an entire edition of the ordinary volume of poems, and this three years after its publication. I would feel badly indeed if I thought this response came to an incorrect carrying on of the teachings of the Old Master.

Thank you for the sweetness of heart you give me when you tell me of the Fore Nature understanding. That is what I thought I had; and, in spite of Arthur Waley's strictures against my text, still think I have.[1] To you, dear friend, I owe it, and I never forget my debt. Well I remember meeting you at Berkeley and hearing you point some comment with a quotation from a T'ang poet; and the eleven years together, exchanging texts and making them better each time, till finally the book evolved which Waley himself called "better" than his own. He was a very generous man at that time; and I am wondering why, since I told in my preface the fact that I lacked your help or that of someone like you, he did not grant me the inner sense of rightness which I feel went into the book. You do it, and I love you for it.

I have written your wife that I shall be most happy to receive a copy of your autobiography and render whatever assistance I may to its proper presentation in English.[2] With my own influential friends dead who might help us in the Oriental sphere, I grasp at empty air when I try to think of how to help you physically. All I can do is to wish that they make life more comfortable for you and eventually let you out. Waley wrote me some time back that he thinks you "too important a Quisling" for any of us to be able to help you.[3] I know well that you are not a "Quisling." You were concerned with the intellectual interests of your people and nothing political. I have tried hard and in many connections to bring this conviction to bear in quarters where it might be of service to you. At the moment all I can do is to say that however free one's feet may be, one's mind and spirit dwell close; and a small room may as well be a universe.

1. Waley did not admire WB's translation of Laotzu. It was too simple and direct for him and, as a scholar of Chinese literature, not as authentic as he thought it should be. It was for WB deliberately an "American version" written for the period of democratic recovery after World War II, which may have been what most disturbed Waley. The language and the syntax of the translation have not dated and the translation still has the immediacy that WB sought.

2. WB never received the autobiography.

3. A "quisling" is a traitor who serves as the puppet of the enemy occupying his or her country. The name comes from Vidkun Abraham Lauritz Quisling (1887–1945), a Norwegian army officer and political leader who was executed for treason.

WB and Hunt went to New York in November to hear a song cycle, composed by the pianist Victor Babin (1908–73), based on eleven poems from The Beloved Stranger, *performed at Town Hall on November 28. They had thought to stay in New York, but instead accepted an invitation to stay at John Dewey's house in Key West, where they remained for most of December.*

TO MR. AND MRS. RALPH HODGSON[1]

c/o John Dewey
Key West, Florida
December 19, 1948

This is the first time I have been more or less alertly alone since I left you. We sped to New York. There was a concert, my words to good music well sung, and then a party of a hundred friends of the composer, the singer and the poet; and then parties breeding from that party, so that I barely saw my brother who lives there but who is himself so saturated with New York that he hardly knew the difference. We had planned a month there; but at the end of a fortnight I was nearly at the end of myself and made a plunge out. New York is not a pleasant place, God wot. . . .

And I suppose New York would have been good too, if I had learned the wisdom of focusing, instead of stepping into the kaleidoscopic vertigo. It happened, though, that I remembered a friend whom I had not seen in twenty-eight years. The last glimpse had been in Peking. He is now ninety years old. I thought of him as the rock of ages and telephoned him. He bade me to his apartment, where he was serving and drinking huge, strong old-fashioneds of whiskey; and he suggested that I run away to a retreat of his in Key West. So here I am, tanned and untired at the end of a week and facing another week of sea and sun before returning to New Mexico. And then it shall be old Mexico again, where at last I can work. The old-time friend was John Dewey,[2] legs less likely than they were in Peking but face more relaxed, less set on solvings, more salved with mirth. It gave me a deep breath of content. . . .

✳✳✳

1. Ralph Hodgson (1871–1962) was born in England, where he published five volumes of verse, which were collected in 1917. He taught in Japan, settled in the United States, and did not publish another book for almost forty years. He then published two more volumes. WB greatly admired his poetry and visited him in Ohio whenever he was able.
    2. John Dewey (1859–1952) was in Peking in 1920, and he and WB were involved in various social activities, including a visit to a school run by ricksha men for their children.

WB last saw Dewey in 1948, when he lent WB his house in Key West for Christmas and New Year's.

TO MIRANDA MASOCCO LEVY [1]

c/o John Dewey
Key West, Florida
December 25, 1948

. . . We have been busy too, mostly doing nothing. The daily diary would have reported, from me at least, breakfast at ten, a bask on the beach with frequent dips in a mellow sea till four, a lazy shave and a few nips till five and then a cocktail party at houses where the genial people of today look just like the genial people of yesterday but aren't. A few of them emerge in one's vision, like the ex-Mrs. Hemingway [2] and her two sons. But usually I might have been doing what I did this afternoon, turn away from a woman whom I met here forty years ago, to meet newcomers, turn back to continue the conversation, saying, "So I was in your house in Islamorada and Homestead in 1909," only to be nudged and to hear a voice say, "No, no, this is someone else," and to look up and see a woman well under thirty. My poor eyes, my poor mind! [3] But why do so many people now seem identical to me? Is it an embarrassing penalty of age? I judge so, except that age mercifully saves one from feeling embarrassed. I said to my hostess this afternoon, "How well you manage these introductions!" She said, "I have white hair too, but I am not your hostess, I am the daughter of John Dewey, in whose house you are staying." And I said, "Am I?" meaning "Are you?" or something.

✳✳✳

1. Miranda Masocco Levy (1919–), usually called "Mirandi," was born in Venice, Italy, and arrived in Santa Fe as the youngest of four orphans when her mother died on a train en route to San Francisco. She was raised in the St. Vincent's Orphanage and WB early took an interest in her. She showed character and style and eventually became a designer of jewelry and clothes. For many years she introduced the more interesting younger people in Santa Fe to WB and acted as a means to his continued engagement with new friends at a time when he and Hunt were tending to withdraw. In 1958 she married Ralph Levy (1919–), a Hollywood movie and television director, and has since lived in New York, London, various parts of Europe, and Hollywood. She was instrumental in helping to establish the Santa Fe Opera.
2. WB refers to Pauline Pfeiffer, Ernest Hemingway's second wife.
3. In his later years WB had severe trouble with his eyes, losing the sight in one in 1951 and by the end of his life most of the sight in his other eye.

TO IDELLA PURNELL STONE

Chapala
June 20, 1949

You have been a golden friend,—taking all these pains. Only a moment ago, I came to the final page of the manuscript.[1] There will be more touches of course here and there; but at least the whole thing is in legible shape for copying. And I'm a dead dog. I was determined to finish the job before going back to Santa Fe; and through six to eight hours of work a day it is done. There may be no audience for it except a few like you and me; but I had to get it off my chest. Almost everything you have sent me is incorporated. The poem was a puzzle. Seeing it again, I have not felt it good enough to use in toto, with all the variants; so I have used two of your original stanzas and four or five of the second collaborative version.[2] If you'd prefer my using all or none, say the word and I'll throw it out. But I think it's O.K. as I've done it.

As to the sex talk, I heave a big sigh. Naturally I've heard all sorts of things about Lawrence, and about myself. I agree with you that such considerations are "personal and private." I did express in *Eden Tree* as much as I thought necessary to express about my own tendency toward men. It used to worry me; but life and Dr. Kinsey have shown me that such a tendency is very common and not a thing to be worried about if taken naturally and respectably.[3] So I have sailed smooth. If the young man who spoke to you seduced me, he knows more about it than I do. I have usually found that people who like to talk of such matters do so because of their own predilections. For myself I have little or no curiosity as to the sex life of others.

In Lawrence's case, in what I have written about him, I should have stayed aside from considering what he felt sexually and toward whom, if his own written stresses on sex had not made necessary a chapter called "The Phallus."[4] However, I think you will like it. I believe that he was a person of mixed nature; and I have heard that he once did experience a strong attraction toward a man, a case with which he deals in the autobiographical *Sons and Lovers;* but I do not for a moment think the term homosexual, with its loose implications, should be applied to him. Psychologists might find implications in my original strong dislike for him; but they are welcome to the trouble of probing such problems. I prefer wholesomer occupation. He and I never mentioned the subject, except once when he spoke with distaste of some "pederast" who constantly took photographs of naked boys at or near Taormina, I think,—in Italy somewhere. And I have since wondered if his objection to our swimming with the bootblacks may not have had a basis of this sort, a fear lest people might misconstrue the friendliness. You may remember his checking Frieda's initial habit of changing clothes in one of our hotel rooms and my amazement when he explained the ban with "What will people say?" This seemed the last sort of consideration to have lodged in Lawrence. But he was an odd fish. I may finally mention the slight homosexual tinge in him, before my manuscript is copied; but I think not. He tells enough about it, I should say, in his books: in his frequent frank admiration of masculine physique. Why humor busybodies with what would seem to me morbid guesses?

Your novel sounds to me tiptop and I hope that you find a way to publish it.

✳✳✳

1. This refers to WB's book on D. H. Lawrence, *Journey with Genius* (1951).
2. Idella Purnell Stone had written a poem on D. H. Lawrence that WB had used in part in his book on Lawrence.
3. Alfred Charles Kinsey (1894–1956) as head of The Institute for Sex Research at Indiana University published major studies on sexual behavior and was one of the earliest to document the facts of homosexuality as a part of human sexuality. This was done in *Sexual Behavior in the Human Male* (1948).
4. WB believed there was a strong homoerotic quality in Lawrence and in his writing. WB discusses this idea in the chapter he eventually called not "Phallus" but "Comrade" in *Journey with Genius*. In Lawrence's *Sons and Lovers* (1913), the protagonist, Paul Morel, has a strong relationship that is both loving and antagonistic with his rival, Baxter Dawes.

The controversy mentioned in the following letter involves the granting of the $1,000 Bollingen-Library of Congress award to Ezra Pound for his Pisan Cantos *as the finest book of poetry in 1948. Pound had been accused of treason and many people thought the granting of this award to a "traitor" by a semiofficial government committee was outrageous.*

TO ROBERT M. DUNCAN[1]

Santa Fe
July 18, 1949

Dear Mr. Duncan:

Although I have heard a good deal about the controversy in the *Saturday Review* and elsewhere, I have not yet read the various presentations, and because of an eye infection cannot at present dig into the *Saturday Review* awaiting me here.[2]

My present view would be first that the *Pisan Cantos,* despite occasional jewel-like passages, do not in any way warrant the award. If the judges had said that they were recognizing an outstanding literary influence over many years, the case would have been different; but I am convinced that even then such would have been an inept gesture, as made through the Library of Congress. My guess is that at least some of the judges were out to shock the bourgeoisie, and that fact in itself is poor business.

I might add that I personally, from my first meeting with Pound forty years ago in New York, to my hour with him two years ago at St. Elizabeths Hospital in Washington, have regarded Pound as insane. The doctor at St. Elizabeths confirmed my impression, saying that insanity had always been in the man and would never be out of him. I have a sort of feeling that if Italy had been his birthplace, he might have exiled himself to the States and inveighed as extravagantly against the one country as he did against the other. I do not think, however, that his later writing justifies his having received the award.

1. Robert M. Duncan (1919–   ) was a professor in the Modern Languages Department at the University of New Mexico.
2. The *Saturday Review of Literature* reported on the controversy that arose when the Bollingen-Library of Congress award was given to Pound and published letters from readers giving their varied opinions.

TO BRUCE PORTER[1]

Chapala
May 4, 1951

***

Before it was too late I spent six months last year in Egypt, North Africa, Greece, Sicily, Italy, France and England. Perhaps I overdid, walking sometimes five or six hours a day. Or perhaps, without the overdoing, it was due that my heart should misbehave, misconnect with my pulse and mistreat me generally as it has been doing since my return. I have learned, however, to go more slowly, to let others do the walking, to manage pretty well on a minimum of medicine and to find that prose is good exercise. One eye is confusingly fogged; but it may revive, as it did once before, and the other keeps well. At seventy I have no complaint to make on my own account—and I try not to be too sad over the ailing world. As to the deaths of friends, which feels like loss of one's own blood, I ponder Santayana's[2] answer when I questioned him on that score in Rome. First he said: "I go nowhere now. Where should I go when I have no friends left anywhere?" Then he said: "But all my life I moved from place to place, left friends behind, was separated from them; and I have come to feel when friends have left me that it was not death but absence. That feeling has been the best I could do about it."

I saw the wonderful old fellow twice in Rome. He was very deaf ("If I don't hear you, I won't try to"), a bit remote now and then but suddenly back, close and gleaming with a sunny wit. He warmly praised my *Way of Life*. "Who knows how much it is Laotzu? But it is you, and I did not think—though I have enjoyed your earlier work—that this was in you." Norman Douglas,[3] too, whose writings I have never liked with my heart, was so lusty, so true to himself, that I was happy to see him several times at Capri. These old fellows, each in his way, were far more alive than the young men I met, like Stephen Spender,[4] Arthur Waley was another who delighted me—as firm and fine as his work. Osbert Sitwell[5] was better to meet than to read. Alfred Noyes,[6] with whom we stayed on the Isle of Wight, was blinded by glaucoma and somewhat by self-esteem but stoical physically and still a sturdy poet.

1. Bruce Porter (1865–1953), a painter, designer, and writer in San Francisco was married in 1917 to William James's daughter Margaret. WB was the best man.
2. George Santayana (1863–1952), the philosopher, poet, critic, and novelist, had been a professor of WB's at Harvard and remained an acquaintance. WB visited him at the convent in Rome where Santayana spent his last years.
3. Norman Douglas (1868–1952), the English writer, was the author of *South Wind* (1917) and other novels.
4. Stephen Spender (1909–   ) is a well-known English poet and critic.
5. Sir Osbert Sitwell (1892–1969) was the author of poems, short stories, novels, and memoirs. He was the brother of Dame Edith Sitwell and Sir Sacheverell Sitwell.
6. Alfred Noyes (1880–1958) was an English poet known for his traditional lyric verse.

Gladys Ficke had given money to Yale University for a five-year study of the psychology of artists, in memory of Arthur Ficke. WB's response to her announcement is an indication of his antipathy to the psychological approach. The concepts of Freud were never taken seriously by WB. He later wrote to Gladys Ficke: "Perhaps someday through understanding Freud better, I'll understand Lawrence better and myself too; but I cannot yet feel the need of that approach to any of us. Life, as I grow older, seems to me simpler rather than more complicated."

TO GLADYS FICKE

Chapala
May 6, 1951

As you know, the direction of psychoanalysis or psychiatry has always puzzled me. My own instincts have been centrifugal, not centripetal. "First to thyself be true" and therefore know thyself. Yes, I can see that; but truth and knowledge of truth have seemed for me to consist in simplifying the complicated rather than in complicating the simple. One is a tiny blood vessel in the tremendous force of life and feels and serves that force by letting it run cleanly through one and not by becoming swollen, exaggerated. A poor metaphor! It's simpler to say that the best insight comes from looking outside one's self, rather than inside. One learns best about one's self by watching and understanding what others do. But probably that's only the half of it.

In any event you are accomplishing at Yale something which Arthur would have liked and which you yourself like; and that, as you say, "ought to be enough to satisfy you."

Stan's move interests me immensely and I wish him all success.[1] How I sympathize with his preference of country to city! In the early twenties of one's life sidewalks give one's legs happy prickles. After that, lanes! Someday in the summertime Bob and I will reach Hardhack and I'll see the old house again—and the new house.

This goes to Hardhack and will, I hope, welcome you there.

✱✱✱

1. Stanhope B. Ficke (1912–75) was Arthur's son by his first marriage, to Evelyn Blunt. He was an architect who at this time had moved his practice to the area around Hillsdale, New York.

TO ANSEL ADAMS[1]

Santa Fe
July 18, 1953

Thanks for the great batch of W.B.s,—all of them very interesting to me, some of them very fine indeed, and the two taken outdoors flattering enough to be of excellent use for publicity if ever I manage to pull another book through to the finish. I'll write again specifying the five or six which seem to me and to others who know me best to be the chosen group. Henriette Hurd,[2] for instance, is dining here tonight,—she of the portrait,—and with several other friends from Roswell, and shall have a look at them. But how the devil am I going to designate for you which I chose,—shall I have to return the prints you sent? On the backs of them are places for numbers, but no numbers.

I am having a rare time now rewriting my version of *Iphigenia in Tauris*, made for Isadora in 1915. Request has come for its inclusion in a series of Greek plays in English versions to be published by the Chicago University Press; and while changing "thees" and "thous" I found that I could not resist radical changes in the text throughout, which will make the play considerably more human and presentable than it was in 1915, though the partly colloquial text seemed then a rather drastic departure.[3]

Also Bob and I have been working on a partly old and partly new volume of verse to contain only lyrics; and then comes in Mexico a definite beginning of some portion of memoirs, probably college and the four years at *McClure's* magazine. In writing a review for the *New Mexico Quarterly* of three books on Willa Cather,[4] I found myself kindled into vivid memories of that period, setting down, apart from the review, a number of pages on my own account about Willa,—and they're something!

***

1. Ansel Adams (1902–84) was a friend of WB's from the Berkeley days. They met through Albert Bender. Adams took many pictures of WB and his Santa Fe house on his visits to the Southwest.

2. Henriette Wyeth Hurd (1907–) painted WB's portrait in 1939. It is now in the Roswell Museum and Art Center in Roswell, New Mexico.

3. The new version appeared in *The Complete Greek Tragedies, Volume II: Euripides*, edited by David Grene and Richmond Lattimore (1956).

4. The volume of verse was called *Book of Lyrics* (1955); the prose memoirs were never completed; the review appeared in the Autumn 1953 issue of the *New Mexico Quarterly* and is reprinted in *The Works of Witter Bynner: Prose Pieces*.

TO GLADYS FICKE

Santa Fe
November 21, 1953

***

I have just read Edmund Wilson's chapters on Edna Millay,[1] and Vincent Sheean's *Indigo Bunting*.[2] Both boys seem to be too sentimental, but I suppose they couldn't help being so. She deserves, however, better treatment. A calm, square facing of her would be to her advantage.

Why don't you do it yourself? From the writing in your novel, which has persistently stuck with me, I know how well you could set down your pages,—I know how well you knew the girl and how rightly you could combine, in an account of her, truth and compassion.

***

1. Edna Millay had died in 1950. The essay by the critic Edmund Wilson, "Edna St. Vincent Millay: A Memoir," was published in *The Nation* on April 19, 1952; it was reprinted as "Epilogue, 1952: Edna St. Vincent Millay" in *Shores of Light: A Literary Chronicle of the Twenties and Thirties* (1952).
2. Vincent Sheean (1899–1975), the correspondent, historian, and novelist, wrote *The Indigo Bunting* in 1951.

TO MIRANDA MASOCCO LEVY

Hollywood
February 3, 1954

Your letter soon followed your voice and we feel a little bit in touch; but I wish it were more. We miss those daily hullos with you like the devil and look forward to their resumption when we return on our way to another separation. But perhaps next time you'll flee with us!

What have we been doing? We're both so tired that we hardly know, and any real account of it will have to wait till the three of us rejoin.

We found Frank Lloyd Wright[1] sixteen miles out of Phoenix in his eyrie on the rocky hillside; and we liked both the man and the place. I had feared that he would be a very peacock of egotism; but he has mellowed much since the days thirty years ago when I used to see him in Tokyo. He has a kind of beauty now that he didn't have then. And the place, photographs of which had set me against it, is a mixture of the spirits of Japan and Mitla presiding over a fitting abode. Gerard (sp?)[2] ought to see it, especially the gentle interiors. Wright said that the whole place is built in the flow of Laotzu. He has my version. He also has a vivid memory of Bob's mother: "She was a doll—the glass of fashion—other women copied her." And he boasted (quite falsely) "I put Myron into architecture." (They were contemporaries.) And he called Bob "Young Myron."[3]

We had two hours of him alone; but when he asked us to stay for dinner and then hear his wife play Gurdjieff music[4] on the harp, with other music from some of his sixty apprentices, we decided that we had better press on to Indio to see a friend who had owned the land on which La Quinta is built and a share of the hotel. I had seen him there thirty years before and had a great time with him. But La Quinta had changed hands; and the Chamber of Commerce, seeking through the Post Office and the oldest inhabitant, could find no trace of him. Tempus! Tempus!

***

1. Frank Lloyd Wright (1869–1959) first met WB when Wright was in Tokyo for the building of the Imperial Hotel, which was constructed from 1916 to 1922. It was razed in 1967. WB had visited Wright at his home and studio called Taliesin West.
2. WB refers to Alexander Girard (1907–1993), a designer and collector of folk art.
3. Myron Hunt (1868–1952), Bob Hunt's father, was one of the major architects in Los Angeles in the early twentieth century.
4. This refers to the music of George Gurdjieff, the mystic, who relied on music he and an associate composed and used with ritual dance and exercise to further self-discipline.

Where We Are
to Where You Are
February 18, 1954

The telephone talk connected us—and I'm glad you knew that it was coming. Of course it was coming. Stravinsky [1] asked me, "Do you see her often?" I said, "Every day. It's a ritual." And his funny little body and his funny little nose approved. You are a part for him and me of the world that matters. You should have seen—and felt—him guiding me, his arm in mine, down the path from his house to the car, loving my blindness. He had said, "They liked my early work, and now they like only my early work. They liked me too soon. But I know that I like what I do now— and they will be liking it sometime, but I like it now. I am ahead of them. And I will always be ahead of them. That is what makes it happy. Because I know. And I don't have to know through anybody else." And I told him my own odd feeling often when I wish and try to write: that poetry is a horse on which I sit like St. George with a lance, and there is a lank dragon under me with claws up toward me and a long jaw of teeth and I have to fight him down to save myself and the horse. And he said, "That is a good figure for what we feel." I was glad that I had confided. The thing was instantly true between us, with no strangeness. With somebody else, even Bob, I should have felt pompous and odd. He knew, quickly and even better than I did, what I meant.

Bob just looked into the room. It's four a.m. Pleasant creatures have gone their way, from his evening and from mine, separate. He had disturbances in his, I only strangeness and age to disturb mine. But he says in the doorway, hearing the typewriter: "Do I disturb your style?" I wonder why that peculiar wickedness in Bob? Except that I know. He is always a little jealous of my connecting with others—or even with myself. And of course I treasure that jealousy.

Sometimes I think I know what it is all about: that in Bob I have captured the beauty of evil and that he, hating cats, has a feline consciousness of that curious fact in our relationship and likes it: that it relieves him of being evil. But to no one except you could I ever try to express the strange and finally beautiful fact: our two beings, adverse but mutually needed, making sound fact and liking it. Either of us without the other would be insincere, incomplete. We correct each other's lies. It's a good team and, by some happy chance, a respectful and comfortable team blessed with the boon of warmth. We are lucky and—now I am sententious—we owe, because of our luck, a lot of patience.

If Bob hadn't looked in and said, "Do I disturb your style?" I shouldn't have used my style as I have done in that paragraph. It's his fault. But it's fun—with you.

✳✳✳

1. Igor Stravinsky (1882–1971), one of the great composers of the twentieth-century, first met WB in August 1950 and usually saw WB whenever he came to conduct at the Santa Fe Opera.

TO HERBERT BROWNELL, JR.[1]

Santa Fe
January 13, 1958

Understanding that there are steps again toward the release of Ezra Pound from detention in St. Elizabeths Hospital, I should like to put in my word urging such action.

Having known Ezra nearly fifty years, I realize that certain of his aspects might not seem normal to the ordinary observer but I have never thought him any less balanced than William Blake and have felt that outside his odd balance he might not have been similarly gifted.

Since I have never heard the broadcasts which occasioned his difficulties with our government, I cannot judge as to the charges of treason but I feel certain that he was only continuing his characteristic and, it would seem to me, harmless outbursts against whatever authorities and beliefs that be. And I am also certain that his actions outside of St. Elizabeths would not be seriously prejudicial to the safety of society.

In other words, I heartily join with other citizens in hoping that he may be, after these years, set free.[2]

***

1. Herbert Brownell, Jr. (1904–   ) was the U.S. Attorney General from 1953 to 1957. WB sent an identical letter to his successor, William P. Rogers (1913–   ).
2. Pound was allowed to leave St. Elizabeths Hospital later in 1958 and lived the rest of his life in Rapallo and Venice, Italy.

TO WILLIAM CARLOS WILLIAMS[1]

Santa Fe
October 27, 1960

Just as I was about to give my secretary an answer to the letter you wrote me, there arrived from Win Scott a copy of the letter you wrote him, paragraphs in both of which concerned my *New Poems 1960*.

I had had an idea that you would like this book and am much pleased to hear that I was right. And I am wondering if you would mind my quoting from your letter to Win—his permission already given: ". . . one of his best, he got hold of something and let himself go. The result was an unqualified piece of work that will be hard to equal for many a long day."

So far, the critics as well as my friends have without dissent liked these poems.

You ask about the physical, perhaps mental, effects of old age, and I readily answer that they are tough on one's living and doing. My remaining eye is only partly here; with drops and magnifiers I still get a good many glimpses—not only of people but of print—and am grateful. Operation on a cataract is apparently made more difficult by glaucoma. Soon I go to the California specialist again and I hope he will manage to retain for me what sight I still have. There is little, I guess, that we can do about the forgetting business. I find myself in the night rehearsing the names of people, places, books, phrases for use on following days, only to have the list dissipate in daylight. But I am still setting down poems more or less in the dark and enjoying the process.

The poem you enclose[2] is so brutally candid that it is hard for me to take—and yet I remember when my brother and I stood by my mother's deathbed and he murmured, "Take it easy, Mother," she responded firmly, "How can I, when it's hard to take?"

Anyway, thanks for the poem and for the cheering letters, one to Win and one to me.

***

1. William Carlos Williams (1883–1963) was an acquaintance, but not a close friend of WB's. They met in New York in the twenties and saw one another in Santa Fe in the 1950s.
2. Williams later asked WB to destroy this poem. Nothing is known about it.

TO GEORGE KENNEDY[1]
MIRANDA MASOCCO LEVY
FRANK FENTON[2]

Santa Fe
August 29, 1962

I have not written you about a bad time Bob has been having with his heart because the doctor advised me to have him write his family and you all himself. He is doing that this afternoon, having spent five days in the hospital, and will tell you about his experience and I imagine with a soft pedal.

Briefly, from my angle, let me say that on last Thursday Bob was bothered at the lunch table by pain and had to leave without reading the mail. Half an hour later, despite nine nitroglycerin and several peritrate tablets, Bob was in the sharpest kind of trouble and was the color of clay. After calling several doctors, we got a "yes" from a woman doctor, Dr. Bobb, who had been here before for my shingles. When she arrived at about 3:30, she told us that Bob must be moved to the hospital in an ambulance, not risking even the shallow steps of the front walk. It happened that Paul Horgan was on the premises. He and Dorothy had to use heavy persuasion to get Bob onto the stretcher. Paul rode down with him in the ambulance and said that he had physically to keep Bob lying down. At any rate, we got him back yesterday with heated protests again against the stretcher and ambulance.

Dr. Bobb tells me that what he had was a small coronary artery occlusion. The first day, he had had extremely low blood pressure, which is now still low but stable. The daily cardiograms have continued disturbing, and the doctor doesn't want her patient climbing even the six stairs between his bedroom and the dining room. I am telling you these facts in addition to what he will himself write you.

He had been having many attacks of what they call angina pectoris, but nothing comparable to this one. Dorothy asks me to say that she has seen many people in pain but never anything like Bob's state that day. I am still numb and bothered, but doing all I can to keep him quiet and to keep well-wishers away. The season, with opera and with various welcome visitors, had obviously been too heavy for him. I'll try to post you news again soon.

✶✶✶

1. George Kennedy (1907–91), who worked at *The Hollywood Reporter* for more than thirty-five years, had been a close childhood friend of Robert Hunt's, and remained a friend for life of both WB and Hunt.
2. Frank Fenton (1901–72) was a friend of both WB and Hunt. Fenton was a professor of English and head of the department at San Francisco State University, the University of Hawaii at Hilo, and the University of Nevada. He served as interim president at San Francisco State University from 1961 to 1962.

TO CARL VAN VECHTEN

Santa Fe
February 11, 1963

Bob and I both appreciated your inquiry after what you heard from Bernardine Fritz.[1] For months now, his illness has kept me in a general daze as to what I have done or not done—reported to friends or not reported. On the other hand, Bob naturally did not want me to be sending danger signals about him to our friends. . . .

It is good to report that for several weeks, although tiring easily, he has been more like himself—though still on occasions looking suddenly gaunt and having to be very careful. The whole period as you may judge has been frightening; but I have a feeling that the scare has finally made Bob realize that he must lead a quiet life. Mine was already quiet, what with the eye trouble and continuing shingles, so that as far as daily living goes the house is in step.

Virgil Thomson[2] was here for part of the opera season and brought us a good report of Fania and yourself, although I had not realized that she like you had become deaf. Let me say incidentally that I have just given up trying out a Dahlberg hearing aid (made by Motorola, I believe) and am now testing a Zenith contraption. Bob has to be both eyes and ears for me a good deal of the time.

Let me end this note with a grim tale about Taos from Virgil. Just after Mabel's death, he came by and reported: "I was on my way to see Mabel

in Taos yesterday, but she saved me the trouble." You have heard I sup-
pose that only a few days ago Tony followed Mabel. I had not seen him
in many months but am told that he was and looked for a long time very
ill.[3]

***

1. Bernardine Szold Fritz was married to Otto Liveright, the literary agent, was in
Europe, especially Paris, in the twenties, and then for a long period in China, where she
married again and where she worked on the *China Critic*.
2. Virgil Thomson (1896–1989), composer, critic, and organist, wrote two operas based
upon librettos by Gertrude Stein: *Four Saints in Three Acts* (1928) and *The Mother of Us All*
(1947).
3. Mabel Dodge Luhan died in August 1962 and Tony Luhan, her American Indian
husband, early in 1963.

TO KATHLEEN HESLER[1]

Santa Fe
February 4, 1964

***

I don't think I have told you the final details about Bob. He had just
been upstairs to apply witch hazel on my back to ease shingles, as he
has been doing every morning for many months; and then I heard John
Meigs[2] at the phone saying: "Please be quick!" I arrived downstairs and
there was Bob unconscious on the floor with John giving him artificial
respiration. Dorothy[3] reminds me that John phoned her at 12:20 and
that she, unable to summon either of Bob's heart doctors, called the hos-
pital and then an ambulance. She and Bill arrived here just as they were
putting Bob on a stretcher. It would appear that quicker medical service
would have done no good. There was almost no breath left, but the face
was beautifully calm. Dorothy went with him in the ambulance and says
that everything was done that could be at the hospital by a doctor and
others on the spot; but my own doctor, McGoey, told me that prompter
treatment would have done no good.
This was better of course than if the poor man had collapsed on the trip
or in Chapala. The end came only an hour or two before Bill Hooten[4]
was starting to drive him to Albuquerque for the plane.
I give you these details because there is something of solace in them, as
in the fact that his face was at peace instead of being distorted as in the
other attack—with what he called the worst pain he had ever experienced.

This is the fullest description I have written anyone about what happened, but I think the facts are due you and may help as they helped me.

1. Kathleen (Cassy) Hesler was a close friend from Chapala.

2. John Meigs (1916–), a painter and designer, has for many years lived close to the Peter Hurds in San Patricio, New Mexico.

3. Dorothy Chauvenet (1904–1994) became WB's secretary late in 1945 and remained with him for the rest of his life. During the later years she had the responsibility for running the house.

4. William J. Hooten (1922–1988) was then the manager of a guest ranch and restaurant in Santa Fe and the assistant to the president of St. John's College. He arranged for Hunt's house to be given to St. John's as a residence for the president.

Bibliography

WORKS BY WITTER BYNNER

Against the Cold. New York: Alfred A. Knopf, 1940.
The Beloved Stranger: Two Books of Song & a Divertisement for The Unknown Lover. New York: Alfred A. Knopf, 1919.
A Book of Love, translated from the French of Charles Vildrac. New York: E.P. Dutton & Company, 1923.
Book of Lyrics. New York: Alfred A. Knopf, 1955.
A Book of Plays. New York: Alfred A. Knopf, 1922.
Cake: An Indulgence. New York: Alfred A. Knopf, 1926.
A Canticle of Pan and Other Poems. New York: Alfred A. Knopf, 1920.
A Canticle of Praise. San Francisco: John Henry Nash, 1918.
Caravan. New York: Alfred A. Knopf, 1925.
Eden Tree. New York: Alfred A. Knopf, 1931; revised and reprinted in *Selected Poems* (1936).
Grenstone Poems: A Sequence. New York: Frederick A. Stokes Company, 1917; revised and reprinted New York: Alfred A. Knopf, 1926.
Guest Book. New York: Alfred A. Knopf, 1935.
Indian Earth. New York: Alfred A. Knopf, 1930.
Iphigenia in Tauris, translated from the Greek of Euripides. New York: Mitchell Kennerley, 1915; reprinted in *A Book of Plays* (1922); revised and reprinted in *The Complete Greek Tragedies: Euripides II,* edited by David Grene and Richard Lattimore. Chicago: The University of Chicago Press, 1956.
The Jade Mountain, A Chinese Anthology: Being Three Hundred Poems of the T'ang Dynasty, 618–906, translated from the Chinese with Kiang Kang-hu. New York: Alfred A. Knopf, 1929; revised and reprinted 1939.
Journey with Genius: Recollections and Reflections Concerning the D.H. Lawrences. New York: The John Day Company, 1951.

The Little King. New York: Mitchell Kennerley, 1914; reprinted in *A Book of Plays* (1922).

The New World. New York: Mitchell Kennerley, 1915; revised and reprinted New York: Alfred A. Knopf, 1922.

New Poems 1960. New York: Alfred A. Knopf, 1960.

An Ode to Harvard and Other Poems. Boston: Small, Maynard & Company, 1907, revised and reprinted *Young Harvard: First Poems of Witter Bynner.* New York: Alfred A. Knopf, 1925.

The Persistence of Poetry. San Francisco: The Book Club of California, 1929.

Pins for Wings, by Emanuel Morgan. New York: The Sunwise Turn, 1920.

Selected Poems, edited by Robert Hunt with a critical preface by Paul Horgan. New York: Alfred A. Knopf, 1936.

The Sonnets of Frederick Goddard Tuckerman. New York: Alfred A. Knopf, 1931.

Spectra: A Book of Poetic Experiments, published with Arthur Davison Ficke under the names of Emanuel Morgan and Anne Knish. New York: Mitchell Kennerley, 1916.

The Spectra Hoax, by William Jay Smith. Middletown, Connecticut: Wesleyan University Press, 1961.

Take Away the Darkness. New York: Alfred A. Knopf, 1947.

Tiger. New York: Mitchell Kennerley, 1913; reprinted in *A Book of Plays* (1922).

The Way of Life According to Laotzu: An American Version. New York: The John Day Company, 1944.

The Works of Witter Bynner: Selected Poems; Light Verse and Satires; The Chinese Translations; Prose Pieces; Selected Letters, general editor James Kraft. New York: Farrar Straus Giroux, 1978–1981.

CRITICAL WORKS ON WITTER BYNNER

For a complete history of Bynner's works and articles on him, see the book by Robert O. Lindsay listed below. Since the publication of this bibliography, there has been little written about Bynner. The book on *The Spectra Hoax* listed above contains an extensive essay by William Jay Smith. Each of the volumes in *The Works of Witter Bynner* contains a critical essay: in *Selected Poems* by Richard Wilbur and James Kraft; in *Light Verse and Satires* by William Jay Smith; in *The Chinese Translations* by Burton Watson and David Lattimore; and in *Prose Pieces* and *Selected Letters* by James Kraft.

The companion volume to *The Selected Witter Bynner* is the biography, *Who is Witter Bynner?,* by James Kraft, also published by The University of New Mexico Press in 1995 . It contains extensive biographical and critical commentary.

The following is a representative selection of works on Bynner that reflects various aspects and different periods of his career:

Austin, Mary "Soil of New Mexico," *New York Herald: Books,* pp. 5–6.

Benét, William Rose "The Phoenix Nest: Contemporary Poetry," *The Saturday Review of Literature,* June 1, 1935, pp. 18–19.

———— "The Phoenix Nest: Contemporary Poetry," *The Saturday Review of Literature,* December 5, 1936, p. 40.

Blackmur, Richard P. "Versions of Solitude," *Poetry,* January 1932, pp. 217–21.

Boorman, Howard L. *Biographical Dictionary of Republican China, Volume I,* New York: Columbia University Press, 1967; see "Chiang K'ang-hu" (or as WB wrote, "Kiang Kang-hu"), pp. 338–44.

Chauvenet, Dorothy M. "Secretary to Witter Bynner," *The Santa Fean,* November 1981, pp. 8–9.

Colony, Horatio "Witter Bynner—Poet of Today," *The Literary Review,* Spring 1960, pp. 339–61.

Day, Douglas "The New Old Poetry of Witter Bynner," *Shenandoah,* Winter 1961, pp. 3–11.

Deutsch, Babette "Bitterness and Beauty," *The New Republic,* February 10, 1926, pp. 338–39.

———— "Two Solitudes," *The Dial,* October 4, 1919, pp. 301–2.

Ficke, Arthur Davison "The Luminous Chinese Sage," *Poetry,* April 1945, pp. 40–42.

Fitts, Dudley "Mr. Bynner's Nimble Versification," *The New York Times Book Review,* June 15, 1947, p. 4.

———— "Poetry and Tradition," *The Saturday Review of Literature,* October 26, 1940, p. 16.

Flanner, Hildegarde "Witter Bynner's Poetry," *University of Kansas City Review,* June 1940, pp. 269–74.

Francke, Kuno Dr. *Young Harvard: First Poems of Witter Bynner,* Foreword by Dr. Kuno Francke, New York: Alfred A. Knopf, 1925.

Haber, Tom Burns (ed.) *Thirty Housman Letters to Witter Bynner,* New York: Alfred A. Knopf, 1957.

Horgan, Paul "Details on Greatness," *The Saturday Review of Literature,* August 18, 1951, pp. 9–10.

———— "In the Autumn of a Poet's Life a Second Flowering," *The New York Times Book Review,* October 16, 1960, p. 20.

———— *Selected Poems,* by Witter Bynner; Critical Preface by Paul Horgan, New York: Alfred A. Knopf, 1936.

Jarrell, Randall "Poets: Old, New and Aging," *The New Republic,* December 9, 1940, pp. 797–800.

Lindsay, Robert O. *Witter Bynner: A Bibliography,* Albuquerque: The University of New Mexico Press, 1967.

Long, Haniel "Mr. Bynner's Philosophy of Love," *Poetry,* February 1920, pp. 281–83.

Masters, Edgar Lee *Grenstone Poems: A Sequence,* by Witter Bynner; Introductory Note by Edgar Lee Masters, New York: Alfred A. Knopf, 1926.

Monroe, Harriet "The Little King," *Poetry,* May 1915, p. 97.

———— "Mr. Bynner in the South-West," *Poetry,* August 1930, pp. 276–78.

———— "New Books of Verse," *Poetry,* December, 1915, pp. 147–48.

Pearce, T.M. "Guest Book," *The New Mexico Quarterly,* August 1935, pp. 211–12.

——— "Selected Books," *The New Mexico Quarterly*, February, 1937, pp. 68–70.
Reedy, William Marion *The Beloved Stranger*, by Witter Bynner, Preface by William Marion Reedy, New York: Alfred A. Knopf, 1930.
Rodman, Selden "Classic and Modern," *The New York Times Book Review*, January 1, 1956, p. 4.
Rudnick, Lois Palken *Mabel Dodge Luhan: New Woman, New Worlds*, Albuquerque, N.M.: The University of New Mexico Press, 1984; see Chapter 7 on Luhan and Bynner.
Schorer, Mark "'People Dislike Me'," *The New York Times Book Review*, July 29, 1951, pp. 3, 18.
Scott, Winfield Townley "Nothing is Static," *The Nation*, November 5, 1960, pp. 352–53.
Slack, Claudia "A Centennial Party for Witter Who?" *The Santa Fe Reporter*, August 20, 1981, pp. 23–24, 26.
Smith, William Jay "Witter Bynner" in *The Penguin Companion to American Literature*, edited by Malcolm Bradbury, Eric Mottram, and Jean Franco, New York: McGraw-Hill, 1971.
Stanford, Donald E. "The Best of Bynner," *The Hudson Review*, Summer 1983, pp. 389–98.
Tate, Allen "Verse," *The Nation*, December, 1925, p. 680.
Tietjens, Eunice "From the Chinese," *Poetry*, February 1930, pp. 289–92.
Udall, Sharyn R. *Spud Johnson and "Laughing Horse"*, Albuquerque, New Mexico: The University of New Mexico Press, 1994.
Untermeyer, Louis "A Christmas Inventory," *The Bookman*, pp. 495–96.
——— "Frustrated Adam," *The Saturday Review of Literature*, October 10, 1931, p. 186.
Van Doren, Mark "Books: Anglo-Saxon Adventures in Verse," *The Nation*, June 26, 1920, pp. 855a–857a.

Location of Letters

The largest collection of Bynner letters, more than seventeen thousand to and from him, is in the Houghton Library at Harvard University. There are original letters and carbons in this collection and both have been used in preparing the present edition. Unless otherwise indicated, the Houghton Library is the source of any letter or journal entry that appears in this volume. If a letter is available in the original in a library or private collection other than the Houghton, its location can be found in the following listing.

All letters referred to as at Yale University are in the Collection of American Literature, Beinecke Rare Book and Manuscript Library, Yale University. The letter to Marianne Moore is in the Dial Papers.

Those letters listed as at the University of Texas are in the Harry Ransom Humanities Research Center, University of Texas at Austin.

Those letters listed as at the Mills College Library are in the Albert M. Bender Collection of that library.

The Haniel Long Papers are in the Department of Special Collections, the Research Library, University of California, Los Angeles.

Date	Recipient	Location
January 12, 1910	Edna Kenton	Columbia University Rare Book and Manuscript Library
August 1, 1916	Woodrow Wilson	Library of Congress, Manuscript Division
January 21, 1922	Alice Corbin Henderson	University of Texas
April 5, 1922	Arthur Davison Ficke	Yale University
September 29, 1922	Mabel Dodge Luhan	Yale University

April 19, 1923	Willard Johnson	University of Texas
July 3, 1923	Alice Corbin Henderson	University of Texas
July 30, 1925	Marianne Moore	Yale University
November 10, 1926	Idella Purnell Stone	University of Texas
January 19, 1928	D.H. Lawrence	University of Texas
February 24, 1929	Albert M. Bender	Mills College Library
November 12, 1930	Arthur Davison Ficke	Mills College Library
January 27, 1939	Arthur Davison Ficke	Yale University
October 28, 1944	Arthur Davison Ficke	Yale University
January 26, 1948	Alice Corbin Henderson	University of Texas
June 20, 1949	Idella Purnell Stone	University of Texas
May 6, 1951	Gladys Ficke	Yale University
February 11, 1963	Carl Van Vechten	Yale University

Index

gan, 262; letter to Robert Hunt, 265–67, 270–73, 283–85; letter to Henry James, 237–38; letter to Willard Johnson, 256–57; letter to George Kennedy, 301–2; letter to Edna Kenton, 244; letter to Kiang Kang-hu, 259–61, 287–88; letter to D. H. Lawrence, 266–67; letter to Miranda Masocco Levy, 301–2; letter to Haniel Long, 246, 252; letter to Edna St. Vincent Millay, 250; letter to Hersilia A. Mitchell-Keays, 239–44; letter to Marianne Moore, 262; letter to Albert Bigelow Paine, 247–48; letter to Margaret Sanger, 261–62; letter to Idella Purnell Stone, 264–65; letter to Carl Van Vechten, 302–3; letter to William Carlos Williams, 300–301; letter to Woodrow Wilson, 249; loss of hearing, 302; at *McClure's* magazine, 4, 143–50, 237; as Emanuel Morgan, 1, 4, 165, 167, 249, 262, 262n3; as Mountain Antelope, 179; as poet, 4–8; as politician, 264n5; politics and, 5–6; portraits by Ansel Adams, 295; quoted, 268–69, 281–82; relationship with Annie Louise Bynner, 261; relationship with Willa Cather, 4; relationship with Cecil B. De Mille, 3; relationship with Isadora Duncan, 246–47; relationship with Arthur Davison Ficke, 4, 249, 285–86; relationship with Alice Corbin Henderson, 167–72; relationship with O. Henry, 4; relationship with A. E. Housman, 4; relationship with Robert Hunt, 5; relationship with Henry James, 152–56, 237–38; relationship with Alfred A. Knopf, 5; relationship with D. H. and Frieda Lawrence, 5; relationship with Haniel Long,

244–45; relationship with S. S. McClure, 144–45; relationship with Edna St. Vincent Millay, 249; relationship with Ezra Pound, 4, 150–51; religion and, 266; resignation from *McClure's* magazine, 148; role in U.S. China Relief, 282, 282n4; in Santa Fe, 5, 251, 271; sense of humor, 7–8; *Spectra* poems, 1, 4, 6, 35–39, 164–65, 249; support of African American writers, 6; translation of Chinese poetry, 188–99, 217; translation of Euripides' *Iphigenia in Tauris*, 233–34; translation of Laotzu, 230; travels, 143, 147, 227, 237, 257, 286, 289–90, 293; travels in China, 4, 190, 196, 227–29; travels with Arthur Ficke, 286; at University of California, 5, 226; views on prostitution, 162; views on waste, 224–25; visits to New Mexico, 168, 273; visit to Chapala, 258

Caballeros, San Juan de los, quoted, 184
Cake, 59–65, 242, 262
Canticle of Pan, A, 43–49
"Canyon, The," 42
Caravan, 52–58, 254
carbolic acid . . . , 51
"Carl Sandburg," 50
Carswell, Catherine: quoted, 174–75; *Savage Pilgrimage, The*, 147
Cathay (Pound), 228
Cather, Willa, 144, 296, 296n4; at *McClure's* magazine, 144; relationship with Bynner, 4; "Sculptor's Funeral, The," 144; *Troll Garden, The*, 146
Cat-tail standing in the ice, . . . , 53
Cease from the asking, you receive the answer . . . , 126

Chambers, Jessie, 175
Chang Tao-lin, 219
Chapala still remembers the foreigner . . . , 69
Chauvenet, Dorothy, 303, 304n3
Chinese Art (Bushell), 188
"Chinese Drawings," 46–48
"Chinese Drawings: A Father," 46–47
"Chinese Drawings: A Horseman," 48
"Chinese Drawings: A Lady," 48
"Chinese Drawings: A Lover," 47
"Chinese Drawings: A Painter," 47
"Chinese Drawings: A Scholar," 48
"Chinese Drawings: A Tea-Girl," 47
"Chinese Drawings: A Wanderer," 47
"Chinese Drawings: Vendor of Rose-Bushes," 47
Chinese Literature (Giles), 215
Chinese magicians had conjured their chance, . . . , 48–49
"Chinese Notes," 45–46
"Chinese Notes: In Manchuria," 45–46
"Chinese Notes: In Peking," 46
"Chinese Notes: In Shantung," 46
"Chinese Notes: The Ming Tombs," 46
Christianity, 227–28; relationship with Taoism, 219
Chuangtzu, as disciple of Laotzu, 218–19
"Circe," 129
"City, The," 53
"Clouds," 129
Clouds dream and disappear; . . . , 53
Cocteau, Jean, 272, 272n2
Colored Stars (Mathers), 195, 229
Come, warm your hands., 32–33
"Comrade," 265n2
Confucius, 219–20; on Laotzu, 214; quoted, 214
"Congo, The" (Lindsay), 280n2
Cool, moving, fruitful and alive I go, . . . , 130

Corbin, Alice. *See* Henderson, Alice Corbin
Corle, Edwin, 274, 275n8; *Burro Alley,* 274, 275n8
"Correspondent," 110
"Countryman, A," 68
Cranmer-Byng, L.: *Feast of Lanterns,* 195; *Lute of Jade,* 195
Crist, Mrs., 177–78
Critic, The, 155–56
Criticism of Some Recent Methods of Dating Laotzu (Hu Shih), 215
Crumble me with fire into the desert sand . . . , 127
"Cycle," 242

"D. H. Lawrence," 50, 54, 254
Damrosch, Walter, 246, 247n2
"Dance for Christ, A," 71–72
"Dance for Rain, A," 72–74
Dawn came— . . . , 74–78
Day, John, 284
"Dead in the Philippines," 125
Dead in the Philippines are they . . . , 125
"Dead Loon, The," 3, 33
Debs, Eugene, 205
"Defeat," 7, 125
De Mille, Cecil B., 243–44; relationship with Bynner, 3
Der Ling, Princess, 197
Despair comes when all comedy . . . , 35
Dewey, John, 289n2, 289–90
"Dial, The," 262
Dim twilight throws a deeper shade across the windowscreen; . . . (Giles), 193
Dixon, John, quoted, 183
Douglas, Norman, 175–76, 294, 294n3
"Down Chung-nan Mountain to the Kind Pillow and Bowl of Hu Ssü," 85
Down the blue mountain in the evening, . . . , 85
"Driftwood," 32–33

Pound, Ezra, 150–51, 276, 276n1, 284, 287, 287n1, 299; Bollingen-Library of Congress award to, 292–93; *Cathay*, 228; insanity, 293; letter from Bynner, 276; *Pisan Cantos*, 293; *Provença*, 150; quoted, 172; relationship with Bynner, 4; *Ripostes*, 150; *Sonnets and Ballate of Guido Cavalcanti*, 150
"Prayer," 126
Preparing me chicken and rice, old friend, . . , 92
"Processional," 119–20
Prophet, The (Gibran), 279
prostitution, Bynner's views on, 162–63
Provença (Pound), 150
Prowling in a corridor, . . . , 54–56
Psychoanalysis and the Unconscious (Lawrence), 255
Pueblo Indians, 181–83; dances of, 169, 184–87
Pulido, Ysidoro, 278, 278n2

quisling, use of term, 288n3

Rainbow, The (Lawrence), 175
"Red Indian" (Lawrence), 178
Red leaped . . . , 42
"Remembering My Brothers on a Moonlight Night," 87
Rhoades, Lourinda, 280, 280n1
rhyme, in *Tao Teh Ching*, 217
Rice, Alice Hegan, *Mrs. Wiggs of the Cabbage Patch*, 147
Rice, Carl Young, 147
Ripostes (Pound), 150
Road to Damascus, The (Mitchell-Keays), 238
"Robert Frost," 50, 139
Robinson, Henry Morton, quoted, 270, 271n1
Roseboro, Viola, 145

Roses have been his bed so long that he . . . , 112
Rossetti might have quarreled with Burne-Jones . . . , 110–11

Saint-Gaudens, Augustus, 239–42; home in Cornish, 238; sculptures of, 241–42, 242n3
Saint-Gaudens, Carlota, 238
Saint-Gaudens, Homer, 238
Samossoud, Clara Clemens, 248, 249n1
Sanger, Margaret, 261–62, 262n1; letter from Bynner, 261–62
Santa Fe, 173–80, 254, 271; writers in, 169
"Santa Fe," 138
Santa Fe Citizens' Committee on Atomic Information, 222–23
Santayana, George, 294, 294n2
Sarton, May, 245; *World of Light, A*, 245
Saturday Review, 292–93, 293n2
Savage Pilgrimage, The (Carswell), 174
Scott, Win, 300
"Sculptor's Funeral, The" (Cather), 144
"Seeing Li Po in a Dream," 87–88
Seiffert, Marjorie Allen, 166
Selected Poems, 276
Seton, Marie, 274, 274n4
Sex in the Arts (Taft), 270, 271n1
Sexual Behavior in the Human Male (Kinsey), 292n3
Shakespeare, William, 202
"Shalako," 81–82
Shaw, Anna Howard, quoted, 224
She does not see the tea her servant brings . . . , 48
Sheean, Vincent, *Indigo Bunting*, 296, 297n2
She had lied from the first moment when she said . . . , 113